D0886850

Police Corruption

Preventing Misconduct and Maintaining Integrity

Advances in Police Theory and Practice Series

Series Editor: Dilip K. Das

Police Corruption: Preventing Misconduct and Maintaining Integrity
Tim Prenzler

Police Corruption

Preventing Misconduct and Maintaining Integrity

Tim Prenzler

CRC Press
Taylor & Francis Group
Boca Raton   London   New York

CRC Press is an imprint of the
Taylor & Francis Group, an **informa** business

CRC Press
Taylor & Francis Group
6000 Broken Sound Parkway NW, Suite 300
Boca Raton, FL 33487-2742

© 2009 by Taylor & Francis Group, LLC
CRC Press is an imprint of Taylor & Francis Group, an Informa business

Library of Congress Cataloging-in-Publication Data

Prenzler, Tim.
    Police corruption : preventing misconduct and maintaining integrity / Timothy Prenzler.
        p. cm. -- (Advances in police theory and practice)
    Includes bibliographical references and index.
    ISBN 978-1-4200-7796-4 (hardcover : alk. paper)
    1. Police corruption--Prevention. 2. Police corruption--Australia--Prevention.
3. Police ethics. 4. Police ethics--Australia. 5. Police administration. 6. Police administration--Australia. I. Title. II. Series.

HV7936.C85P74 2009
364.1'323--dc22   2009003715

Visit the Taylor & Francis Web site at
http://www.taylorandfrancis.com

and the CRC Press Web site at
http://www.crcpress.com

*This book is dedicated to the memory of
Pastor Martin Frederick Prenzler,
1927-1999.*

He dedicated his life to helping people in need.

Table of Contents

Series Preface

While the literature on police and allied subjects is growing exponentially, the impact upon day-to-day policing remains small. The two worlds of research and practice of policing remain disconnected even though cooperation between the two is growing. A major reason is that the two groups speak in different languages. The research work is published in hard-to-access journals and presented in a manner that is difficult for the lay person to comprehend. On the other hand, police practitioners tend not to mix with others and remain secretive about their work. Consequently, there is little dialogue between the two and almost no attempt to learn from one another. Dialogue across the globe, among researchers and practitioners situated in different continents, are, of course, even more limited.

I attempted to address this problem by starting the IPES where a common platform brought the two together. IPES is now in its 13th year and has been organized in all parts of the world. Several publications have come out of these deliberations and a new community of scholars and police officers has been created whose membership runs into several hundreds. Another attempt was to begin a new journal, aptly called *Police Practice and Research* that opened the gate to practitioners to share their work and experiences. The journal has attempted to focus upon issues that help bring the two on a single platform. The journal is now completing eight years and is in its 35th issue.

Clearly, these attempts, despite their success, remain limited. Conferences and journal publications do help create a body of knowledge and an association of police activists but cannot address substantive issues in depth. The limitations of time and space preclude larger discussions and more authoritative expositions that can provide stronger and broader linkages between the two worlds.

It is this observation that has encouraged many of us to conceive and implement a new attempt in this direction. We are embarking on a book series that seeks to attract writers from all parts of the world, to find practitioner contributors, and to create a series that makes a serious contribution to our knowledge of the police as well as to improve police practices. We are interested not only in work that describes the best and successful police practices, but also one that challenges current paradigms and breaks new ground to prepare police for the twenty-first century. We are looking for comparative analysis that highlights achievements in distant parts of the world as well as one that makes an in-depth examination of specific problems confronting a particular police force. We hope that through this series we will accelerate the process of building knowledge about policing and help bridge the gap between the two worlds.

We invite police scholars and practitioners across the world to come and join us in this venture.

Dilip K. Das, PhD
Series Editor

Foreword

Welcome to the inaugural text in the new series "Advances in Police Theory and Practice," published by CRC Press/Taylor & Francis. *Police Corruption: Preventing Misconduct and Maintaining Integrity* fulfills the primary aims of the series by advocating innovative practice, connecting research to best practice, and addressing contemporary needs in policing.

With its easy-to-read style and focus on practical strategies, the book bridges the gap between research published in academic journals and reports and the real world needs and constraints of police managers, supervisors, and policy makers.

The book begins by taking us on a journey through the often sordid world of police corruption. While many police officers undertake their work conforming to the highest ethical standards, we must also face the facts about the recurring problem of police officer misconduct—however much these facts may challenge our preferred, benign image of the police. Tim Prenzler's analysis of the types of unethical behaviour leads appropriately into an analysis of the structural causes of problem behaviour in policing—causes that lie largely outside the individual officer.

These topics form the content of the first two chapters in the book. They could be appropriately described as diagnostics. The remainder of the book is dedicated to an exploration of applied strategies designed to maximise ethical conduct and identify and prevent corruption. This entails a wide range of approaches, including articulating standards, measuring and monitoring behaviour, recruitment screening tests, ethics training, complaints investigation and discipline, informal resolution of complaints, research-based risk management techniques, advanced techniques (including covert surveillance and integrity tests), the creation of independent oversight bodies, and the development of ethical leadership.

Wherever possible, in keeping with one of the key aims of the new series, Prenzler takes a global perspective on his subject matter. Policing, it seems, is prone to the same potential problems of corruption and misconduct everywhere in the world. And, as the author points out, the fact that advanced democracies have experienced major problems with serious and extensive police corruption highlights the importance of establishing robust and enduring anti-corruption systems in new and emerging democracies. In that regard, the model comprehensive integrity system set out in the book makes a major contribution to the goal of global ethical policing.

I would like to thank Tim Prenzler for his contribution to the series and for setting a high standard for those who follow.

A number of other people have been closely involved in the development of this series who also must be thanked. As Acquisitions Editor, Carolyn Spence has done an excellent job in soliciting authors and helping with the assessment of submissions. Amber Donley has also done a sterling job as project coordinator in editorial project development at Taylor & Francis Books.

Many thanks are also due to the anonymous reviewers who gave of their time to provide feedback on book proposals; and to the authors who have joined the team and committed themselves to the often arduous task of writing a book.

I encourage readers to consider making their own contributions to 'Advances in Police Theory and Practice'.

Dilip Das, PhD
Series Editor

Preface

In the mid-1980s I was an impoverished university student working part-time delivering pizzas on Australia's Gold Coast. On occasion, a pizza had to be delivered to a brothel. The brothels were in converted houses on major streets. The buildings were discreet but all the pizza drivers knew where they were. (There was some competition for these assignments!) I knew that prostitution was completely illegal. After all, the government was run by puritanical Christians. So how was it that the brothels were thriving? I figured police simply weren't interested in enforcing the law because the brothels didn't cause any trouble, and presumably the politicians didn't know they existed. But in 1987 a major corruption inquiry was launched. It turned out police were receiving payments from the brothel owners in a system that went so far back in time it could not be properly traced. The police commissioner went to jail on a 14-year sentence for accepting bribes. An assortment of other police and crooks were also jailed, along with six politicians, on a range of corruption-related convictions.

These events opened my eyes to the dark side of policing, and to the role of government in police corruption. Within a short time, caught up in the subsequent wave of reform, I had a job teaching ethics to police recruits. Here again my eyes were opened to the diversity of police views on ethical issues. I was impressed by the apparent integrity of many recruits. But I will always remember a session run by one police officer. She gave the scenario of an officer pulling over a speeding vehicle. The driver turns out to be the officer's mother. What would the recruits do in this situation? I was amazed at how a vocal minority were completely hostile to the idea of writing a ticket, even ridiculing anyone who would breach a family member. There were also deep divisions over issues like free entry for recruits to nightclubs, informing on colleagues, and the treatment of ethnic minorities. These experiences taught me several things: ethical reasoning only takes us so far, police must be made to comply with ethical standards—and special attention needs to be paid to the defiant minority!

During this period—the 1990s—my home jurisdiction of Queensland became a world leader in police reform initiatives with the creation of a powerful external watchdog agency and a range of initiatives, including whistle-blower legislation and integrity testing, designed to stamp out corruption. A number of other jurisdictions in Australia soon went through the same cleaning out process as efforts intensified to put a stop to decades of serious and systemic corruption. My teaching and research interests shifted from a focus on "solving" ethical problems in policing to identifying effective techniques for facilitating and enforcing compliance. This took me on a worldwide search, examining police corruption reports from many different places, continuously looking for fair and effective prevention strategies.

This book is the culmination of that 17-year quest. Unfortunately, one of the outcomes of these inquiries is an extremely cynical attitude toward the commitment of governments and police leaders to genuine accountability. Reform in my home jurisdiction has foundered on the rocks of government secrecy, indifference, and party politicking. Both sides of politics continue to take a weak approach to the proper implementation of reform. I have also been extremely disappointed at the reactionary and ignorant response adopted by the leadership of the main police union in Queensland. However, we do see some responsible leadership in police unionism in Australia, and there can be little doubt that enormous improvements have been made in Australia and many other jurisdictions that give hope for a slowly evolving application of the science of police integrity management. Certainly we now have a strong knowledge base about what is required.

This book focuses on practical strategies to prevent police corruption. Recurring major scandals around the world, the large volume of complaints against police, and the steady stream of criminal convictions of police demonstrate the extent of the problem and the need for an instructive text that brings together everything that is known about best practice measures to reduce misconduct. The book includes some historical observations, but the main sources of information derive from the last four decades of experimentation and learning about effective integrity management.

I have sought to make this book easy to read, free from academic waffle, and as accessible as possible to the widest readership, including police, students, policy makers, and lay readers. I have also sought to make the book as international as possible. My optimism in that regard was dampened by the fact that research in this area is dominated by the duopoly of the United States and the United Kingdom, with substantive contributions from only a few other countries. Nonetheless, one of the key target audiences for this book is police managers, politicians, and lawyers in emerging and developing democracies who are committed to democratic and ethical policing. There is a great deal to be learned from the many innovations and the many failures in established democracies. At the same time, we need more empirical research on what works in police integrity management from a wider range of different countries and jurisdictions.

The book follows a logical sequence by first describing and explaining types of police misconduct, their effects, and different causal factors. Chapter 1 examines diverse examples of corruption from a range of jurisdictions, with a focus on the more extensive and extreme manifestations in order to demonstrate the potential for policing to fall into complex and highly destructive forms of misconduct. Chapter 2 looks at different ways of categorizing misconduct, its impacts on the community and police themselves, and the main theories about why police become corrupt. This section underscores the need for a sustained commitment, and a large-scale and sophisticated infrastructure, to combat corruption and close off corruption opportunities over the long term. This is followed by a chapter that deals with the converse of these problems: establishing universal ethical principles that police everywhere should follow, oriented toward addressing the key areas of ethical decision making for police. Chapter 4 then assesses ways of identifying and measuring misconduct problems and the ethical climate of a police department, with a focus on a diagnostic approach oriented toward tailor-made preventive interventions.

Chapter 5 discusses best practice procedures in recruitment for selecting ethical applicants, and preservice and in-service training methods for imparting departmental values. This is followed by a chapter on the essential elements of an advanced complaints and discipline system. The emphasis here on "getting tough" is then balanced by a discussion in Chapter 7 of alternative strategies for dealing with complaints and misconduct, including informal resolution, local and managerial resolution, and mediation. Chapter 8 is concerned with risk reduction strategies and system controls, including early warning and early intervention systems, which employ a range of indicators to identify and preempt developing patterns of unethical behavior. Attention then shifts in Chapter 9 to "advanced strategies" for combating more hidden and entrenched forms of corruption. These strategies include drug and alcohol tests, integrity tests, and the use of undercover agents. The foregoing sections are focused on internal measures. Chapter 10 examines the role of independent external oversight bodies that audit police strategies and have the capacity to conduct their own investigations. The final chapter on ethical leadership emphasizes the need to go beyond a checklist of rules and technologies with leadership that values, requires, and models integrity in all aspects of police work. At the same time, the chapter emphasizes how the ultimate test of ethical leadership is the extent to which all aspects of a comprehensive integrity system are properly implemented and maintained.

I am keen to thank the many people who provided direct or indirect assistance with this project. Writing this book has been an ambition for many years, but it was Dilip Das who convinced me to take action and submit a proposal to CRC Press. Having a deadline with a reputable publisher is a great motivator. Thank you, Dilip, and thanks also Carolyn Spence and Amber Donley for your assistance in production. Thanks are also due to my employer, Griffith University, for giving me the time and resources to write the book. The research for this book was also supported by an Australian

Research Council Linkage Grant, An Integrity System for Victoria Police, managed by the Centre for Applied Philosophy and Public Ethics, Charles Sturt University; and by the Australian Research Council Centre of Excellence in Policing and Security. I am pleased to be able to acknowledge colleagues who have provided inspiration and help over many years, as well as specific help with aspects of the research and editing for this book: Stuart Macintyre, Rick Sarre, Hennessey Hayes, Janet Ransley, Peter Grabosky, Seumas Miller, David Bradley, John Kleinig, David Bayley, Arch Harrison, Keith Bryett, Frank Rynne, David Brereton, Vince Henry, Colleen Lewis, Louise Porter, Janet Evans, Lorraine Mazerolle, Michael Briody, Glen Dawson, Elspeth Wilson, Sandra Smith, Jackie Chapman, and Brigitte Bouhours. Finally, special thanks to three special, funny people: Linda, Alex, and Grace.

About the Author

Tim Prenzler is Chief Investigator of the Australian Research Council (ARC) Centre of Excellence in Policing and Security (CEPS) at Griffith University, Brisbane, Australia. He also teaches in Griffith's School of Criminology and Criminal Justice. Prenzler has developed and taught courses in crime prevention, security management, and ethics and accountability in criminal justice. His main research interests are in the areas of police ethics and integrity, the history of women police, gender equity in policing, the work and regulation of the security industry, crime prevention, and police and security officer safety.

The Misconduct Problem in Policing

1

Is it possible to think of a whole police force, or a unit within it, as an organized criminal gang? This, in fact, is how police have at times acted—running extortion rackets, trafficking in narcotics, systematically stealing from the public, beating up the opposition, and even engaging in torture and murder. The account of police protection of prostitution outlined in the preface to this book is a common story. However, it is a relatively benign version of the much more complex, sometimes sinister story of police corruption. One of the characteristics of this recurring social malaise is that it takes highly diverse forms, ranging from free coffee and doughnuts to protection of vice to fabrication of evidence, and on to drug trafficking and murder. Police misconduct has a deeply corrosive effect on society, undermining the system of democratic authority and threatening the security of ordinary citizens. It fosters organized crime, government waste, public disaffection, resistance to authority, and noncooperation with police.

This chapter provides a brief history of the problem, describing findings from famous judicial inquiries and some academic research, and then provides accounts of particularly notorious cases of police malfeasance that have drawn public outrage and notoriety. It concludes with a discussion of the problem of ambiguity in police misconduct cases.

Historical Background

In *Forces of Deviance: Understanding the Dark Side of Policing*, Kappeler, Sluder, and Alpert (1998) observe that, "Since the creation of the first law enforcement agencies, police have engaged in misconduct. ... To study the history of police is to study police deviance, corruption and misconduct" (p. 28).

One of the first systematic attempts to address this problem occurred with the creation of the New Police in England in the 19th century. Modern concepts of ethical policing are based on the model adopted with the formation in 1829 of the London Metropolitan Police. Up to that point, policing was generally corrupt, as well as amateurish and often incompetent. As one example of corruption, a traditional practice by which constables received a percentage of fine monies simply served to stimulate false prosecutions and extortionate threats of prosecution (Kappeler et al., 1998, p. 32). Corruption of the offices of sheriff and constable was part of the endemic corruption of the English judiciary, as well as the parliament, military, and civil service—key

1

institutions that operated through bribery, favoritism, and a trade in positions and influence. The chief proponent of the New Police, Robert Peel, lobbied for a police force where corruption and incompetence would be minimized because officers would be vetted, trained, salaried, supervised, subject to a disciplinary regime, and detached from politics.

Despite the seeming merit of Peel's proposal, it was deeply unpopular due to fears the new force would be militaristic and oppressive. Part of the reason for this concern was that the military provided support to the civil police against populist unrest. "Peterloo" and similar atrocities were fresh in the minds of English people. The Peterloo Massacre occurred in Manchester in 1819 when cavalry charged political protestors, killing 11 and injuring many hundreds. The protest—involving tens of thousands of people supporting an enlarged franchise and lower food prices—was intended to be peaceful. A large number of women were among the injured. Many people were trampled by horses or hacked with sabres. The event caused outrage and galvanized opposition to the authorities. Advocates of professional policing were, therefore, faced with widespread fear that a standing police force would be militaristic and use violence to oppose the movement for democracy, as well as routinely harass and intimidate ordinary citizens (Critchley, 1967).

Partly in response to these concerns, the New Police walked the beat without a firearm, equipped only with a strengthened hat, a truncheon, and a rattle (later a whistle) (Critchley, 1967, p. 51). A strong emphasis was placed on officers being courteous and helpful. Instructions also emphasized that force was to be used as an absolute last resort, and police were meant to focus on prevention rather than prosecution. Recruitment emphasized "moral character," as well as intelligence, good health, and physical agility (Kappeler et al., 1998, p. 35). The new standards presented an enormous challenge in implementation. Thousands of officers were dismissed or resigned in the first years. Drunkenness on duty was a particular problem, and other problems, such as bribery and neglect of duty, quickly surfaced.

Nonetheless, the new professional model took hold and quickly found widespread popular support and adoption by other forces in Britain. In contrast, in the same period, frontier societies like the United States, Canada, and Australia suffered from the continuation of different blends of customary and military models. Lack of supervision of frontline officers and high levels of discretionary freedom made for highly arbitrary law enforcement and unreliable protection of citizens. Police became enmeshed in crooked local politics; in the racist, sometimes genocidal policies of the time; in the brutal suppression of labor strikes; and in organized protection rackets involving alcohol, gambling, prostitution, and abortion. The beating and torture of suspects became a routine way of administering justice for minor crimes and extracting confessions for serious crimes (Kappeler et al., 1998). The adoption of the professional model in the latter part of the 19th century in many countries saw some improvements, but many of these were undermined in the 1920s and 1930s with the rise of alcohol-related organized crime in the prohibition period.

It would seem to be almost universally the case that police corruption flourishes where the professional model is not present in any substantive form. Consequently, the history of any police force, as Keppeler et al. argue, will inevitably reveal forms of corruption. The examples provided so far are from democracies, considered advanced for their time, with judicial and parliamentary scrutiny of public offices. Where any form of democracy is absent, police are almost inevitably corrupt as key components of a dictatorial or totalitarian system. In a "police state," police typically lack a properly developed impartial community-oriented crime prevention and law enforcement role. They are deeply morally compromised by their role as agents of the ruling elite—as spies, assassins, and torturers. Under the right political and social conditions, police agencies rapidly morph into the stuff of nightmares, organized under euphemistic titles such as "state security police." Some of the worst examples include the Gestapo (a contraction of Secret State Police) in Nazi Germany, the KGB (Committee for State Security) in communist Russia, the SSC (State Security Council) in Apartheid South Africa, and the IIS (Iraqi Intelligence Service or Mukhabarat) in Saddam Hussein's Iraq. Many secret police agencies in dictatorships in Central and South America after World War II carried out systematic human rights abuses, often with the support of the U.S. government and Central Intelligence Agency (CIA) in the interests of large American capital, exploiting resources and workers south of the U.S. border. In the case of the CIA, its description as a "rogue elephant" derived from the fact that it was insulated from control by Congress, acting with a free hand to carry out illegal covert operations, such as assassinations, and providing aid to brutal police regimes (Prados, 1986).

The following sections examine a variety of contemporary corruption cases that have galvanized public attention, and serve to highlight the magnitude of the police misconduct problem.

Major Judicial Inquiries and Associated Corruption Cases

The Knapp Commission in New York City, from 1970 to 1972, marked a turning point in modern consciousness about police misconduct. Global media reports publicized the unfolding revelations of bureaucratically organized corruption in the New York Police Department (NYPD). Events were given flesh and blood in the dramatized books and films, *Serpico* (Maas, 1973) and *Prince of the City* (Daley, 1978). The widespread corrupt practices in the NYPD at the time were based on the exploitation of routine functions such as ticketing parking violations and prosecuting illegal gambling. Police abused their authority to create a system of extortionate gratuities from restaurants and business owners. Knapp famously described two types of officers: "grass-eaters" and "meat-eaters":

> The overwhelming majority of those who take payoffs are grass-eaters, who accept gratuities and solicit $5, $10, and $20 payments from contractors, tow-truck operators, gamblers, and the like, but do not aggressively pursue corruption payments. Meat-eaters, probably only a small percentage of the force, spend a good deal of their working hours aggressively seeking out situations they can exploit for financial gain, including gambling, narcotics, and other serious offenses that can yield payments of thousands of dollars (Knapp, 1972, p. 65).

In a study of international trends in police corruption, Prenzler (2002) compared the findings of the Knapp Inquiry with those from the other side of the world 25 years later in the 1997 Wood Inquiry into the New South Wales Police Service—the largest police force in Australia. An expanded list of findings is contained in Table 1.1, showing a remarkably similar set of themes. Known as "the best police force money can buy," by the time of the Wood Commission the New South Wales Police had become fairly sedate compared to the "roaring twenties" style policing of the 1970s and 1980s when officers franchised armed robberies and gangland killings (Wood, 1997, chap. 3).

In addition, both the New York and New South Wales reports identified problems with the sale or disclosure of confidential information, interference with internal investigations, theft from dead bodies, kickbacks from tow truck operators, and internal corruption in overtime and sickness benefits. In New York there was also extensive police corruption in building construction permits, parking and liquor regulations, and a trade in preferred assignments.

Many other jurisdictions underwent similar, often painful exposés of corruption through judicial—or public—inquiries that used a variety of techniques including compelling testimony, offering indemnities to corrupt officers who provide information, and undercover operations. The problems revealed by these inquiries and associated investigations were varied—although many common elements are apparent, as the following examples show.

- In 1981, the Scarman Inquiry, following the Brixton riots, revealed a systemic problem with police harassment of racial minorities by London Metropolitan Police officers (Scarman, 1986).
- The 1982 McDonald Commission investigation into the Security Service of the Royal Canadian Mounted Police (RCMP) found it engaged in a "dirty tricks" campaign against separatist groups. The illegal actions included arson, burglaries, interference with mail, and data theft. The Criminal Investigation Branch of the RCMP was also found to engage in similar tactics (Rosen, 2000; Royal Commission, 1981).

Table 1.1 Statements From the Knapp Inquiry in New York City and the Wood Inquiry in New South Wales

	Knapp (1972)	Wood (1997)
General	"Police corruption was found to be an extensive, department-wide phenomenon, indulged in to some degree by a sizeable majority of those on the force" (p. 61).	"The Royal Commission disclosed a very serious state of corruption that was widespread and of long-standing origin … the state of corruption found can only be regarded as systematic and entrenched" (p. 161).
Gratuities	"The most widespread form of misconduct the Commission found was the acceptance by police officers of gratuities in the form of free meals, free goods, and cash payments. Almost all policemen either solicited or accepted such favors in one form or another. … Many thousands of free meals were consumed by policemen each day and the sheer numbers created problems for the most popular eateries" (pp. 170, 172).	"There was abundant evidence of the ready availability of various forms of gratuities ranging from small amounts of money to free liquor, meals and sexual services on both a casual and regular basis, particularly among those police whose duties took them to the clubs and premises where they might have been expected to enforce vice, gaming, licensing and drug laws"(p. 95).
Opportunistic corruption	"An extortion attempt by police officers is sometimes the end product of careful surveillance of a target. … Most often a police officer seeking to score simply keeps for himself all or part of the money and drugs confiscated during a raid or arrest" (pp. 98-99).	"In a disturbingly large number of cases, the Royal Commission received complaints of money and property having been stolen by police in the course of routine police work. … Theft and extortion from criminals had become regular features of policing in some sections" (p. 114).
Process corruption	"The most common court-related payoffs were those made to policemen to change their testimony so that a case was dismissed or the defendant acquitted." … Drug-related process corruption included "'flaking,' or planting narcotics on an arrested person and 'padding,' or adding to the quantity of narcotics found on an arrested person in order to upgrade the arrest" (pp. 187, 91).	"In almost every segment of the evidence called, the issue of process corruption reared its head, comprising variously: perjury, planting of evidence, verbals in the forms of unsigned records of interview and note book confessions … assaults and pressure to induce confessions" (p. 84).

Table 1.1 Statements From the Knapp Inquiry in New York City and the Wood Inquiry in New South Wales (continued)

	Knapp (1972)	Wood (1997)
Vice and gambling	"Organized crime is the single biggest source of police corruption, through its control of the city's gambling, narcotics, loansharking, and illegal sex-related enterprises. … The collection of tribute by police from gamblers has traditionally been extremely well organized and has persisted in virtually unchanged form for years" (pp. 68, 70).	"The protection of clubs and vice operators was at Kings Cross conducted on much the same basis as that for the drug suppliers. Key members … admitted to the regular payment of corrupt monies for these purposes" (p. 123).
Alcohol	"In the course of its investigation into bars, Commission investigators could not help but observe numerous police officers imbibing free drinks—both on duty and off … there was plenty of drinking on duty" (p. 176).	"Drinking on duty, and covering for police affected by alcohol while on duty, was an entrenched and expected practice" (p. 98).

Source: From *Report of a Commission to Investigate Allegations of Police Corruption and the City's Anti-corruption Procedures,* by W. Knapp, 1972. New York: The City of New York, adapted with permission; and *Royal Commission into the New South Wales Police Service: Final Report* by J. Wood, 1997, Sydney: NSW Government Printer, adapted with permission.

- The River Cops scandal in Miami in the 1980s led to the conviction or dismissal of over 90 officers for involvement in a highly lucrative cocaine "skimming" and resale racket, involving murder and attempted murder (Kappeler et al., 1998, p. 55).
- In 1985, the Key West Police Department in Florida was declared a "criminal enterprise" under the U.S. federal government Racketeering Influenced and Corrupt Organizations Act (RICO). The deputy chief and chief-of-detectives were jailed for 30 years on 17 counts including bribing a witness, conspiracy, racketeering, and cocaine possession with intent to distribute. A sergeant of detectives and a lieutenant of detectives also received long sentences, along with an attorney, his wife, and eight other drug traffickers. The main witness testified he regularly delivered cocaine "in Burger King bags and Chicken Unlimited boxes" to the deputy chief in his office in city hall ("3 Ex-cops," 1985, p. a10; "Key West," 1984).
- The 1987-1989 Fitzgerald Inquiry in Queensland, Australia, revealed "top to bottom" corruption centered on the protection of gambling

dens and brothels, extending to tampering with evidence and institutionalized sex discrimination (Fitzgerald, 1989).

- The Christopher Commission in 1991 identified widespread brutality in the Los Angeles Police Department (LAPD), and systematic extra-legal "punishment" of suspects by police. It followed the bashing of African American Rodney King, revealed through a citizen's covert video recording. King, lying defenseless and unmoving on the ground, was repeatedly kicked by a group of officers while another group stood by and watched (Christopher, 1991).
- In New Orleans, in the early to mid-1990s, up to 200 police were associated with a series of crimes including drug trafficking, bank robbery, motor vehicle theft, assault, and murder (Kappeler et al., 1998, p. 57).
- The Rampart Scandal in Los Angeles in 1997-1998 involved serious crimes by a small number of officers, including armed robbery, theft of drugs, assaults on detainees, and fabrication of evidence (Board of Inquiry, 2000).
- In 1997, in the state of Victoria, Australia, an investigation by the Ombudsman—codenamed Operation BART—revealed a system of illicit payments to police who bypassed a roster system for assigning emergency repairs to burgled premises. The system was believed to have been operating for at least 20 years. Approximately 550 serving officers were implicated (Ombudsman Victoria, 1998).
- The 1999 MacPherson Inquiry into the inadequate investigation by London Met officers of the murder of a black teenager again sparked widespread revelations of systemic racism in English forces (MacPherson, 1999).

Academic Research

Using social science research methods, academic research at times also reveals significant corruption problems. Barker (1978), for example, used an anonymous survey to ask officers in a U.S. city police department about their perceptions of colleagues' involvement in corruption. He found respondents estimated that 40% of officers had engaged in excessive force against a prisoner, 23% had committed perjury, and 31% had had sex on duty!

Other researchers have observed routine misconduct simply by melting into the background as they accompanied police at work. In a famous pioneering study conducted in the early 1960s, Jerome Skolnick (1994) obtained permission to act as a participant-observer in the police department of a U.S. city. He conducted numerous interviews and rode along on patrol shifts, accompanied detectives and specialist squads, and attended court. He was quickly accepted by police and even given a considerable amount of hands-on work. Although Skolnick did not find much in the way of graft, his main finding was that law enforcement was highly discretionary, selective, and racially biased. Justice was not administered in an impartial or efficient manner. This was a product partly of the cynical white male police culture, partly of strict rules of evidence, and partly of the inherent difficulty of obtaining evidence. Police fell back on a principle of "positive deviance," focusing their efforts on the appearance of productivity, especially in relation to crime clearance figures. The process included an excessive and unfair reliance on deal making with criminals and protection of criminal informants.

Other academic studies have revealed different forms of corruption. Also in the United States, Jennifer Hunt's (1990) participant-observation study identified extreme and endemic sex discrimination and harassment in internal police relations. David Johnson (2004) used interviews and documentary sources to challenge the myth of Japanese police integrity, highlighting embezzlement, kickbacks from the pinball industry, and tolerance of the organized crime group, the Yakuza. A recent study in Uttar Pradesh state in India—with a force of 180,000 officers—mapped out the presence of almost every type of misconduct imaginable. Beatrice Jauregui (2007) spent 12 months observing and interviewing police. She concluded that all aspects of policing were deeply corrupted. All citizens understood that they were expected to pay police, whether they were reporting crime or were suspects. The fabrication or destruction of evidence to mislead the courts was standard practice. Generally, capacity to pay determined whether the victim or offender received the most favorable police response. Officers were also locked into a system of payments to superior officers to avoid persecution and obtain favored postings and promotion. Preferred postings were where protection payments were most lucrative. Applicants could pay up to eight times a constable's annual salary for a place in the academy, with the expectation that much of this money would be recouped from bribes. All police actions were driven, not by impartial fact-finding and application of the law, but by complex customary obligations to relatives, associates, and persons of power and standing in civil society and government. (For a collection of country reports see Klockars, Kutnjak Ivkovic & Haberfeld, 2004.)

Notorious Cases

At times, police misconduct can take on particularly extreme forms, with devastating consequences. The following provides a sample of cases, some older and some more recent, with a more personalized orientation.

The Irish Miscarriages of Justice Cases

In England in the 1970s, pressure on police over Irish Republication Army (IRA) terrorist bombings stimulated a rash of serious miscarriages of justice cases. One of the worst involved the Birmingham Six, when six men were detained and tortured by police over a pub bombing in Birmingham. They were convicted and served 16 years in prison as a result of false confessions, as well as false testimony by police and baseless scientific evidence. The Guildford Four and Maguire Seven cases mirrored the Birmingham case. The "Four" were harmless hippies detained at length by Guildford police under Draconian anti-terror laws and tortured into making false confessions. Following a trial littered with errors by the prosecution, they served 15 years in jail. The Maguire Seven were relatives of Gerry Conlon, the supposed Guildford Four ringleader, who were convicted of supporting the alleged bomb plot. The seven included Conlon's father, who died in prison, and a boy of 14, who was sentenced to four years in jail (Rozenberg, 1992).

Ruby Ridge

In 1992 the Federal Bureau of Investigation (FBI) and U.S. Marshals Service were involved in a deadly siege with a reclusive antigovernment group living in the bush at Ruby Ridge, Idaho. The tragedy began when six marshals entered the Weaver family property to engage in covert reconnaissance. The action was directed at informing an arrest strategy against Randy Weaver, who had failed to appear in court over weapons law violations. Accounts differ over who fired the first shot, but when Weaver, his 13-year-old son Sammy, and a friend, Kevin Harris, came out to investigate their dog barking, a shootout started, resulting in the deaths of one of the marshals (shot by Harris) and Sammy, who was shot by a marshal in the back as he fled. The FBI then initiated a siege, adopting a shoot-to-kill policy against any persons seen with weapons. There was no attempt to communicate with the occupants, who were fired on despite the absence of return fire. Weaver was wounded and Harris was severely wounded as they retreated from a failed attempt to retrieve Sammy's body. The same bullet that hit Harris as he entered the cabin killed Weaver's wife, Vicki, who was standing behind the cabin door. The two men and Weaver's three surviving children held out in the cabin for eight days until surrendering. At trial, Harris argued he had no idea who the marshals were and was deemed to have acted in self-defense. Weaver eventually received minor convictions over the weapons offenses. A federal court dismissed manslaughter charges against a federal sharpshooter, but a Department of Justice report uncovered a litany of procedural and policy errors that led to the three deaths (USDoJ, 1994).

Abner Louima

In 1997, a Haitian immigrant, Abner Louima, while helping break up a fight outside a Brooklyn nightclub, was mistakenly arrested for an assault on a police officer. En route to the police station, Louima was beaten with fists, batons, and handheld radios. At the station he was beaten again. In the station bathroom, with his hands cuffed behind his back, he was kicked in the testicles and anally raped with the wooden handle of a drain plunger. The main perpetrator, Officer Justin Volpe, had paraded through the station with the bloodied plunger. The day after the assault the severely injured Louima was taken to the hospital. His bladder and colon injuries required several operations, and he spent two months in the hospital. His teeth were also badly damaged from the plunger being shoved into his mouth. Volpe was convicted of several offenses and received a 30-year sentence (Matthews, 2007).

The Dutroux Affair

In 1989, Belgian Marc Dutroux was convicted of the abduction and rape of five girls. Following early release from prison he became a professional criminal, purchasing seven houses with the proceeds from serial muggings, fraud, and the sale of illicit drugs and stolen cars. In the mid-1990s, he kidnapped, raped, and tortured six girls between the ages of 8 and 19. He kept the girls in three of his houses, including in a dungeon built in a basement. Dutroux made videos of the girls being sexually violated and tortured. Two of the girls starved to death when Dutroux was in custody for several months on other matters. Two other girls were murdered, and two were rescued. The crimes caused outrage across Belgium, particularly because of flaws in the investigation into the disappearances. Police were widely suspected of direct complicity in the crimes, and public dissatisfaction with the whole justice system culminated in a 250,000-plus protest march in Brussels. Although a parliamentary commission found no involvement by police, it found that the pedophile ring received a form of indirect protection from entrenched incompetence and laziness. Police failed to put Dutroux away despite his blatant criminal lifestyle, and in the abduction investigations they failed to share information, failed to search the houses properly, and dismissed important leads. The commission report found that better procedures could have saved the lives of several of the girls. The report included a wider assessment of gross negligence in Belgian policing (Associated Press, 1997; Bates, 1998; Landuyt & T'Serclaes, 1997).

Police Death Squads

The last 15 years have seen a growing problem with police in impoverished South and Central American countries engaging in extrajudicial killings of youth gang members. In Honduras, Mexico, Guatemala, and El Salvador, a rapidly escalating gang problem, brought on by extreme poverty and over-crowding, has been attacked by police by executing suspected gang members, often on the basis of supposed identifiers such as tattoos or hand signals. Police night patrols shoot victims on the spot and leave the bodies in the street. In other cases, victims have been kidnapped and taken to the city outskirts for execution. In El Salvador, police and soldiers formed "antigang task forces" that became little more than "hunting expeditions" (Bermúdez, 2005, p. 2; see also Huggins, 1997, on the history of Brazilian police death squads that evolved into organized crime gangs, and the section on extrajudicial killings in the 2005 Commonwealth Human Rights Initiative report on police accountability [CHRI, 2005]).

"Mafia Cops"

In 2006, two retired New York detectives, Louis Eppolito and Stephen Caracappa, were convicted of criminal offenses covering the period from 1979 to 2005. The decorated officers lived double lives working as informants and hired killers for the mafia Lucchese family and crime boss Anthony "Gaspipe" Casso. They were convicted of eight murders. The pair received payments of $4,000 per month for supplying information, with payments of up to $75,000 for murders. Other charges included money laundering, kid-napping, and obstruction of justice. In one instance it was revealed that the duo supplied wrong information on a target that led to the shooting death of an innocent man. They tipped off the mafia to police informants, and on one occasion arrested a member of the mafia then handed him back to the Mob, who tortured and killed him. The men were also convicted of trading in methamphetamines while in retirement in Nevada (BBC News, 2006; Lawson & Oldham, 2006).

The Problem of Ambiguity

In a number of the cases described above, the police who were involved escaped criminal convictions, sometimes after being charged. Miscarriages of justice perpetrated by corrupt police show how criminal trial outcomes are far from reliable. This process can also operate in reverse, where patently cor-rupt police are acquitted after being charged with criminal offenses. Despite prosecutions, no police were ever convicted in the Guildford Four and Maguire Seven cases. An FBI sharpshooter at the center of the Ruby Ridge shootings escaped manslaughter charges despite apparent flagrant breaches of procedure. In a related problem, judicial inquiries frequently make sweep-ing statements about corruption that appear to be belied by the relatively small number of criminal convictions that result. Even when convictions of corrupt police are obtained, this is often considered as, at best, a partial success, with the protracted process leaving victims of police abuses and their families and communities deeply dissatisfied. In the Abner Louima case, for example, two officers received criminal convictions but one of the assault convictions was overturned and the officer was convicted of a lesser perjury charge. Two other officers associated with the incident were convicted of conspiracy to obstruct an investigation, but these convictions were overturned. A fifth officer was charged but found not guilty of a cover-up.

The upshot of this is that police corruption allegations often involve considerable legal indeterminacy and controversy. Investigations often fail to identify clear-cut criminal conduct, but instead identify a series of slips, misjudgements, and poor decisions that add up to disaster. Such cases also illustrate the very difficult dilemmas faced by law enforcement officials in the field (see Chapter 3) and the difficulty of establishing procedures to prevent errors. The case study in Sidebar 1.1 of the infamous Waco Siege further illustrates this problem for the law enforcement and for the accountability of police.

Government enquiries absolved the FBI and ATF of legal culpability but indicated that the approach taken had contributed to the deaths. The ATF allegedly bungled the initial raid through sloppy surveillance that alerted the

Sidebar 1.1: The Waco Siege

In 1993, agents from the U.S. Bureau of Alcohol, Tobacco, and Firearms (ATF) entered the property of the Branch Davidian religious sect outside Waco, Texas, with a warrant to arrest several leaders and search for suspected illegal firearms. The occupants took shots at the approaching ATF agents and a firefight broke out, with the result that four agents and six Davidians were shot dead, and 16 agents were injured. The FBI then launched a siege of the complex that lasted 51 days. Approximately 120 people were surrounded. The FBI assembled an arsenal of high calibre weaponry. Armoured combat vehicles were used to crush surrounding buildings and vehicles. Agents cut off all power and water and played loud distorted noises through loudspeakers, including during the night. The siege came to a climax when FBI commanders formed the view that the group was about to commit mass suicide. Armoured vehicles punched holes in the walls and pumped in tear gas to force out the occupants. Fires broke out, probably lit by some of the occupants. Nine people escaped the rapidly escalating massive inferno but many were trapped inside a concrete bunker. The bodies of 75 people, including 25 children, were found in the remains (Danforth, 2000; Stone, 1993).

occupants, resulting in an ambush. The ATF then persisted with the operation, despite being informed that the Davidians were heavily armed and prepared to repel them. It was also alleged that the cult's leader, David Koresh, should have been apprehended on one of his frequent jogging excursions outside the compound. Furthermore, the FBI, wrongly it seems, treated the case as a hostage situation. A number of children and adults had been permitted to leave the complex at different times. However, the occupants' distrust of the Bureau was compounded when they learned that the children were separated from their mothers and some of the adults were arrested. Conflict also emerged between FBI negotiators, who favored a negotiated solution, and tactical commanders, who favored "pressure tactics" and an assault. Scholars advised that the "pressure tactics" were escalating the cult members' sense of apocalypse and willingness to die in a perceived battle of good against evil. Survivors later testified that it was almost impossible to get out of the burning complex. Exits were blocked with debris and smoke, and they feared being shot (Danforth, 2000; Heymann, 1993; Stone, 1993).

Conclusion

This chapter focused on many of the more extreme cases of misconduct. This was done to drive home the message of the potential for policing to deteriorate into extremely harmful and widespread deviant behaviors. Many police departments operate over generations without such high levels of corruption, but some are plagued by extensive intergenerational corruption. Policing is also highly prone to technical and procedural errors that result in serious injury and loss of life. The next chapter, "Understanding Police Misconduct," elaborates on the variety of misconduct types and applies a set of theories to explain why misconduct is such an enduring feature of police work.

Understanding Police Misconduct

2

The previous chapter described highly diverse and sometimes extreme forms of police misconduct. However, the range of misconduct types is not infinite. Police duties have evolved into a common form all around the world, and with this comes a common set of pressures and opportunities for misconduct. These factors can be analyzed, and the misconduct problem categorized and understood. There is now a large body of knowledge about the nature and causes of police misconduct, which this chapter summarizes. Most importantly, there is also a very sound knowledge base about what is needed to eliminate, or at least minimize, police misconduct. As in medicine, effective treatment relies on accurate diagnosis.

The present chapter therefore covers a broad diagnosis of police misconduct, focusing on two main areas formulated in terms of "structural" and "cultural" factors. It starts by describing a six-part set of misconduct categories, then outlines the main negative impacts, and concludes with a review of the scholarship on causal factors.

Categorizing Police Misconduct

The misconduct case studies in Chapter 1 illustrated something of the range and possible severity of police misbehavior. Scholars have produced different typologies and terminology that attempt to meaningfully differentiate between varieties of misconduct and cover the full spectrum of police misconduct types (e.g., Barker, 1983). Typologies help to explain corruption and develop targeted preventive strategies. Police departments and civilian oversight agencies that monitor police conduct also have their own categories for the purposes of formal investigations, adjudication, and discipline. These categories are usually contained in statute law, and often involve a hierarchy of seriousness, moving from the most serious criminal offenses down to more intermediate types of misconduct through to relatively minor disciplinary offenses. It should also be noted that there is considerable overlap in common usage of the key terms "corruption" and "misconduct." Misconduct is often used as a broad, all encompassing term, with corruption carrying a more narrow meaning focused on illegal material benefits (see Punch, 2003, p. 171). However, in practice the terms are frequently used interchangeably.

The following is a six-part typology of police corruption and misconduct (adapted from Prenzler, 2002). The six categories are designed to capture both the breadth of possible misconduct and also discrete types. As noted, apart from helping to focus analysis of causes, they also have utility in developing prevention efforts aimed at preempting all possible misconduct types.

1. **Graft or "classic corruption"** involves officers misusing their position for personal benefit. Bribery, for example, involves payment for officers not doing their duty. Graft of this type may be highly organized, as in a "protection racket," where police receive a regular fee from a brothel or gambling den for not raiding premises and prosecuting the proprietors. This is a common type of misconduct found by judicial inquiries. Graft can also be irregular and "opportunistic," such as taking cash "on the spot" for not charging an apprehended drug dealer or a speeding motorist. Corruption is often consensual, but it can involve police extorting money from criminals, in the form of "shakedowns," or from legitimate businesses or the public. Classic corruption may also include police obtaining a benefit through theft of goods from a crime scene or theft of property from persons in custody, or from reselling seized drugs or selling confidential information. In some accounts, classic corruption includes gifts and discounts (gratuities). These are sometimes called *"petty corruption"* because they are usually small in value but entail an expectation of favorable treatment by police to the gift giver (Sigler & Dees, 1988).

2. **Process corruption** involves tampering with, or fabricating, evidence, as revealed in miscarriages of justice cases. The victims of this type of corruption may be innocent or guilty of crimes, but police pursue a conviction in court through fraudulent means. Process corruption involves any perversion of the course of justice, including police lying in the witness box, withholding contrary evidence, or coercing suspects into making confessions. It can also occur in the investigation phase, when information is obtained by illegal searches or wiretaps, or when suspects are not informed of their rights or are denied legal advice.

3. **Excessive force** or "brutality" covers the wide range of forms of unjustified force. This can be anything from "rough handling"— such as excessive frisking—through to serious assault, torture, and murder. Verbal abuse, intimidation, and threats of violence also belong in this category, as do dangerous high-speed vehicle pursuits (which pose a physical threat). The capacity of police to use force is normally restricted to "minimal," "reasonable," or "proportionate" force, required when police intervene to protect people, arrest resisting suspects, or act in self-defense. Actions such as shooting fleeing suspects or arbitrarily frisking people are normally illegal.

4. **Unprofessional conduct or miscellaneous misconduct** is a broad category covering other types of deviance directed toward the public—sometimes grouped together in typologies as "misconduct" or "disciplinary offenses." This area is distinguished from graft in that there is no clear or direct material benefit to the officer involved. Unprofessional conduct can include harassment and incivility, racial or sexual discrimination, inaction and laziness, misuse of confidential information (e.g., looking up the address of a person for nonwork-related reasons), and neglect of crime victims or detainees. It can include refusal to cooperate with other law enforcement agencies. And it can extend to decisions in investigations and prosecutions that deliberately favor relatives or friends—"nepotism" and "cronyism"—and discriminate against "enemies," including political parties or other activist organizations or social groups. (These actions might be described as "corruption" in some accounts.) The use of police status in pursuit of private disputes also belongs in this category.

5. **Internal corruption or workplace deviance** includes harassment of police employees and discrimination or favoritism in assignment and promotion (including sexual harassment and discrimination of the type documented by Hunt, 1990). It can include payments for favorable postings or promotion, along with abuse of sick leave, being intoxicated on the job, and lower level misuse of departmental time and resources. The category also includes criminal offenses against the police organization or on the job, such as embezzlement and illicit drug use.

6. **Unbecoming or unprofessional conduct off duty** includes criminal offenses and inappropriate behavior committed off duty but deemed to reflect adversely on the officer's work—such as drunk driving, assault, and abusive language.

Impacts

Police misconduct has highly variable effects. People can be seriously injured and killed when excessive force is used in raids, sieges, and crowd control operations. Although police protection of some forms of vice, such as prostitution, is sometimes seen as a victimless crime, in many cases it facilitates the cruel exploitation of women and children. Illegal abortions, gambling, illicit drugs, and alcohol can all have devastating physical, emotional, and financial effects on individuals and families. Police protection rackets inevitably involve supply of illegal substances and services through organized crime gangs, who frequently enlarge their activities to include extortion, kidnapping, and gang warfare. Where police misconduct involves neglect of duty, members of the public become victims of crime, whether it is theft, robbery or armed robbery, domestic violence, rape, or assault. For instance, in one area of New York, the Knapp Commission found a particularly strong correlation between high crime rates and low arrest rates. Observations revealed the crime rate was attributable to the fact that police were drinking in bars instead of working the streets (Knapp, 1972, p. 146).

One of the worst outcomes of police corruption is a miscarriage of justice. Apart from the conviction and punishment of innocent persons, miscarriages of justice include the failure to prosecute guilty parties, or the acquittal of guilty parties, as well as excessively lenient or excessively harsh penalties. The latter can result from corrupt police reducing charges or "loading up" an accused person with an excessive number of charges. The most extreme aspect of wrongful convictions is the execution of innocent people. In the United States, between 1973, when executions were resumed, and April 2, 2008, 128 people on death row were exonerated and freed (DPIC, 2008). The inescapable conclusion from this is that thousands of innocent people lost their lives over the 19th and 20th centuries as a result of the death penalty and wrongful convictions. Thousands more spent many years in prison on death row. Analyses of exonerations and assessments of the quality of evidence in case histories in different jurisdictions and over different time periods yield different results about police complicity (Kappeler & Potter, 2005, chap. 14). However, in almost every case, the process of wrongful conviction begins with incompetent or corrupt police work.

Unethical practices by police can also provoke a backlash that generates further crime and disorder. Human rights activists have blamed police death squads and repressive antigang tactics for driving young people away from social services and into the arms of crime gangs (Bermúdez, 2005). Police repression and racial discrimination have been identified as key trigger factors in major destructive riots in blighted inner-city areas (Perez, Berg & Myers, 2003; Scarman, 1986). The beating of Rodney King by LAPD officers and subsequent acquittal of officers by a white-dominated jury provoked six days of rioting in Los Angeles in which 55 people were killed, over 2,000 were injured, and 800 buildings were destroyed by fire (BBC News, 2002; Parks & Smith, 1999)

Survey research also shows that perceptions of corruption adversely affect public confidence in police, and this is particularly the case for ethnic minorities who feel neglected or persecuted by police (Weitzer, 2004). The Knapp Commission observed that "[y]oungsters raised in New York ghettos, where gambling abounds, regard the law as a joke when all their lives they have seen police officers coming and going from gambling establishments and taking payments from gamblers" (Knapp, 1972, pp. 89-90).

An added effect of this is that law enforcement and crime prevention become more difficult when high crime communities are reluctant to cooperate with police. Survey research also shows that "[v]iews about police legitimacy do influence public cooperation with the police, … and those who view the police as more legitimate are more likely to assist police to control crime. The key antecedent of legitimacy is procedural justice" (Murphy, Hinds & Fleming, 2008, p. 136).

A recent review of police accountability issues in commonwealth countries noted that when people do not trust police, because of corruption and incompetence, the rich turn to private security for protection and the poor often resort to vigilante justice (CHRI, 2005, p. 9).

The public also bears the financial costs of taxpayer-funded responses to police misconduct. Major judicial inquiries into corruption or related issues can run for years and cost many millions of dollars. One of the official investigations into the Waco Siege " … lasted 14 months, employed 74 personnel, and cost approximately [US]$17 million. The Office of Special Counsel interviewed exactly 1,001 witnesses, reviewed over 2.3 million pages of documents, and examined thousands of pounds of physical evidence" (Danforth, 2000, p. 4).

Lawyers are the main financial beneficiaries of these inquiries. Civil litigation by aggrieved citizens also imposes a huge burden on taxpayers, both in defending claims and paying successful litigants. Rodney King won US$3.8 million from the City of Los Angeles (BBC News, 2002). Abner Louima's suit against the New York City Council resulted in a US$8.75 million settlement (Matthews, 2007). Each year, large police departments need to hold millions of dollars in contingency liability funds to cover litigation costs.

Within policing, corruption can also have a devastating effect. The workplace is poisoned by shared guilt, suspicion, and secrecy (Daley, 1978; Maas, 1973). Nonconformists or whistle-blowers are usually subject to intense pressure to join in corruption. When peer pressure and isolation fail, threats and persecution are sometimes employed, including death threats. Police internal witnesses often have to receive protection and go into hiding until trials are completed. Some need to start whole new lives under witness protection.

When corruption is exposed it usually takes many "victims" among police, but also among politicians and lawyers who were parties to offenses. When these people are dismissed, disbarred, or imprisoned, their professional lives are ruined, liberty can be lost for a period, and families shamed and financially hurt. Police suicides following allegations of misconduct are a well-known fact, often reported in the media, although poorly documented (Barron, 2007). The general problem of corruption and the potential for corruption has many victims. Even when accused officers are acquitted, the process of investigation and trial is usually protracted and extremely stressful. A U.S. Department of Justice review into investigations into the 1992 Ruby Ridge shootings identified a nine-year process involving seven separate inquiries. The 2002 review found that the previous investigations and disciplinary outcomes were all deeply flawed (USDoJ, 2002).

Causes of Police Misconduct

Just as the forms of misconduct are diverse and complex, the causes of police misconduct are also diverse and complex, and scholars have produced different models and categories of causal factors. Most modern accounts are concerned with identifying causes other than individual moral failure. Personal moral failure is often a vital element in initial decisions to engage in corruption. However, the continuation or enlargement of corruption is then normally related to factors larger than the individual (Punch, 2003). This usually involves a combination of elements within the police organization—primarily inadequate accountability mechanisms—as well as outside, in the wider social and political realm. Any protracted or widespread corruption is therefore normally "systemic" within the organization. Part of this problem has been a state of management disbelief or denial concerning the intrinsic nature of corruption risks. The pervasiveness of the simplistic "bad apple" theory of individual moral failure meant police departments lacked infrastructure—properly resourced with committed staff—for dealing with information about corruption and operating preventive programs (Knapp, 1972; Newburn, 1999). The following section sets out a two-part explanation of police misconduct, based on the concepts of primary structural and cultural influences.

Structure

A structural—or "structural-functional"—perspective focuses on the nature of police work, or the "task environment," and the ways in which police are "structured" into larger social systems and institutional roles (e.g., as one element of the criminal justice system) (Bennett, 1984; Kappeler et al., 1998). From this perspective, primary corruption opportunities derive directly from the police law enforcement function. Police work involves frequent contact with criminals who are motivated to trade benefits for immunity from prosecution. This "economic" demand-and-supply scenario applies to any illegal behavior coming to police attention, and may result in corruption in limited forms with individuals acting opportunistically. The scenario has also led to acute problems of long-term corruption networks, particularly where there is a high demand for illegal commerce in "vice": drugs, liquor, prostitution, pornography, and gambling.

Historically, police protection rackets have frequently been a by-product of a political process in which minority lobby groups successfully influenced politicians to criminalize activities in demand from sections of the populace. Criminalization and subsequent corruption produced a "steady state," achieved when the lobbyists have their morality enshrined in law, consumers are able to satisfy their desires, suppliers make a living, politicians maintain their power, and police augment their income while keeping their political masters satisfied. The steady state is threatened from time to time if vice becomes too public and difficult questions are asked. The system therefore requires occasional adjustments in the form of token police raids or prosecutions, with some scapegoats among the suppliers. But, overall, the system can endure for many decades with limited maintenance.

An additional factor in this equation is that police work is necessarily highly dispersed, with limited management reach into the everyday tasks of frontline officers. Patrol officers and detectives typically enjoy very low levels of supervision and high levels of discretion that give them wide scope to bend or break laws and evade detection (Barker, 1983). In this regard, modern policing retains many of the features of frontier policing discussed earlier. Even when managers initiate reform, or are pressured to clean up a department, the task is often undermined by the inability to ensure genuine change at operational levels (Reuss-Ianni, 1983). The Knapp Inquiry famously identified an approximately 20-year cycle of scandal, reform, and decay. A major challenge, therefore, for the reform and professionalization of policing is to install accountability mechanisms and instill attitudes that will endure over the long term. A crucial element of this will be to counteract the traditional freedom from scrutiny enjoyed by operational police.

A structural approach also explains variations in police deviance related to different units and tasks. Police work is organized in a division of labor that is highly compartmentalized. Detective squads are notorious for process corruption because their work is focused on the detailed investigation and prosecution of crimes. Officers in specialist licensing or vice squads are more likely to engage in organized graft. Traffic officers often have limited opportunities for regular or serious graft, but are presented with numerous low-level misconduct opportunities, especially in terms of cash payments or harassment of citizens. Officers in drug squads and armed holdup squads frequently engage in the most lucrative forms of corruption through exposure to large quantities of cash and valuables.

Patrol officers are more likely to engage in a range of low-level forms of misconduct as their work is constantly shifting and episodic, usually restricted to a quick response to diverse incidents. There is some scope for theft from crime scenes, brutality, and some involvement with protection rackets. There is also scope for a wide range of other forms of unprofessional conduct and internal corruption such as work avoidance, incivility, discrimination, and benefit fraud. Patrol officers are also subject to more frequent provocations from persons who challenge their authority. Offenders often engage in highly provocative and dangerous actions such as spitting in the face of officers or attacking them with needles or other weapons (Prenzler & Sarre, 2009b). This aspect of the working environment tempts police to engage in preemptive violence or to use violence as a form of personal payback (Human Rights Watch, 1998; Mollen, 1994).

A structural perspective is also useful for developing a more complex understanding of process corruption and miscarriages of justice. Pressure to fabricate evidence comes from a number of sources, including political and community pressure to bring offenders to justice in a short space of time—particularly for more terrifying or repugnant crimes. The media often plays a particularly insidious role in this process. In the English miscarriages of justice cases in the 1970s, fears about IRA terrorism provided a major catalyst for breaches of human rights by police and prosecutors. Researchers in this field have identified a process by which detectives begin a case with open minds, but then quickly zero in on the most likely suspect. This shift engenders "tunnel vision." The investigators become preoccupied with making a quick case against the apparent best suspect (or suspects) and other leads are abandoned (Ransley, 2002).

Another structural factor that has influenced police procedural deviance over a long period has been the conflict between the adversarial justice system (especially in English-speaking countries) and the application of crime "clearance rates" as a police performance measure (Skolnick, 1994). Even where police are genuinely concerned with finding the right offender, the task of matching offenders to offenses sets police against the standards of the criminal courts. Corrupt process can be a direct response to police frustration with due process constraints, such as suspects' right to silence or the high standard of proof—beyond reasonable doubt—in criminal cases. Ironically, the system has provided something of an open door to police abuses by grossly overvaluing confessions (Punch, 2003). A further structural aspect of miscarriages of justice is the difficulty of the appeal process. Police who fabricate evidence have traditionally been protected by the many barriers to appeals. The barriers are partly legal, in the form of laws requiring substantive fresh evidence, or institutional, as in the absence of properly resourced standing commissions to reinvestigate questionable cases (Ransley, 2002).

Police brutality is also influenced by perceived or actual pressures for summary punishment—or "street justice"—on behalf of society (Mollen, 1994, p. 49). This is associated with cynicism about defendant safeguards and sentencing policies. Frustrated with the courts and public prosecutors, police simply subsume the roles of "judge, jury, and executioner" under the utilitarian principle of the greater good for society. This situation has given rise to the concept of the "Dirty Harry syndrome," glamorized in the character of a Hollywood screen detective who defies his supervisors and breaks the law to protect innocent citizens from predatory criminals (Pollock, 2007). It has also been argued that brutality follows from the fact that police are given an impossible task of controlling crimes caused by social factors such as unemployment and poverty (Scarman, 1986). Officers who feel powerless may be tempted to exceed their powers and use threats, harassment, and beatings to deter criminal behavior. The ultimate expression of this approach is police death squads.

Some attention has already been given to the political context of police work in relation to vice. Politicians are also often themselves part of the money chain in protection rackets. Alternatively, they can simply fail to exercise proper oversight of police—usually as part of a more arms length quid pro quo arrangement. Politicians will turn a blind eye to police deviance in return for police support and for police action against political enemies (Fitzgerald, 1989). Police unions have also been notoriously defensive of corrupt colleagues. They form a powerful political lobby willing to trade loyalty to politicians for freedom from interference.

Many of the factors listed above apply in other occupations. Members of security staff are subject to provocations and temptations to use excessive force. Procurement officers have numerous opportunities for kickbacks from preferred suppliers. Inspectors in areas such as health and safety may be offered bribes to overlook infringements. However, many of these corruption opportunities are limited. What is arguably unique about policing is the breadth of opportunities and pressures for misconduct that apply across the task environment (Wood, 1997).

Culture

The second main area of theory related to police misconduct concerns the concept of organizational culture (Crank, 1998; Kappeler et al., 1998). Culture refers to group identities, values, attitudes, beliefs, traditions, unwritten codes, symbols, rituals, and habits. The police occupational culture—or "subculture"—has been subject to an enormous amount of research. Secrecy and protective solidarity are central to this perspective—the so-called "blue wall" or "blue curtain" of silence. The 1994 New York City Mollen Inquiry devoted a large chapter to dissecting the relationship between culture and corruption. Twenty years after the Knapp reforms, Mollen found that the NYPD's internal accountability mechanisms had collapsed. Serious criminal behavior by police was entrenched in some sectors, protected by the blue wall:

> The code of silence and other attitudes of police officers that existed at the time of the Knapp Commission continue to nurture police corruption and impede efforts at corruption control. Scores of officers of every rank told the commission that the code of silence pervades the Department and influences the vast majority of honest and corrupt officers alike (1994, p. 51).

This sentiment is echoed repeatedly in the findings of inquiries and reviews all over the world. As the New South Wales Wood Commission found:

> One of the greatest obstacles identified by the Royal Commission has been the code of silence and solidarity in the face of any form of criticism of the Service or prospect of internal investigation. In some quarters this has been referred to as the brotherhood which supports those who close ranks and punishes viciously those who place duty first. It has become so powerful a feature of the police culture that it rarely requires express enunciation. Rather, it has been understood, accepted and blindly followed without regard to the harm to the Service it causes, or to the risks it creates for honest police (Wood, 1997, p. 134).

The culture of solidarity and cynicism provides important moral justifications for corruption—"techniques of neutralization" (Sykes & Matza, 1957)—and emotional rewards and reinforcements. Material rewards from corruption are justified as compensation for undervalued work. Victims of police abuses are characterized as deserving "social garbage." Poor role modeling by supervisors, and disinterest or even support, reinforces these attitudes. Solidarity extends to a seemingly chronic inability of police to dispassionately investigate and discipline their own members. Internal units set up to investigate complainants have typically served rather to deflect and bury complaints.

The traditional police subculture of support for corruption begins with recruitment and training that produces a narrow conformist type of officer (Prenzler, 2002). Traditionally in many countries, recruitment has been almost exclusively from among poorly educated males. In racially divided societies, police were often predominantly or exclusively white, contributing to an "us versus them" mentality. Training was often perfunctory, focused on law, fitness, and physical control techniques. The inevitable effect of this was that police developed a socially isolated "macho" culture that encouraged violence and supported disdain toward women and ethnic minorities.

However, fixing recruitment and training will not solve the larger problem. Survey research indicates that many recruits bring high moral standards with them to police work (partly as a result of rigorous selection). These standards rapidly deteriorate during academy training or on the job (Brown & Willis, 1985; Wortley & Homel, 1995). This is commonly seen as a reaction to dealing with some of the worst elements of society, but it is also widely attributed to on-the-job socialization (Alain & Grégoire, 2008; Brown & Willis, 1985; Mollen, 1994, p. 62). The concept of a police subculture includes the "slippery slope" theory of corruption. The theory is used in a number of ways—for example, to apply generally to all police when minor misconduct opens the way for more serious corruption. It is also applied to a socialization technique by which rookie officers are "inducted" into the informal system through peer pressure to accept gratuities, and then introduced gradually to more serious corruption (Sherman, 1977). Within a short time, personal moral standards are deeply compromised.

Many aspects of the traditional police culture are closely associated with structural-functional influences. For example, inaction by police in the Dutroux affair was related to the highly segmented organization of Belgian policing. Dutroux's criminal activities occurred across small police units that failed to communicate with each other. At the same time, the inquiry found that "[t]he police hierarchy on the whole encourages and maintains rivalries and tension between police services. … A central database is available to all police services, but the will and, above all, the necessary culture are lacking to exchange information" (Landuyt & T'Serclaes, 1997, pp. 110, 120).

Another example of structural-functional influences on culture is the way the need for confidentiality to protect sensitive operations translates into habits of protective secrecy. A further example is the way the camaraderie deriving from the stress and danger of police work translates into the covering up of corruption. The problem occurs when positive values, required for effective policing, mutate into secrecy and defensiveness. The common problem of racism is similarly closely related to conflict between police and minority groups in the arena of street crime—a structural conflict that has its origins in larger social forces. However, brutality and discriminatory policing also follow from the cultural dimension of biased recruitment, the pervasiveness of racist and sexist jokes and stereotypes, and inadequate management support for cultural sensitivity.

As previously noted, many aspects of policing can be found in other occupations. In regard to the issue of organizational culture, other government departments, businesses, and even charities have been seen to deteriorate into dysfunctional and abusive practices and supporting values, including protective solidarity. Nonetheless, commissions of inquiry have claimed that organizational solidarity has taken on a particularly acute and entrenched form in policing (e.g., Wood, 1997, p. 135). Whatever the case, it is clear that policing is highly prone to the development of undesirable cultural traits that encourage or even require corruption as "normal" practice.

Conclusion

Policing is only one occupation prone to corruption and misconduct, but it is possibly unique in the variety of opportunities, temptations, and pressures that generate widespread deviance. Unfortunately, this means that a powerful, complex, and expensive prevention system needs to be instituted and maintained over the long term. Partial or short-term interventions will not do the job because corruption will quickly resurface. An effective integrity system begins with the removal of ambiguity about the type of behavior that is tolerated or expected, through a clear articulation of ethical standards. This is the topic of the next chapter—"Setting Standards."

Setting Standards

3

Corruption and misconduct entail breaches of ethical standards. The previous chapters described different types of abuses without going into detail about the standards broken in the process. The current chapter focuses on these standards, and takes a more positive approach to the issue of police integrity by describing best practice in different areas of decision making. A written description of ethical standards and communication of those standards to police is a key component of a comprehensive integrity system. At a practical level, police cannot be expected to comply with ethical requirements if they do know what they are. Additionally, it is simply unfair to expect officers to follow rules they have not learned. Clear detailed standards should also help identify and stop management hypocrisy in issues of ethical leadership and discipline.

The current chapter begins by emphasizing the importance of police ethics with reference to the value of the police role in society, as well as emphasizing the importance of police political legitimacy. It then outlines the role of codes of conduct, including their practical role in training and discipline. The final part of the chapter uses the United Nations (UN) *Code of Conduct for Law Enforcement Officials* and the *Law Enforcement Code of Ethics* of the International Association of Chiefs of Police (IACP) to elaborate key universal standards for ethical policing. These are related to the areas of discretion, due process, torture, graft, loyalty and whistle-blowing, gratuities, confidentiality, force, cooperation between policing agencies, custody, striking and moonlighting, and personal conduct.

The Importance of Police Ethics

Police ethics are important because policing is important. The police role is typically summarized as preventing crime, enforcing the law, maintaining order, and providing emergency assistance. The creation of the New Police in London in 1829 and the spread of the professional model shifted law enforcement and crime prevention from a "potluck" affair for ordinary citizens to a universal service delivery model. Echoing the original aspirational statements of the New Police, the International Association of Chiefs of Police describes the police role in terms of the following personal oath of an officer:

As a law enforcement officer, my fundamental duty is to serve the community; to safeguard lives and property; to protect the innocent against deception, the weak against oppression or intimidation and the peaceful against violence or disorder; and to respect the constitutional rights of all to liberty, equality and justice (IACP, 2002, p. 35).

This means that police exist to protect people from crime: from murder, assault, sexual assault, robbery, theft, fraud, and many other types of threats to people's well-being and property. One could hardly think of a more valuable task—one that must surely rate as high as those of medicine and the military defense of a nation. Police are also there to minimize people's fear of crime and the restrictive and stressful effects that can have. Police are therefore an essential institution in the realization of fundamental human values of freedom, security, equality, and justice. In modern policing systems ordinary persons can pick up the phone and have a police officer rush to their location to provide assistance. The speed and quality of responses will vary depending on numerous factors, but the basic service is in place as a mainstay of public safety. From a historical perspective, this is an extraordinarily positive addition to civilization. In addition to crime prevention and intervening to stop the continuation of a criminal event, police are also essential to the realization of justice after a crime has been committed in helping fulfill the social demand that offenders be brought to trial and subjected to community sanctions.

Police Powers

Police ethics are also important because of police powers and their potential negative effects. Police are rightly called "the gatekeepers of the criminal justice system" in that most prosecutions arise from their activities and discretionary decisions. There is therefore an enormous amount at stake for any citizen confronted with the possibility of a police arrest decision—ranging from inconvenience and embarrassment, to a fine, loss of employment, and short- and long-term jail time, and even to execution in some jurisdictions. Police also have broad powers to protect citizens or curtail their activities without having to resort to arrest.

To perform policing functions, especially those that involve restraint of citizens and use of force, police use a variety of legal powers. These powers are drawn historically from the general powers of all citizens to arrest offenders and to use force to protect people and property (depending on factors such as the severity of the offense or threat). Police are merely delegated a task that can be undertaken by, or was in fact the obligation, of all citizens. What distinguishes police from ordinary citizens in part is that police are employed and trained to enforce the law. They are also equipped with a range of weaponry. Legislators in most jurisdictions have also passed specific laws giving powers to police above those of ordinary citizens. These include such things as authority to arrest on suspicion, the capacity to hold people without charge for limited periods, the authority to demand a person's name and address, "move-on" powers, and the authority to disperse crowds or to apply to install a listening device or conduct a search (Prenzler & Sarre, 2009b). Police are also generally accorded higher levels of protection against mistakes in their work. Their actions therefore have direct impacts on the freedoms and the experiences of justice of numerous stakeholders, including suspects, victims of crime, witnesses, and the general public. As with any delegated authority there is always a potential for misuse that needs to be countered by adequate accountability mechanisms.

Police Legitimacy

Police ethics are inextricably linked to police legitimacy. Unethical policing is illegitimate policing, but the institution of policing itself requires legitimacy. Police legitimacy derives from the legitimacy of the whole criminal justice system, whose core power is the capacity to detain, try, and sanction individuals. More broadly, the system's legitimacy—or "authority"—entails an "entitlement to be obeyed" (Pollock, 2007, p. 193). This in turn derives from the authority of the state. The main modern justification for political force was developed by Enlightenment philosophers and is termed "social contract theory." It argues that

> [t]he state of nature is a "war of all against all" and, thus, individuals give up their liberty to aggress against others in return for safety ... law is a contract— each individual gives up some liberties and, in return, is protected from others who have their liberties restricted as well (Pollock, 2007, p. 132).

This is the moral and philosophical basis of democratic government and law. Policing, theoretically, is a product of the will of the people. Police accountability is always ultimately to the people, and police ethical standards are about ensuring the highest quality of *democratic policing*. (Some added pressure in that regard comes from the fact that, as employees of the state, police wages are derived from money compulsorily acquired from citizens through the tax system.)

This is the ideal political arrangement for policing and the justice system. In practice, democratic lawmaking in many countries is deeply flawed. A variety of factors are responsible for this, but the main ones are:

- The delegation of authority to parliamentary representatives who have their own personal agendas;

- Distortions of the principle of "one vote one value," for example, through unequally sized electorates and single-member geographically based electorates that do not provide for overall proportional representation of voters;
- The discipline of political party machines that requires representatives vote along party, not popular, lines; and
- Secrecy in government, where government information and decision-making processes are concealed from voters.

A prime example of electoral distortion occurred in the U.S. presidential election in the year 2000, under a system in which popular votes are mediated through an "electoral college" (FEC, 2001). The "winner" in the election received 50,456,002 popular votes or 47.87%. The runner-up received 50,999,897 votes or 48.38%! Thus, in theory, from 2000 to 2004, the federal administration, including the Justice Department and federal policing services, were "illegitimate."

Police legitimacy is also called into question by social inequality There is a left-wing critique of policing in mixed capitalist economies which argues that the secret primary function of police is as a "reserve army" of ruling elites. The first loyalty of police is not to protect "the people," but to protect the power and interests of the ruling class. The reserve function is activated when strikes, popular riots, and revolutionary action threaten the property and power of the governing elites in business and government. Even on a day-to-day basis the equality principle of criminal law and policing disproportionately benefits the rich because they have more property—property "stolen" from exploited workers. There is also an argument that under traditional policing systems state resources are directed "downstream," away from the social causes of crime, so that police effectively are engaged in persecution of the poor and marginalized citizens who are pressured into crime by their circumstances (White, 1998).

Police Legitimacy and Ethical Policing in Unequal or Nondemocratic Societies

Can we say that police in a democracy, like Canada or India, are "legitimate" and that police in a dictatorship, like China or Saudi Arabia, are "illegitimate"? The answer is more complicated than a simple "yes" or "no," and involves the issue of degrees and nuances of legitimacy. As we have seen, electoral systems and political accountability are distorted in all sorts of overt and covert ways in modern democracies. It is rare or impossible to find a parliament, a system of laws and punishments, and a police force that are the product of the equal say and equal votes of all members of a community. However, this does not mean that we should automatically abandon faith in police. Just as there are degrees of distortion, so are there degrees of legitimacy.

Let's consider this issue by going back to the left-wing critique of policing and law enforcement. It is true that low social capital and disadvantaged social locations are key factors in crime causation, and that the majority of people convicted in the criminal justice system are from the lower classes (Hayes & Prenzler, 2007). At the same time, in prosperous welfare states, where there is a cushioning of economic need, personal psychological motives and opportunity factors are also important in crime causation (Cornish & Clarke, 1986; Gabor, 1994). Consequently, different types of deterrence-oriented and incapacitative strategies involving police remain important for preventing crime. Furthermore, while police do inevitably act as guardians of ruling class property and power, they are also engaged in one of the most egalitarian and direct forms of democracy by responding to calls for assistance regardless of the status of the caller.

Michael Buerger (1998) picks up on these contrary tendencies and makes an important argument about (a) the potential variability of police legitimacy as a function of police decision making, and (b) a standard for judging police legitimacy. Drawing on the social contract theory, he argues that "police authority is weakest when officers act on their own initiative, and strongest when they act on behalf of citizens requesting assistance" (Buerger, 1998, p. 93). This makes the response to "calls for service" a key yardstick of egalitarian democratic policing. Given that crime reports typically include the address of the caller and some personal details such as gender, the extent to which policing reflects community diversity and addresses community needs can be fairly accurately mapped—and public surveys can also be used to evaluate police responsiveness. There is an important caveat that needs to be applied to Buerger's theory. We know that many crime victims, such as victims of child abuse or domestic violence, are intimidated into silence. Egalitarian policing therefore also requires police to show initiative in intervening in crimes in certain circumstances.

A major challenge for police integrity systems concerns "exporting" ethical standards from more advanced democracies to emerging or developing democracies. This raises the issue of "cultural fit" in societies where there are powerful traditions of institutionalized graft, social obligation, and gift giving of the type described in the Indian study by Jauregui (2007) in Chapter 1. Can we set down principles of ethical policing that apply everywhere in the world? Or is this a form of cultural imperialism? A culturally tolerant attitude might accept minor graft as a widespread and harmless custom in many socities. However, an important distinction needs to be made here between cultural traditions that are essentially harmless and those that are discriminatory, patriarchal, and unjust. In the case of police gratuities, for example, these are rarely harmless, but entail abuse of position and biased policing that should not be disguised behind euphemisims of "cultural traditions." This is a key finding of Jauregui's study: that "gratuities" were extortionate and intrinsic to the corruption of the whole policing system. The same can be said about the question of social obligations: customs that require police to defer to relatives, friends, or prominent persons always entail discrimination against other groups.

Where cultural sensitivity is required is not in compromising standards in principle, but in the pace of implementation of standards, the level of punitiveness associated with breaches, the amount of attention given to ethical standards in training, and the degree of education required of the wider community. In a report commissioned by the U.S. Department of Justice, *Democratizing the Police Abroad: What to Do and How to Do It*, David Bayley identified four basic norms that need to be pursued in order for police anywhere to be genuinely accountable and "democratic":

1. Police must give top operational priority to servicing the needs of individual citizens and private groups.
2. Police must be accountable to the law rather than to the government.
3. Police must protect human rights, especially those that are required for the sort of unfettered political activity that is the hallmark of democracy.
4. Police must be transparent in their activities (Bayley, 2001, pp. 13-14).

Bayley also argues, however, that accountable policing entails responsiveness to local needs and conditions. Police need to be sensitive to local customs, while actively educating their consituency in principles such as the avoidance of favoritism. There can be little doubt over the need for these norms and standards. The challenge lies in putting them into practice.

The challenge is particularly fraught with difficulty for honest police in dictatorships. In this situation officers have to do what they can to serve the community equally, without compromising ethical standards in investigations and by depoliticizing their role as much as possible. They need to create as many direct lines of communication as they can with ordinary citizens and use what discretion they have to prioritize the needs of these citizens. Inevitably they will be faced with difficult decisions about defying or subverting orders that breach international conduct standards when these actions might put them at risk for being dismissed or being persecuted themselves. In many cases it may simply be impossible to practice ethical policing. In such cases, persons with ethical standards probably need to seek employment in less sensitive and less compromised fields.

Constabulary Independence and the Separation of Powers

"Constabulary Independence" and "the separation of powers" are key principles of ethical policing designed to stop politicization. Constabulary independence refers to the freedom of police to enforce the law as they feel is appropriate, without directions in specific cases from politicians or senior police. It works with the idea of the separation of powers, which is a division of labor designed to prevent one person or group from holding a monopoly of power in the criminal justice system—in effect, becoming "judge, jury, and executioner." Under the separation of powers, the courts test the quality of evidence presented by the police, and are necessarily in a partially adversarial relationship with them. This is essential to prevent miscarriages of justice that might arise from police bias or corruption. Similarly, corrective services apply penalties; police and t,he courts do not. Judges and corrective services officials do not normally investigate crimes. Some hypothetical examples of breaches of the separation of powers involving police include the following (Prenzler & Sarre, 2009a, pp. 262-263):

1. A senior politician in a low crime, but marginal, electorate tells the police chief to increase police numbers ahead of an election because a survey shows people want more police.
2. A juror on a criminal case and a detective giving evidence in that case keep secret a personal relationship that might influence the juror to favor the prosecution.
3. A judge secretly attempts to influence a parliamentary committee appointing a new police commissioner.

The Role of Codes of Ethics

What constitutes corruption and misconduct is normally defined in criminal law and in police administration and police powers legislation. Ethics is usually considered as something broader, informing the direction of the law and operating more as "the spirit" rather than "the letter" of the law. Over time, police have refined professional codes of ethics to more clearly define expected behaviors. There is now a strong consensus at the official level about core principles that should direct and constrain police decision making. Two of the best expressions of this consensus are the *Law Enforcement Code of Conduct*, developed by the International Association of Chiefs of Police (IACP, 2002), and the United Nations *Code of Conduct for Law Enforcement Officials* (UN, 1979). These codes address specific issues or areas of ethical decision making, and are developed in the following sections.

Code positions, and the rationale behind them, can be usefully built into police preservice and in-service training (Chapter 5). But they also have value when they are enforceable as part of the complaints and discipline system. The clearer the standards and the greater the number of examples, the more police can be confident about how to behave when faced with ethical dilemmas. Similarly, the clearer the code, the more confident decision makers on disciplinary panels should be when evaluating officer conduct once the facts have been ascertained. A code of conduct should therefore be much more than a set of ideals. It should be a very clear set of standards, applied in a very practical way, as part of the day-to-day operations of a complaints and discipline system. The code should also be comprehensive in covering all areas of police ethical decision making and areas of public concern, including the separation of powers, gratuities, the management of demonstrations, hot pursuit policies, and the use of discretion. Codes should also be enforceable; otherwise, they will most likely end up as little more than wishful thinking. The weighting of different code provisions can also be communicated through links to a disciplinary matrix of offenses and sanctions (Chapter 6).

Although codes are generally seen as universal and timeless, they can require maintenance and some updating. A recent example, discussed below, involves what constitutes torture in a police interrogation. The post-9/11 War on Terror has brought this to attention. Other issues may involve the deployment of new use-of-force technologies, such as stun guns and capsicum spray, or be triggered by particular problems, such as deaths in custody or injuries from high-speed pursuits. A standing ethics or professional standards board, with community representation, should monitor the relevance of police ethical standards as they relate to current social issues and changing values, seeking improvements where necessary (HMIC, 1999b, p. 110). This work can be enhanced through surveys of police, the public, and key stakeholders.

Discretion

The most important of the general principles in police codes is the requirement to enforce the law and assist the public equitably, without discrimination. In the words of the IACP code, the first duty is impartiality:

> A police officer shall perform all duties impartially, without favor or affection or ill will and without regard to status, sex, race, religion, political belief or aspiration. All citizens will be treated equally with courtesy, consideration and dignity. Officers will never allow personal feelings, animosities or friendships to influence official conduct (2002, p. 36).

Discretion does, nonetheless, present difficult choices for police. Resource limitations and competing demands mean police must prioritize responses —to put additional resources into cold cases, for example, or focus on fresh cases, or to resource street crime over white-collar crime or vice versa. Frontline police also have dilemmas of discretion. They normally possess considerable scope across a discretion continuum from full enforcement to partial enforcement to issuing warnings to welfare responses to ignoring offenses. They frequently need to make on-the-spot decisions about what is most expedient or in the public interest. This is particularly applicable where offenders are themselves victims of abuse or addictions. In some of these cases a welfare-oriented response, such as connecting offenders to welfare services, might be more appropriate and justifiable from a public interest perspective than arrest. What must be kept in mind is that the more policing is biased in favor of one group, or the more police abuse their position to benefit themselves, the less legitimate and more harmful they become.

Scenarios about police discretion can involve scores of variations (see Pollock, 2007). Some of the principles identified above that should guide the exercise of discretion in different situations are developed further in the IACP code:

> A police officer will use responsibly the discretion vested in his position and exercise it within the law. The principle of reasonableness will guide the officer's determinations, and the officer will consider all surrounding circumstances in determining whether any legal action shall be taken.
>
> Consistent and wise use of discretion, based on professional policing competence, will do much to preserve good relationships and retain the confidence of the public. There can be difficulty in choosing between conflicting courses of action. It is important to remember that a timely word of advice rather than arrest—which may be correct in appropriate circumstances—can be a more effective means of achieving a desired end (2002, p. 36).

Due Process, Including Deception and Entrapment

This is perhaps the best-known ethical dilemma for police and one that provides a staple plot element in police dramas. The "Dirty Harry syndrome" or "noble cause corruption" occurs when police are tempted to use illegal or ethically questionable means to obtain justice, such as pressuring a suspect to confess or misrepresenting their powers to coerce people into compliance (Pollock, 2007). "Formalist ethics" generally prohibit all such actions because coercion and deception, in this view, cannot be made into precedents for normal human relations. People may be willing to apply it to others but don't want it applied to them. "Consequentialists," on the other hand, are likely to argue that the higher goals of justice and public safety justify violations of the rules, including threats and physical pressure, in some cases, and may justify legalized forms of undercover operations.

Generally, though, there is a consensus among police ethicists that the gains that might be achieved through illegal means—finding the location of a serious criminal by torturing an accomplice, for example—are not worth the miscarriages of justice that can result from such actions (Kleinig, 2008). This view is elaborated in the IACP code. Article 4, "Utilization of Proper Means to Gain Proper Ends," states unequivocally that

> [t]he law enforcement officer shall be mindful of his responsibility to pay strict heed to the selection of means in discharging the duties of his office. Violations of law or disregard for public safety and property on the part of an officer are intrinsically wrong; they are self-defeating in that they instill in the public mind a like disposition. The employment of illegal means, no matter how worthy the end, is certain to encourage disrespect for the law and its officers. If the law is to be honored, it must first be honored by those who enforce it (2002, p. 38).

Torture

Torture is a variant of due process violations because in a law enforcement setting it normally involves the infliction of pain to obtain evidence. (It also has application in use-of-force scenarios related to rescue.) The UN position is particularly important here in relation to the post-9/11 War on Terror, given controversies over the use of torture by security agencies when interrogating terror suspects. One particularly valuable aspect of the UN code is that it explicitly directs all agencies involved in any sort of policing, including "military authorities" or "state security forces" (Article 1), to abstain from torture. In contrast to efforts by some authorities to justify torture on the basis of the threat posed by terrorism, the UN code is unambiguous about rejecting this, as shown in Sidebar 3.1. This black and white position is adopted because of the problem of the "slippery slope" or precedence: A minor violation or an

Sidebar 3.1: United Nations Code on Torture—Article 5

"No law enforcement official may inflict, instigate or tolerate any act of torture or other cruel, inhuman or degrading treatment or punishment, nor may any law enforcement official invoke superior orders or exceptional circumstances such as a state of war or a threat of war, a threat to national security, internal political instability or any other public emergency as a justification of torture or other cruel, inhuman or degrading treatment or punishment.

Commentary:

(a) This prohibition derives from the Declaration on the Protection of All Persons from Being Subjected to Torture and Other Cruel, Inhuman or Degrading Treatment or Punishment, adopted by the General Assembly ...

(b) The Declaration defines torture as follows:

' ... torture means any act by which severe pain or suffering, whether physical or mental, is intentionally inflicted by or at the instigation of a public official on a person for such purposes as obtaining from him or a third person information or confession, punishing him for an act he has committed or is suspected of having committed, or intimidating him or other persons. It does not include pain or suffering arising only from, inherent in or incidental to, lawful sanctions to the extent consistent with the Standard Minimum Rules for the Treatment of Prisoners'" (UN, 1979, pp. 2-3).

exceptional case creates a justification for further violations until the rule becomes meaningless.

Some police ethicists, such as John Kleinig (2008, p. 42ff) have recognized a problem with the term "severe pain." The section needs to be amended by deleting "severe," as the current terminology can be used to justify quite painful and distressing interrogation methods. For example, "extraordinary rendition" techniques have been used with impunity by CIA affiliates in the War on Terror, including sleep deprivation, hypothermia, and near drowning ("waterboarding") (Human Rights Watch, 2007, p. 531ff).

Some ethicists, like Kleinig, recognize there might be certain extreme circumstances where a significant evil might be averted by torture—to intervene in a "ticking bomb" scenario, for example. Kleinig's answer is that there may be circumstances where a degree of flexibility about torture is justifiable, but that the danger of a rationalization of torture means that law enforcement authorities should never accept the option as an "advance directive" (2008, p. 46).

Graft

A police officer may be offered money or other benefits with the explicit intention that the officer will not prosecute the offender who makes the offer. This is clearly a bribe. Acceptance would be a criminal act. But even a well-intentioned police officer may be tempted if the offense seems minor (keeping a hotel open past the prescribed closing time, for example) and the officer feels he or she is deserving (he or she may feel underpaid and have a large family to support). In such cases there is a basic conflict between a formalist duty to the law and a consequentialist concept of relative benefits and harms to different people. Police ethical codes, however, respond to this issue by simply and unequivocally affirming that any kind of bribery entails a breach of duty and is therefore entirely unacceptable.

Article 7(b) of the UN code also emphasizes how the rejection of corruption is something that is rightly expected of police regardless of the law in their jurisdiction. In other words, a legal system that allows official corruption does not provide a moral excuse:

> While the definition of corruption must be subject to national law, it should be understood to encompass the commission or omission of an act in the performance of or in connection with one's duties, in response to gifts, promises or incentives demanded or accepted, or the wrongful receipt of these once the act has been committed or omitted (1979, p. 4).

Article 7 also asserts that officers should not only refuse to engage in corruption but "shall also rigorously oppose and combat all such acts." This shifts the ethical position from a somewhat passive position of nonparticipation to one requiring active involvement in anticorruption to the point of taking the initiative in anticorruption efforts. This position underlies the position on whistle-blowing in the next section.

Loyalty and Whistle-Blowing

As we have seen, the danger and stress of police work make solidarity an important part of the coping mechanisms of police. But solidarity can easily become a cloak of silence and secrecy behind which corruption flourishes. Police who witness misconduct then become torn between their duty to reveal the truth and help stop corruption, and group pressures to keep silent. The latter pressures can be extremely intense, including octracism, bullying, and even death threats. However, the importance of police integrity and the difficulties of detecting integrity make it essential that police make disclosures about observed or suspected misconduct, and this has also become a basic ethical position, as in Article 8 of the UN code shown in Sidebar 3.2.

Sidebar 3.2: United Nations Code on Loyalty and Whistle-Blowing

"Law enforcement officials who have reason to believe that a violation of the present Code has occurred or is about to occur shall report the matter to their superior authorities and, where necessary, to other appropriate authorities or organs vested with reviewing or remedial power."

Commentary:

(b) The article seeks to preserve the balance between the need for internal discipline of the agency on which public safety is largely dependent, on the one hand, and the need for dealing with violations of basic human rights, on the other. Law enforcement officials shall report violations within the chain of command and take other lawful action outside the chain of command only when no other remedies are available or effective. It is understood that law enforcement officials shall not suffer administrative or other penalties because they have reported that a violation of this Code has occurred or is about to occur.

(c) The term 'appropriate authorities or organs vested with reviewing or remedial power' refers to any authority or organ existing under national law, whether internal to the law enforcement agency or independent thereof, with statutory, customary or other power to review grievances and complaints arising out of violations within the purview of this Code.

(d) In some countries, the mass media may be regarded as performing complaint review functions similar to those described in subparagraph (c) above. Law enforcement officials may, therefore, be justified if, as a last resort and in accordance with the laws and customs of their own countries and with the provisions of article 4 of the present Code, they bring violations to the attention of public opinion through the mass media" (UN, 1979, p. 4).

It is significant that the code identifies alternative avenues for disclosures when police do not trust internal channels. One related issue that is not addressed is that of self-identification. In cases where police feel particularly threatened as a result of coming forward there may be a case for them making anonymous disclosures.

Gratuities

Gratuities have already been touched on in this chapter, but some elaboration of the issue is important. It is generally acknowledged that gratuities represent something of a gray area for police ethics. A gratuity is a gift, usually of a minor nature, offered to a police officer where there is no direct communication of an expected return favor. A typical example is where a police officer may be offered a discount meal by a café owner in a situation where the intentions of the person offering the benefit may be unclear. The intention might simply be to express appreciation for the fact police do a difficult job, or it might entail the unspoken expectation that police will overlook offenses by the café owner or provide better security by frequenting the café to obtain the discount. Ethically, the idea of gratitude is used to justify the arrangement. This type of arrangement in relation to hamburger and doughnut outlets has received a great deal of attention in popular culure and sullied the police image. Over time, small gratuities can add up to many thousands of dollars in value.

The research evidence shows very clearly that any standing offer of gratuities is far from innocent. The intention is usually to obtain cheap security in violation of the principle of equitable service. One study in the United States found that stores offering gratuities did receive a disproportionate, if limited, amount of police presence (Wells & DeLeon-Granados, 1998). An Australian survey of police officers found that the majority—57%—were willing to ignore a serious traffic violation in favor of persons who had provided gratuities, in direct defiance of statutory obligations and departmental policy (Macintyre & Prenzler, 1999).

A number of opinion surveys also show that the public sees gratuities as an exploitation of a public service position that can skew the police presence and lead to favorable treatment of gift givers. People are generally opposed to police receiving all but the most minor and *incidental* gratuities, such as a glass of water or cup of coffee outside a commercial arrangement (Jones, 1997; Prenzler & Mackay, 1995; Sigler & Dees, 1988). The prohibition should extend to all the possible "perks" police can be involved in, including free parking, free travel on public transport, and free entry to nightclubs. One way to equalize responsibility in this area is to prohibit the public from offering police gratuities, as well as prohibiting police from accepting them.

A related area concerns corporate gifts. Proposed donations to police or sponsorhsips from the corporate sector need to be assessed in terms of public perceptions and possible unfair obligations, with strict written guidelines and conditions. Decisions need to be made at a high level and recorded in detail. Gifts related to tendering processes, however, should be totally prohibited. Police are often major purchasers of private sector products, such as motor vehicles, weapons, and computers (Ayling &

Grabosky, 2006). It is essential here that common private sector practices of tenderers "wining and dining" potential clients and offering gifts, such as corporate ticket boxes at sporting stadiums and theater productions, are completely prohibited. These are transparently designed to influence purchasers by means outside objective business and public interest criteria. The IACP position in Article 9 on gifts and favors is therefore justifiably strict:

> The law enforcement officer ... shall ... guard against placing himself in a position in which any person can expect special consideration or in which the public can reasonably assume that special consideration is being given. Thus, he should be firm in refusing gifts, favors, or gratuities, large or small, which can, in the public mind, be interpreted as capable of influencing his judgment in the discharge of his duties (2002, p. 39).

Confidentiality

Confidentiality is another area where police may be tempted to bend the rules. An inquiry by a police officer about a neighbor who seems suspicious, or an inquiry from a friend about their child's teacher, may seem to be justified from the point of view of safety. However, access to criminal records or other data, such as a person's residential address, constitutes a breach of privacy and can have serious adverse consequences as a result of the misuse of that information, such as for personal revenge or harassment. The commentary on Article 4 of the UN code states that

> [l]aw enforcement officials obtain information which may relate to private lives or be potentially harmful to the interests, and especially the reputation, of others. Great care should be exercised in safeguarding and using such information, which should be disclosed only in the performance of duty or to serve the needs of justice. Any disclosure of such information for other purposes is wholly improper (1979, p. 2).

Chapter 8 of this book, "System Controls and Risk Management," includes a section on procedures for putting these code positions into practice through information security protocols.

Force

Police may be required to apply forms of physical restraint to apprehend offenders, to protect people, or to affect lawful directions. Use of force covers a wide range of options across a scale of severity, including shouting, pushing, holding, tackling, applying capsicum spray, using a stun gun, hitting with a baton, engaging in a high-speed vehicle pursuit, and shooting a person. If insufficient force is used, offenders can escape justice, and victims of crime or police can be injured or killed. But it is also easy to use too much force, also leading to injury or death. The split second nature of many of these decisions makes them even more acute. The IACP code emphasizes that force should be used only as a last resort:

> A police officer will never employ unnecessary force or violence and will use only such force in the discharge of duty as is reasonable in all circumstances.

> The use of force should be used only with the greatest restraint and only after discussion, negotiation and persuasion have been found to be inappropriate or ineffective. While the use of force is occasionally unavoidable, every police officer will refrain from unnecessary infliction of pain or suffering and will never engage in cruel, degrading or inhuman treatment of any person (2002, pp. 36-37).

Article 3 of the UN code, in Sidebar 3.3, emphasizes that this principle surpasses whatever legal provisions apply.

Sidebar 3.3: United Nations Code on Use of Force

"Law enforcement officials may use force only when strictly necessary and to the extent required for the performance of their duty."

Commentary:

(a) This provision emphasizes that the use of force by law enforcement officials should be exceptional; while it implies that law enforcement officials may be authorized to use force as is reasonably necessary under the circumstances for the prevention of crime or in effecting or assisting in the lawful arrest of offenders or suspected offenders, no force going beyond that may be used.

(b) National law ordinarily restricts the use of force by law enforcement officials in accordance with a principle of proportionality. It is to be understood that such national principles of proportionality are to be respected in the interpretation of this provision. In no case should this provision be interpreted to authorize the use of force which is disproportionate to the legitimate objective to be achieved.

(c) The use of firearms is considered an extreme measure. Every effort should be made to exclude the use of firearms, especially against children. In general, firearms should not be used except when a suspected offender offers armed resistance or otherwise jeopardizes the lives of others and less extreme measures are not sufficient to restrain or apprehend the suspected offender. In every instance in which a firearm is discharged, a report should be made promptly to the competent authorities" (UN, 1979, p. 2).

The principle of minimum force obliges police to carefully match the level of force they use to the level of threat, and the principle has wide implications. For example, it has very practical implications for the planning and management of demonstrations. Police have a duty to allow citizens to express their opinions in public protests but not to stand by while people are hurt, legitimate activities are disrupted, and property is damaged. At the same time, police should refrain from extreme actions to disperse unruly mobs, such as bashings, whippings, shootings, and letting dogs loose on demonstrators. Chapter 8 of this book, "System Controls and Risk Management," also includes a section on procedures for balancing the right to protest with public safety measures.

Cooperation Between Policing Agencies

One feature of modern policing with important implications for good police practices is the proliferation of agencies involved in law enforcement. This phenomenon has occurred partly in response to the lack of expertise in conventional police forces—in fighting sophisticated economic crimes, for example. But the existence of multiple agencies can exacerbate jealousies and conflicts over who has jurisdiction or who is in command in different crime cases, or it can produce "buck passing" where no agency wants to take responsibility. Lack of cooperation can mean crimes remain unsolved and criminals remain free to commit further offenses. Hence, the IACP code of conduct states that "[p]olice officers will cooperate with all legally authorized agencies and their representatives in the pursuit of justice. ... It is imperative that a police officer assist colleagues fully and completely with respect and consideration at all times" (2002, p. 37).

The diversification of policing agencies has also involved significant growth in "private policing." Private security services operate on fundamentally different principles from public police, with the private sector focused on selective services to owners and clients. However, the traditional enmity between public and private police needs to be overcome in the public interest. Cooperation can occur in areas such as intelligence sharing. But, again, police need to guard against favoring one private security firm and its clients over others. The IACP code clearly sets out the general spirit under which cooperation between government agencies should occur, and some specific controls. These also have application to relations with private security:

> The law enforcement officer shall cooperate fully with other public officials in the discharge of authorized duties, regardless of party affiliation or personal prejudice. He shall be meticulous, however, in assuring himself of the propriety, under the law, of such actions and shall guard against the use of his office or person, whether knowingly or unknowingly, in any improper or illegal action. In any situation open to question, he shall seek authority from his superior officer, giving him a full report of the proposed service or action (2002, p. 38).

Custody Requirements

The UN code also emphasizes the importance of police providing adequate facilities and care for persons in their custody. This is an area where police can be tempted to act negligently—denying food, drink, or other basic comforts and medical attention to suspects in their care. The worst outcome of this is the phenomenon of deaths in police custody, especially the problem of indigenous deaths in countries with postcolonial societies. Article 6 states that "[l]aw enforcement officials shall ensure the full protection of the health of persons in their custody and, in particular, shall take immediate action to secure medical attention whenever required" (UN, 1979, p. 4). The article also stresses the importance of police deferring to the judgment of health professionals on medical care issues.

Striking and Moonlighting

There are a number of other areas where police face ethical issues and need to follow ethical guidelines. Going on strike is one that is not addressed in the two codes covered in this chapter. Strikes may entail a conflict between leveraging a legitimate industrial demand versus exposing the public to danger. Riots and looting have been triggered by police strikes. In general, negotiation should always be a first option, with an escalation of industrial action only where it is deemed absolutely necessary in support of reasonable demands. The principle of the public interest should, nonetheless, prevail.

"Moonlighting"—taking a second job—is also not addressed in the codes. Police may legitimately wish to improve their income by working in areas such as private security. But this may present conflicts of interest in the form of temptation to use confidential information or exercise police powers when working in a private capacity. Secondary employment needs to be approved by management. Guidelines must require evidence of an absence of conflicts of interest or any potential for secondary employment to interfere with an officer's commitment to their police job.

Personal Conduct

Should police be subject to a higher standard of personal conduct as custodians of the law and role models to the community? For example, should police officers who are caught committing serious traffic offenses off duty be dismissed from their employment? A formalist notion of equal justice would say no. But the argument that police hold a special position in the community is used to justify additional sanctions, including dismissal for actions deemed to bring the profession into disrepute. Under "private life," the IACP emphasizes that

> [p]olice officers will behave in a manner that does not bring discredit to their agencies or themselves. A police officer's character and conduct while off duty must always be exemplary, thus maintaining a position of respect in the community in which he or she lives and serves. The officer's personal behavior must be beyond reproach (2002, p. 37).

Conclusion

This chapter reviewed the main areas of ethical decision making related to police misconduct and integrity, and set out the primary standards using two internationally recognized codes, as well as suggesting areas where additions and refinements are required. Specifying and communicating ethical standards is a key component of a state-of-the-art integrity system. Codes make for useful learning devices when coupled with scenarios and simulations in training programs (chapter 5). They also provide a useful yardstick for measuring police attitudes toward misconduct, as discussed in the next chapter.

Measuring Misconduct and Integrity

4

The previous chapters referred, often indirectly, to the mechanisms through which police misconduct has been revealed. The current chapter looks more closely at these diverse sources and how they can be utilized most effectively for diagnostic and preventive purposes. It is important to note, though, that the title of this chapter is somewhat misleading. There are no true measures of police misconduct or integrity. In other words, there is no way to be 100% sure that all types of misconduct have been identified and their extent and intensity quantified. This is because misconduct is, obviously, generally secretive. Potential witnesses might be intimidated into silence, they might themselves be involved in corruption, and other potential witnesses, such as complainants, may be mistaken or their testimony cannot be corroborated. Police also work in a way that makes it impossible to conduct continuous surveillance of all their activities. Measuring misconduct—or "the measurement of police integrity," to put a positive spin on the topic (Klockars, Kutnjak Ivkovich, Harver & Haberfeld, 2000)—is therefore a very imprecise science. What we are really talking about is developing "indicators" of corruption—that is, pointers, vague signs, and imprecise markers—that might be evidence of real corruption or simply "white noise" that cannot be analyzed as useful information. The evidentiary quality of these indicators, especially in relation to the criminal standard of "beyond a reasonable doubt," is highly variable.

The various problems with measures of police misconduct and integrity should not, however, mean that the mission is abandoned. One thing we can be confident about from the many experiments and innovations in corruption research and prevention from the last 40 years is that a combination of different measures can provide a very useful guide to problems and issues in a police department and to the impact of reform strategies. This chapter therefore looks at the benefits and limitations of available measures, keeping in mind that the greater the number of different measures, the more likely it is to obtain a useful multidimensional picture of police conduct. (In research methods parlance this is called "triangulation," although the layering of data is not necessarily limited to three sources.) The chapter begins by describing the role of inquiries, citizen action groups, and the press as sources of information about police conduct. It then focuses on data related to the complaints and discipline system, including complaint types and trends, and outcomes of case dispositions, such as convictions. An examination is then made of the role of stakeholder surveys and interviews, covering police, complainants, arrestees, and the general public. The value of analyzing litigation trends is also discussed. The final part of the chapter promotes the idea of integrity system assessments. An important component of "measuring" misconduct and integrity involves assessing the risk of misconduct in relation to system controls. In other words, it is not enough just to look for indicators of misconduct, but also to review the quality of the whole integrity system

Inquiries

Estimates of the levels of police misconduct in inquiry reports can provide a baseline measure of the impact of reform strategies. A closely related measure here is the assessment of the integrity system pre-reform, including complaint substantiation rates, disciplinary outcomes, and complainant satisfaction rates. These sources might include data on racial and sexual discrimination and harassment within a department As previously noted, there is often a major disjunction between the global assessment of corruption levels in a report—terms such as "pervasive" or "endemic," for example—and convictions of police in the criminal courts, perhaps in the scores or low hundreds. However, the only efficient and responsible course after an inquiry is usually to prosecute the most blatant cases in the challenging arena of the criminal courts. Dismissals and resignations during and immediately after an inquiry period provide a further measure of probable misconduct. But global judgments about conduct, and also the cultural dimensions of police integrity, provide very important approximate measures for assessing progress from these low points.

Inquiries are an essential reserve tool of government for exposing and thereby "measuring" misconduct. All parliaments need to have a constitutional authority to establish a judicial inquiry when necessary. Because inquiries can be hobbled and "set up to fail" in many ways, to some extent we can judge the reliability of their findings by the extent to which they have been given the right tools. These include the following (Wood, 1997):

- Capacity to extend the time frame of the inquiry so that investigations are not truncated by a short due date imposed by politicians
- Capacity to expand terms of reference to cover other government departments or types of corruption as these might become apparent
- Capacity of the inquiry head to independently appoint investigators and other staff
- Power to demand answers to questions (with criminal sanctions for not answering or for providing misleading answers)

- Capacity to use covert tactics including stings, undercover agents, audio and video recording, and telephone and e-mail taps
- Capacity to "turn" corrupt officers to become witnesses, usually through offers of indemnities from prosecution

The same criteria apply to external oversight agencies, which should permanently hold the same powers as inquiries (see Chapter 10).

The Press

A free press is absolutely essential to police accountability, and it is an important source of information about police conduct. As an independent private or community sector institution, the press should have no formal ties or obligations to police. Their power to communicate with mass society means they have broad social obligations beyond simply selling stories and advertising. They are a vital institution in a liberal democracy. Some of the most important revelations of corruption that have led to major inquiries have come from police whistle-blowers working with investigative journalists. In some cases, investigative journalism entails simply physically observing illegal vice establishments and the interactions of proprietors and police.

The role of the press can cut both ways. Journalists can be party to the covering up of misconduct because they need to maintain a good working relationship with police to produce crime reports. At the same time, the press also has a vested interest in attracting an audience with dramatic stories, and accounts of police corruption usually make good drama. An added advantage is that reporters often have access to police radio scanners, which allows them to follow police actions and observe police behavior in high-risk situations such as sieges, raids, and demonstrations. While media stories about police misconduct often lack context, they can be particularly useful for bringing problem police behaviors to the attention of the public and other groups, such as civil libertarians and politicians (Human Rights Watch, 1998, p. 61).

Citizen Action Groups and Integrated Methods

International human rights groups and civil libertarian groups are also sources of information about possible abuses by police. A major example is the 1998 report by Human Rights Watch, *Shielded from Justice*. The report analyzed excessive force cases in 14 major cities in the United States, concluding that police brutality was "one of the most serious, enduring, and divisive human rights violations in the United States" (1998, p. 1).

The particular value of this report is that it identified patterns of abuse and system failures across a sample of prominent police departments by employing a variety of methods including interviews with victims, police, and lawyers; legal case analyses; and examinations of police records and reports. Reports by international groups can also be important for bringing in an independent eye and providing funds for research in impoverished countries. Transparency International, for example, conducts case study investigations, but it also produces a regular *Global Corruption Barometer* report based on public surveys. The report makes international comparisons that put the spotlight on countries with high levels of police corruption, and because the reports are concerned with all types of corruption, they highlight the relative prominence of police corruption in many societies (e.g., Transparency International, 2004).

Complaints and Discipline Data

Policing attracts large numbers of complaints, and inquiries have repeatedly argued that the failure to properly investigate complaints is a key factor in the concealment of corruption and misconduct. However, complaints are generally a poor source of accurate or verifiable information about police behavior. Formal investigations are expensive, and even independent investigations tend to produce low substantiation rates and low complainant satisfaction—frequently 10% or less (Lersch, 1998; Liederbach, Boyd, Taylor & Kawucha, 2008; Pate & Fridell, 1993; Strudwick, 2003; see Chapters 7 and 10). With most complaints there is simply insufficient evidence to make a confident determination about culpability or even about exactly what happened. In many cases it will come down to the complainant's word against the officer's word, with no independent witnesses or other sources such as closed-circuit television (CCTV) or video footage (Griswold, 1994). Additionally, the very fact that police are involved in stopping people from committing illegal acts that some people want to pursue means that a considerable proportion of complaints will be retaliatory, although such motives are difficult to prove.

Despite these problems there are a number of reasons why complaints should be included in any system for measuring misconduct, and why each separate allegation within a complaint should be subjected to thorough preliminary assessment. One reason concerns the apparent sincerity of complainants. One of the most extensive studies of complainant satisfaction was performed as part of an evaluation of the complaints system for England and Wales operating after the establishment of the Police Complaints Authority. Given the potential problem of vexatious and trivial complaints, Maguire and Corbett (1991) found, nonetheless, that the large majority of complainants appeared honest and genuinely aggrieved. This was partly gauged by the reluctance of many to complain and that complainants on the whole were not vindictive—most sought only an apology or official acknowledgement of their complaint (1991, p. 168; see also Chapter 7).

An additional reason for taking complaints seriously is that there is evidence that, like complaints about consumer products, they represent only the "tip of the iceberg" of public dissatisfaction. Public perception surveys indicate that as many as 90% of people who have felt they wanted to complain about an unhappy experience with police did not do so because they felt it would not achieve anything, or because they could not be bothered, or they were afraid of repercussions (Maguire & Corbett, 1991, pp. 53-55; CMC, 2000a). This "dark figure" of disaffected noncomplainants (Maguire & Corbett, 1991, p. 53) includes victims of police abuses who are themselves implicated in crime (McDonald, 1981). In these cases, it should be kept in mind that just because a complainant has committed a crime doesn't mean their complaint is not legitimate.

Substantiated complaints provide more solid information on corruption and misconduct. The proper investigation of complaints is therefore important, not just to provide justice to victims and remove corrupt officers, but because the outcomes are a vital source of information about types and levels of corruption and misconduct, and changes over time. Again, however, most inquiry reports and reviews criticize the lack of investigative rigor associated with handling of police complaints so that substantiation rates may grossly underestimate the true extent of misconduct. Even with independent processing, the evidentiary problems discussed above mean that substantiation rates in the 10% to 30% range may still constitute an underestimate (Chapter 10).

Another reason for taking complaints seriously is that, taken as a whole, they provide a type of barometer of police-citizen conflict. They therefore provide data both for large-scale diagnostics about police-citizen interactions, and for impact measures of conflict reduction initiatives. Analysis of complaints should be undertaken across as many variables as possible to understand the dimensions of the problem and assist in targeting preventive interventions. Variables should cover the following (Ede, Homel & Prenzler, 2002a; IPCC, 2007c; PONI, 2007c):

- Who makes complaints—in terms of variables such as gender, ethnicity/race, age, social class, and residential location?
- Who was the complaint made against—in terms of variables such as sworn/unsworn status, rank, years of service, station, duties, squad?
- When did the alleged incidents occur—day of the week, time of day?
- Where did the alleged incidents occur—for example, outside nightclub, watchhouse, police vehicle?

- What police operations and procedures did the incident relate to?— for example, arrest, use of capsicum spray, traffic stop, crime investigation, detention, public demonstration.

Viewed over time, complaints can also be key sources of information about possible increases or outbreaks in specific types of misconduct that need urgent intervention, such as a spike in assaults, or they can provide indicators of emerging areas of risk, such as police involvement in the amphetamine trade in nightclubs or a decline in the quality of responses to crime victims.

Policing frequently attracts large numbers of complaints, as many as one for every two officers per year, with a wide variety of complaint types possible within that figure (Prenzler, 2002). Complaints usually entail a larger number of sub-elements in the form of "allegations." To be accurate, allegation is the best term for describing and measuring complaints, and for reporting disposition and substantiation rates. Nonetheless, some complications remain. A simple case is where a complaint is linked to an individual complainant, and the single complaint consists of more than one allegation. For example, an individual complainant may allege an individual police officer (a) ignored a legitimate request for assistance (a type of negligence) and (b) spoke to them in a threatening manner (a type of rudeness or even brutality). One allegation might be substantiated and the other not and thus the complaint itself cannot be tagged in terms of substantiation. However, this approach is not immune from confusion. For example, two complainants can allege that two police officers ignored their request for assistance and spoke to them both in a threatening manner. This could be counted as between one and eight complaints or allegations. Another problem with the terms complaint and allegation is that they denote personal dissatisfaction or victimization. In fact, many people, including police, who simply observe police misconduct or questionable behavior may feel duty bound to report it, but they are not claiming to be victims or even to be personally offended by the behavior. These are more accurately described as "reports" or "disclosures."

One upshot of these issues of definitions, categories, and recording of complaints is that different agencies use different systems. Despite the problems, "complaints" tends to be the favored catchall term, with "allegations" being used increasingly when tracking case dispositions. The following are aspects of complaints dealt with, or overseen by, the Independent Police Complaints Commission for England and Wales for the period 2006-2007 (IPCC, 2007c, pp. vi, 4-11, 30-40; also Bullock & Gunning, 2007, p. 1). These represent a fairly typical profile of complaints against police for many jurisdictions, although there are often considerable variations in the terminology used for complaint categories. The figures also highlight the fact that the majority of complaints tend to be about client service issues and lower level misconduct, as opposed to graft or brutality.

- There were 141,892 police in England and Wales (March 31, 2007).
- 28,998 complaints from the public against police were recorded.
- This was an increase of 10% on the previous year.
- Police numbers increased by 1%.
- The complaints were made by 29,637 people.
- Complainants were classified as "directly affected by the action of the police" (88%), "adversely affected" (8%), "witnesses" (2%), and "representatives" (2%).
- The complaints were made against 32,574 individual police staff members or contractors. Of these, 93% were police officers.
- This amounted to approximately one complaint for every four officers.
- The complaints consisted of 45,883 separate allegations.
- The main categories of allegations were
  - 24%—"other neglect or failure in duty"
  - 21%—"incivility, impoliteness, and intolerance"
  - 15%—"other assault"
  - 7%—"oppressive conduct or harassment"
  - 5%—"unlawful/unnecessary arrest or detention"
  - 5%—"breach of code C of PACE (Police and Criminal Evidence Act) on detention, treatment, questioning"
  - 4%—"lack of fairness and impartiality"
  - 3%—"mishandling of property"
  - 3%—"discriminatory behavior"
  - 2% —"breach of code B of PACE on searching of premises and seizure of property"
  - 2%—"improper disclosure of information"
  - 2%—"other irregularity in procedure"
  - 2%—"irregularity in relation to evidence/perjury"
- 41,584 allegations were processed to completion.
- Of these, 47% went to local resolution, 30% were investigated, 12% were withdrawn, and 10% were subject to a "dispensation" (not proceeded against for various reasons, including insufficient information or an apparent abuse of the complaint process).
- 11% of investigated complaints were substantiated.
- 3,532 appeals were completed.
- Of these, 15% were deemed "invalid" and not proceeded with.
- Of the remaining 2,996 appeals, 61% related to the outcome of an investigation, 26% related to the nonrecording of a complaint, and 12% related to local resolution.
- 24% of "valid" appeals were upheld.

- There are 43 police forces in England and Wales. There was considerable variation in the proportion of complaints per force. The highest was 492 per 1,000 officers in Northamptonshire, and the lowest was 142 per 1,000 officers in Merseyside.

As noted, complaints represent police-citizen conflict and public dissatisfaction. Reducing complaints will therefore be an ultimate aim of any complaints and discipline system. This goal is nonetheless problematic. Falls or rises in complaints are difficult to interpret. An increase could reflect improving public confidence in the system rather than lack of effectiveness (Worrall, 2002). A decrease might show that the system is working to deter misconduct, or it might reflect citizen alienation (Walker & Bumphus, 1992). Consequently, while basic quantitative measures of complaints need to be collected and considered, they must be augmented with more creative assessments of system effectiveness. It is also probably a good idea to establish notional benchmarks below which some tolerance of complaints can be expected as "part of the territory." When complaints go above these levels, concerted efforts should be undertaken to understand the problem and find effective means of making reductions without compromising the work of police.

Surveys and Interviews

The following subsections discuss the contributions of social science research methods, using mainly anonymous survey and interview techniques to identify attitudes, perceptions, and experiences related to police conduct.

Defendant Surveys

Surveys (or interviews) of arrestees, or "defendants," are a potentially useful source of information about police practices. It could be argued that this group is intrinsically antipolice and their responses cannot be trusted. However, useful information and benchmarks can be developed in surveys of a group who are primary targets of police actions. Sidebar 4.1 reports selected results from a Queensland study showing moderately positive outcomes for police, with some scope for possible improvements. Some survey responses can also be tested through other sources—examination of interview tapes, for example (see below)—in order to gauge the gap between survey respondents' claims and more objective criteria. Even if arrestee responses are not entirely accurate, the first one or two surveys provide baseline data so that, if subsequent surveys are conducted in the same way, any major changes can be identified that might require intervention, such as increased allegations of assaults.

Sidebar 4.1: Sample Results From a Survey of Arrestees

The following is a summary of some key findings from the 1999 Defendants Survey conducted by the Queensland Police Service oversight agency, the Crime and Misconduct Commission (formally Criminal Justice Commission). The survey was conducted by interviewing defendants in the waiting areas of eight magistrates' courts across the state. A total of 1,005 persons were asked a total of 139 questions in face-to-face interviews about all aspects of their experience with police.

- Of 483 respondents who were interviewed at the police station, 42% said the interview was videotaped, 38% said it was audio taped, 11% said a written record was taken, 6% said it was not recorded, and 3% were unsure.
- 20% of respondents said that some degree of force was used against them. Of these, the main types of force identified were "tight handcuffs" (46%), "open hand" (20%), and "closed fist" (12%).
- 65% reported that they felt they understood what was going to happen to them after their initial contact with police.
- 45% were not "unhappy" with any aspects of their treatment by police, and 55% were unhappy. Those who were unhappy provided a large variety of reasons. The main reasons were rough treatment (17%), intimidation (9%), unhappy with aspect of search (9%), shouldn't have been charged/arrested me (9%), and assault (7%).
- Of those who were unhappy, only 20% made a complaint.
- Respondents were asked if there was anything positive they wanted to say about their experience. There were 514 specific comments (multiple responses were permitted). Of these, 194 referred to police being "friendly/polite," and 111 said they were "all right/reasonable."
- 47% said they were subject to a personal search. Of these, 69% were satisfied with the way the search was conducted. Of the 31% who were dissatisfied, 19% said the search was "too intrusive/rough," 15% said the search was unnecessary, 13% referred to lack of privacy, 12% felt "embarrassed/humiliated," 11% referred to the unpleasant manner of police, and 9% said there was a lack of information provided.

(CJC, 2000a)

Interviews of arrestees can be highly detailed and carefully designed to cover all aspects of due process related to police questioning, arrest, searches of person and property, and custody. Below are some examples of further kinds of questions that can be asked (adapted from CJC, 2000a):

- Were you told you were under arrest?
  - If yes: Were you told what the charges were?
- Did police take any of your property?
  - If yes: Did you receive a receipt?
- Was a body search conducted?
  - If yes: Was the person searching you the same gender as you?
- Did police inform you that you were entitled to have a lawyer provide advice?
- Did police inform you that you were entitled to have a lawyer present during the interview?
- Were you provided with adequate food and drink?

Public Confidence Surveys

Members of the public are the key constituency of police, and their perceptions of police integrity are an extremely important test of the ethical standing of police. Corruption in a police force can be widely known, and this is often reflected in low levels of public confidence. Conversely, improvements in police conduct should be reflected in higher levels of public trust. Public confidence surveys allow for general measures of public perceptions of police integrity. Within a questionnaire there is scope for more specific questions directed at persons who have had recent contact with police. They also allow for measurement of any gap between numbers of people who had a grievance against police and numbers who complained (Maguire & Corbett, 1991). Some sample results for "perceptions of police integrity" from an Australian survey are shown in Table 4.1.

Apart from these responses on integrity, 66.1% of respondents were satisfied or very satisfied with the services provided by police, with only 9.9% being dissatisfied. However, of people who had had contact with police, 81.0% were satisfied or very satisfied with their most recent contact, with 12.3% being dissatisfied (SCRGSP, 2008, pp. 6.15-6.16). These positive results are from a country with relatively robust anticorruption systems. They can be compared with responses to a public opinion survey about police conducted in St. Petersburg, Russia, in 2002. Gilinsky (2005) found the following:

- 35.5% of respondents felt that unjustified detention on the streets was a serious problem (30.8% said the question was hard to answer).

Table 4.1   Perceptions of Police Integrity, Australia, 2006-2007

Criteria	%
Agree or strongly agree that police treat people "fair and equally"	66.5
Disagree or strongly disagree that police treat people "fair and equally"	17.6
Agree or strongly agree that police perform the job "professionally"	79.7
Disagree or strongly disagree that police perform the job "professionally"	7.8
Agree or strongly agree that most police are honest	76.0
Disagree or strongly disagree that most police are honest	9.7

Source: From *Report on Government Services 2008* (pp. 6.17-6.19, attachment 6, tables 6A.15-17), by SCRGSP (Steering Committee for the Review of Government Service Provision), 2008, Canberra: Productivity Commission. Copyright 2007 by Productivity Commission. Reprinted with permission.

- 41.3% said brutal treatment of detained people was a serious problem (41.2% said the question was hard to answer).
- 46.5% said police taking bribes was a serious problem (43.1% said the question was hard to answer).
- Of people who had been stopped by police on the street or other public places, 69.8% said police were very impolite or impolite, and 25.1% said they were not very polite; 64.9% said police behaved in a way that was absolutely unfair or rather unfair.

Although the questions were not the same in the two surveys, the differences show that in the case of the St. Petersburg Police there is a strong argument for closer analysis of police conduct with a view to addressing any real misconduct and improving police-citizen relations. (For similar results from surveys in other countries see CHRI, 2005, p. 6).

Police Surveys

Another innovation in the area of integrity measurement is surveys of police. In one famous study cited in Chapter 1, Barker (1978) surveyed officers in a city police department about their perceptions of corruption. Respondents alleged that 40% of officers had engaged in excessive force against a prisoner, 23% had committed perjury, 8% had drunk alcohol on duty, and 31% had had sex on duty. How reliable are these findings? They are probably as good as any survey can be, depending on how a survey is constructed and delivered. In this case, anonymity was largely guaranteed by the fact that the researcher, an outsider to the department, personally supervised completion of the questionnaires. In any research like this, there is a risk that a "social desirability effect" will reduce the accuracy of responses. This may be especially applicable in relation to police corruption if officers do not want corruption exposed. On the other hand, anonymity and perhaps a desire to get the problem fixed may motivate police to be honest. Certainly, police survey responses are usually far from "socially desirable" in relation to the code positions outlined in the previous chapter. Cultural factors should also be taken into account when considering the validity of responses. Responses might be more questionable in some countries, such as Japan, where there is a very conformist culture (Johnson, 2004). Responses in other countries might be more reliable—Canada and the United States, for example—where there is a greater level of openness in public life.

One way of building more sophistication into a police survey is to triangulate the sources and then compare the results. An interesting example of this comes from the Royal Commission into the New South Wales Police. A survey found a major discrepancy between serving officers, 33% of who claimed to have personally encountered corruption, and resigned officers, 60% of who claimed to have encountered corruption (AIC, 1996, p. 130). Does this completely confound the study? Not necessarily. Presumably the truth lay somewhere in the middle. Either way—33% or 60%—the results can be interpreted as indicating an unacceptable level of probable corruption.

Surveys can also ask useful questions about police views on the causes of corruption. The results might vary between jurisdictions and have significant implications for prevention, in relation to police salaries, for example, political or administrative pressure to clear up crimes, or the availability of drug money. Interview formats with independent persons as interviewers can allow for follow-up questions and more detailed and frank responses (e.g., Graef, 1990).

Police Ethical Climate Surveys

"Ethical climate" surveys have now become a standard tool of integrity diagnostics. These surveys are focused on police attitudes toward misconduct, but they can also include questions of the type outlined above about perceptions of levels of misconduct by colleagues, levels of management commitment to ethics, and the effects of different anticorruption strategies (see Ede & Legosz, 2002; Frank, McConkey & Huon, 1995; Huon, Hesketh, Frank, McConkey & McGrath, 1995; Klockars et al., 2004; Klockars et al., 2000).

Ethical climate surveys typically ask two main types of questions about (a) officer attitudes to classic ethical issues in policing (along with their perceptions of the attitudes of their colleagues and department), and (b) officer willingness to report breaches (and perceptions of their colleagues' willingness to report). Topics usually include bribery, gratuities, conflicts of interest, use of force, tampering with evidence, and misuse of confidential information. These are usually presented in the form of short scenarios. Respondents are then required to rate the seriousness of a breach of standards included in the scenario, such as acceptance of a gratuity or bribe, application of excessive force, or fabrication or altering of evidence. Ratings are applied using a Likert-style scale. Examples of typical scenarios, and directions for responding, are included in Sidebar 4.2.

Sidebar 4.2: Typical Ethical Climate Scenario Questions

The following scenarios represent areas of ethical decision making that police may face. Please read each scenario and rate the actions according to the accompanying scale. 1 = not serious (i.e., *not unethical*) and 5 = very serious (i.e., *very unethical*).

A police officer pulls over a driver weaving on the road. The driver turns out to be an off-duty senior constable. In an effort to avoid blowing in the alcohol breath-testing device he says to the officer on duty, "I'm on the job."

A local hotel is pulling in large numbers of young people. Local community members begin to complain about noise and traffic congestion. What is particularly strange is that there have been no reported offenses for underage drinking. There is little doubt that a cozy relationship with the local licensing police has developed as evidenced by the fact that police do not pay for meals or drinks at the hotel.

In a pub stouch [fight] a young female probationary constable receives a nasty black eye from a young hood wielding a billiard cue. As the arrested offender is led into the cells, the probationer's team member gives him a savage kidney punch saying, "Hurts, doesn't it?"

An offender is picked up for a particularly nasty rape and assault in a local park. There's no doubt he's the culprit. There's an excellent ID but the offender is streetwise and says nothing. To make matters certain, the words, "OK, I was in the park but I didn't touch the bitch," are falsely attributed to the offender and noted in the arresting officer's notebook.

A young, very attractive lady in a sports car smiles at an officer standing alongside the traffic lights. As she drives away the officer notes her license number. Back at the office he conducts a motor vehicle check on the computer system to find her address.

(Adapted from Frank et al., 1995; Huon et al., 1995)

As indicated, these questionnaires usually request views related to several groups, as well as the issue of willingness to report, so that each scenario question typically involves the following aspects:

- The respondent's personal view,
- What the respondent thinks a typical fellow police officer would think,
- What the respondent thinks is the official police department view,
- The respondent's personal willingness to report the matter (1 = unwilling, 5 = very willing), and
- The respondent's view of a typical officer's willingness to report.

Attitudes do not always equate to behavior. Officers who tolerate or even support forms of misconduct might not be engaging in these behaviors. Ethical climate surveys therefore do not measure misconduct. They measure attitudes that may support misconduct at different levels within a department. They are also useful for identifying gaps between official ethical standards and police officer standards. Consequently, they have significant potential value in informing preservice and in-service ethics training programs, and improving aspects of integrity systems, such as supervisor styles, misconduct penalty grids, and departmental communications, that need improvement (Huberts, Kaptein & Lasthuizen, 2007; Klockars, Kutnjak Ivkovich & Haberfield, 2005).

Legal Professionals

Finally, periodic surveys of judges, prosecutors, and defense lawyers can also be useful for gauging possible police misconduct in the management of accused persons and, especially, in the area of due process (see Ramsey & Frank, 2007). This is particularly important for attempting to identify miscarriages of justice, especially wrongful convictions, where police may have deliberately or accidentally made errors. Again, professionals' perceptions of misconduct in prosecutions and the treatment of detainees do not equate to real misconduct, but findings can provide leads that should be investigated.

Litigation

Litigation against police is a valuable source of information that has been underutilized for measurement and diagnostic purposes (Ransley, Anderson & Prenzler, 2007). The consensus among researchers is that it is difficult to win against police in the civil courts and that civil suits represent an action of last resort for aggrieved citizens. This means that cases that are won or settled provide fairly reliable evidence about both problem behaviors by officers and faults in management and procedures. There also appears to be a growing trend internationally toward increased successful litigation against police across the spectrum of negligence, assault, false imprisonment, trespass, and malicious prosecution (McCulloch & Palmer, 2005; Ross, 2000). There also appears to be an increase in police successfully suing their employers in areas such as discrimination, stress, and negligence (Ransley et al., 2007). Analysis of litigation cases shows that inadequate training and supervision of field officers are key factors in events leading to claims. Case analyses also draw attention to the need for much greater controls in areas such as raids, strip searches, the policing of public demonstrations, and the use of weapons (Ross, 2000; Smith, 2003).

Incident Data

Most modern police departments require that police record significant events such as use of force—including discharge of firearms, use of capsicum sprays and stun guns, high-speed vehicle pursuits, and any types of injuries to police or the public—or incidents such as motor vehicle accidents. These do not provide evidence of misconduct, but a large increase, or consistently high rates above national benchmarks, should give cause for concern and lead to the initiation of research oriented toward reducing such adverse events. Similar use can be made of human resource data, including sick leave, and workers' compensation and stress leave claims. Officer performance reports by supervisors are an additional source of information that can include more specific indicators of misconduct such as reported insubordination, failure to attend court, poor quality of briefs of evidence, poor personal appearance, and charges or complaints related to off-duty behavior. The results of random or targeted drug and alcohol tests, and integrity tests, provide further measures of misconduct and compliance (see Chapter 9).

System Audits

Audits of police systems can also usefully identify misconduct or indicators of misconduct. Audits can be conducted on tapes of interviews with suspects to ensure that due process requirements are complied with (CMC, 2004b). Audits can also be used on the receipt, storage, and return of prisoners' property, and the receipt and storage of evidence. These are areas where there is a high risk of corruption with theft and tampering with evidence. Computer-based audits can also be undertaken to check unauthorized access to confidential information (see Chapter 8). Where audits find breaches of procedure, these might result from human error. However, follow-up investigations should look for patterns of misuse or other evidence that might reveal intentional breaches.

Integrity System Assessments

The final component of measuring misconduct and integrity concerns measuring the integrity system itself. The rationale for this is that if a police department does not have all the basic elements of a comprehensive integrity system in place, including misconduct measurement tools, then there is a high probability that undetected misconduct is occurring. It is essential, therefore, that regular audits of the whole system are undertaken that match the system against a model template, including assessments of the commitment of management to make the system work.

System audits can be carried out by the external oversight agency for a police department. However, given that the external agency is part of a comprehensive system, there should also be occasional audits by other independent agencies, such as private sector consultancy firms or university researchers (Hoque, Arends & Alexander, 2004; Kaptein & van Reenen, 2001; PIC, 2001).

As we have seen, complainants provide a very mixed bag of information about police behavior. However, how police respond to complaints is a significant measure of their commitment to integrity. Consequently, an important method of gauging the quality of a complaints and discipline system is conducting regular surveys of complainants. The first survey provides a baseline measure. Although it is important to be flexible with surveys to ensure that emerging issues are covered, the more questions are retained in their original form, the more accurate comparisons can be made about changes over time. Three-year intervals probably provide for a reasonable schedule. Surveys need to ask probing questions about how the initial review or investigation was conducted, including types of questions asked, the attitude of the investigators, timeliness, and the adequacy of communication (Landau, 1996; Maguire & Corbett, 1991). Surveys also need to be constructed to ensure that they capture important social subgroups, such as young people or ethnic minorities who are more vulnerable to police abuses. Surveys of complainants have provided valuable information about how to improve complaints systems (see Chapters 7 and 10).

Surveys of police officers are also important for obtaining their perceptions of the complaints and discipline system, including its capacity to deter and detect misconduct, its fairness, and the appropriateness and effects of different sanctions and responses. Specific questions should also be addressed to officers who have been the subject of complaints and have had direct experience with the system

Police professional standards units and external oversight agencies also need to have the case files from their investigations and disciplinary decisions regularly audited by an independent group with high-level professional representation, such as lawyers and reputable investigators (Finn, 2001, p. 124; Prenzler & Lewis, 2005). Audit boards should test the quality of investigations and the appropriateness of outcomes. The Rampart Board of Inquiry in Los Angeles recommended that regular audits be done of disciplinary outcomes to stop the widespread practice of a double standard in discipline that favored management (Parks, 2000, p. 339). Auditing can include interviews, where auditors seek explanations for decisions before making final evaluations.

Conclusion

Measuring police misconduct and integrity is an inexact science. Nonetheless, the ideal approach is to deploy multiple measures to obtain the best picture possible of the nature and extent of misconduct problems in a department. A systematic approach to assessing the types and extent of misconduct is also essential for informing managers and policy makers about the impacts of integrity measures and areas that need improvement.

Recruitment and Training

5

When the New Police were established in London in 1829 it was hoped that a new era of professional policing would be built on a strict system of vetting and training. In fact, the New Police were plagued by high turnover rates—around a third of personnel in the first years—partly as a result of dismissals for misconduct. Drunkenness was a major problem. Conditions were also extremely harsh, pay was close to "the breadline," and discipline was often arbitrary and petty. Despite all this, the New Police launched a professional model of policing whose core principles still guide modern aspirations and practices, and proper recruitment and training standards are a core part of this ideal (Critchley, 1967; Kappeler et al., 1998).

Police recruitment and training have evolved significantly since 1829, with some important contemporary innovations. Police departments have adopted a range of tests designed to screen out applicants who have a record of misconduct or who appear vulnerable to misconduct. Aspects of testing also attempt to "select in" potential officers with qualities resistant to the pressures and temptations of police work. Preservice training presents further opportunities to eliminate candidates who display inappropriate behaviors. Once selected, recruits are then normally subject to training systems that communicate, test, and reinforce organizational ethical standards. Although there is little in the way of strong evidence of "what works" in ethics training, there is a range of ethical competencies and knowledge—such as codes of conduct positions and their rationales, and how to manage ethical dilemmas—that in principle should be communicated to all police over their career as part of the accountability obligations of police departments.

Background

It is a generally recognized tenet of police integrity management that it is easier to exclude potential problem officers during recruitment than it is to remove them once they are employed. Hence, recruitment is seen as a crucial means of preventing entry by persons predisposed to crime, violence, deception, emotional volatility, rudeness, and other forms of misconduct or poor service. The importance of integrity screening was brought home by the 2000 inquiry into police corruption in the Rampart area of Los Angeles. The inquiry found that a number of the primary offenders should never have been recruited: "Criminal records, inability to manage personal finances, histories of violent behavior and narcotics involvement are all factors that should have precluded their employment as police officers" (Parks, 2000, p. 332).

In the similarly notorious Miami River Cops scandal of the mid-1980s, involving around 90 officers in drug-related crime, overly hasty and liberal affirmative action recruitment policies, including the relaxation of background checks, underlay the infiltration into police ranks of a large number of persons with strong criminal tendencies (Sechrest & Burns, 1992).

Significant resources are now used in attracting and selecting the right recruits as a vital first step in a comprehensive integrity system. In sum,

> Systematic integrity screening of police applicants is an important mechanism for promoting organizational integrity, along with measures aimed at modifying the attitudes and behaviors of serving officers, reducing opportunities for police to act improperly, enhancing supervision, and reforming the more negative aspects of the organizational culture. ... Improved screening at the "front end" will make it easier to implement these other strategies. It is also much more cost-effective to exclude ethically suspect individuals at the outset than to have to deal at a later stage with problems that may result if such applicants become police officers (PEAC, 1998, p. 66).

What is also widely recognized is that recruitment standards are readily undermined by an academy environment that fails to take ethics seriously and, most significantly, by a working environment in which personal ethical standards can be quickly eroded unless countervailing influences are in place. One of the greatest challenges for police integrity management is to implement strategies that maintain officers' personal commitment to the universal standards of ethical policing. We have seen that a number of factors cause officers' standards to deteriorate post-academy, as a result of socialization into a culture of misconduct and rule breaking, and through the stresses, strains, and frustrations of the job. Ongoing, "in-service" training is seen as one potentially important means of countering this tendency.

Overall, the main elements of progressive recruitment and training for integrity are, therefore,

- Criminal history checks and automatic exclusion for disqualifying offenses;
- Character references, especially from employers;
- Psychological tests that flag possible negative character traits;
- Drug tests;
- Panel interviews that probe applicants' ethical awareness and personal principles, and follow-up investigations of possible adverse indicators;

- Training of recruits in the department's code of conduct and the rationale for these standards;
- Simulated exercises in managing ethical dilemmas;
- Maintenance of ethical competencies through in-service training; and
- Further integrity screening at key career transition points.

These, and associated elements, are developed in the remainder of this chapter.

Promotional Material

Before a potential recruit even makes inquiries or applies to a department, recruitment begins with police career advertising. Police now regularly advertise recruitment rounds in the media, and police careers are promoted through visits to schools and colleges and through academy open days. These venues provide opportunities to communicate the use of selection criteria that include evidence of personal commitment to integrity. This approach is designed to encourage those who may have knowledge of previous misconduct problems in a police department, and to deter those with a predisposition toward misconduct. Integrity messages in promotions, and a more general message about a department's integrity system, also signal to a wider audience that the department has a strong commitment to ethical policing (Mollen, 1994, p. 112).

Criminal History Checks

Checking whether police applicants have criminal records is probably universal in democratic societies. Evidence of past offending is deemed as evidence of a possible future lack of honesty and/or temperament. This approach conflicts with the principle of the "rehabilitation of offenders"—the right of offenders to overcome their past and make a fresh start. Unfortunately for people in this situation, policing is considered too important and too corruption prone to risk relapses. Furthermore, knowledge that some police have criminal pasts could seriously impact public confidence. A "clean" criminal record is therefore a standard requirement in recruitment.

Criminal history checks are fairly straightforward in practice. The applicant's name is run through an electronic database of the jurisdiction's criminal records. A match results in automatic exclusion, unless the applicant can show the record is for another person with the same name. Fingerprinting provides a follow-up mechanism to ensure applicants have not engaged in identity fraud or are not wanted on charges (PEAC, 1998, p. 66ff). One issue is how far to search. Checks should certainly cast the net as widely as possible to include national criminal record databases, as well as country of origin checks where feasible. Checks of this nature can include service records for those who have worked in the defense forces (PEAC, 1998, p. 66). If new arrivals in a country cannot be reliably checked for criminal records, then it is probably safer, unfortunately, to exclude them.

Where police agencies differ is in the degree to which they tolerate evidence of minor criminal behavior. Some agencies take a zero tolerance stand, including in the area of traffic offenses. In other cases, where candidates generally present strong professional suitability standards, departments are prepared to overlook minor convictions of nonviolent and noneconomic types, typically driving offenses. Others may tolerate relatively minor offenses, such as shoplifting, when the criminality occurred during childhood or adolescence and where there is evidence of many years of desistance. These offenses should, however, be noted for consideration as part of the capture of indicative data that might trigger closer investigation of an applicant (PEAC, 1998, p. 67).

Referees

Another practice, common in all employment application processes, is to obtain written references from people who have had experience with the applicant. Questions will normally relate to a variety of qualities desirable for police, with integrity questions focused on character and attitudes. This area is problematic in that referees might not be of good character themselves or might distort reports to favor an applicant for whom they have a personal liking. Reports from relatives or friends are often of little value. Selection panels will therefore need to consider how independent and authoritative the referee appears and engage several referees who have not had contact with each other. Referees are expected to be of good standing, and to have been in positions enabling them to report on the qualities of potential recruits, especially as former work colleagues, teachers, employers, or supervisors. Police agencies also vary in the extent to which they require evidence of the good standing of referees. Doubts can be addressed in part through follow-up interviews with referees, by phone or in person (PEAC, 1998, p. 92). Some agencies expect applicants to include references from police officers, although this appears to be unfair and contributes to a closed society of police.

Panel Interviews

Conducting face-to-face interviews is a common method for examining the motivations, appearance, interpersonal skills, and attitudes of potential recruits. A good panel interview process engages a variety of perspectives that should lead to selection of the best applicants (Stevens, 2000). Variations occur in the training and preparation of interviewers, the composition of interview panels—police, external independent persons, and representative community figures—and interview questions, e.g., the use of behavior-based questions or more theoretically oriented ethical questions.

Panel interviews provide an opportunity to test personal statements made in applications, and even to present applicants with ethical scenarios. Procedural fairness is extremely important where future careers are at stake. Interviewers are vulnerable to forming opinions based on stereotypes (Stevens, 2000), and panel members need to challenge each other as part of the process. The same questions should be asked of all applicants, and all questions must be overtly relevant to policing. (One risk area here is that interviewers will ask intrusive and personal questions for their own inappropriate purposes.) In general, applicants should be allowed time to consider their answers and not be cut short in their replies.

Structured interviews appear to be the most reliable way of selecting candidates who will perform the best on the job (Stevens, 2000). Structuring includes the following content and process dimensions:

> Basing question content on job analysis, asking the same questions of all applicants, limiting applicant questions, reducing the use of prompts or elaboration, ensuring that all interviews are of the same length, and eliminating interviewers' access to background information about applicants received before the interview ... scoring each answer ... taking detailed notes, using multiple interviewers, having the same interviewers rate all applicants, restricting cross-talk among interviewers, using statistical procedures to combine interviewers' ratings, and training all interviewers (Stevens, 2000, pp. 32-33).

Some panels supply interviewees with the questions in advance to give them time to consider their answers. Numerical scoring of applicants across different criteria helps in reducing subjectivity and unfairness. Formal training of all interviewers is essential to ensure proper procedures (PEAC, 1998, pp. 56-69).

Personality and Psychological Testing

Many police departments now require that applicants undertake personality or psychological tests, which can include a strong ethics component. Research has shown that adverse scores on some test measures are predictive of higher numbers of complaints and problem behaviors (Aamodt, 2004; Boes, Chandler & Timm, 1997; Cochrane, Tett & Vandecreek, 2003; Macintyre, Ronken & Prenzler, 2002; Sced, 2004). Popular tests in police recruitment include the MMPI-2 (Minnesota Multiphasic Personality Inventory) and 16PF (Sixteen Personality Factor). These tests can identify a range of desirable and undesirable traits, including emotional stability, honesty, impulsiveness, defensiveness, and aggressiveness, and a range of psychological disorders.

A Victoria Police study illustrates the potential value of psychological tests (Macintyre et al., 2002). In the period before the study was undertaken, MMPI-2 test scores were not used in a strict manner to exclude applicants with poor results. The study tracked the careers of officers with adverse scores. There were 141 officers in the sample who were recruited despite being deemed "undesirable" by psychological assessors. The officers accumulated a total of 956 complaints in a 10-year period, which were estimated to cost many millions of dollars in complaints processing costs and replacement costs of officers who were dismissed.

Generally speaking, psychological tests are used in integrity screening to "flag" possible problem behaviors and attitudes rather than trigger automatic exclusion. This is because tests do not have 100% predictive accuracy. The problem of "false positives" means that applicants could be excluded who would not demonstrate undesirable behaviors in the future. "False negatives" allow inappropriate people to slip through, underscoring the importance of other kinds of checks. High scores on undesirable measures should be used to direct further investigation of an applicant's suitability, such as through an interview-based psychological assessment and wider interviews with associates (Macintyre et al., 2002).

A Recruitment Integrity Committee

The above discussion drew a distinction between matters that are cause for automatic exclusion from recruitment and those that are considered problematic. One mechanism that has been recommended for managing problematic cases is an "integrity committee" (PEAC, 1998, p. 71). The committee should consist of senior staff including top management of the Human Resources Branch and the Professional Standards Unit. The committee can direct that further investigations be made and review all the available evidence related to an applicant's integrity in order to make a final decision on recruitment.

Nondiscriminatory Recruitment, Affirmative Action, and Women Police

A fair recruiting system under modern social justice standards entails a delicate balancing act between strict application of objective selection criteria and "positive discrimination" that favors ethnic minorities and women. These groups have been traditionally excluded under the racist and sexist policies of the past. Nondiscrimination is an obvious essential requirement today, but the application of high educational standards and tough physical tests can exclude many applicants from outside the dominant ethnic male group. A major rationale for affirmative action follows from the argument that police should be representative of the social makeup of the communities they serve. Chapter 1 also noted how the male-dominated culture of policing is a key causal factor in corruption. Given that young males account for about 80% of crime and 90% of violent crime, recruiting exclusively from this group is simply a recipe for misconduct and brutality. Consequently, the idea of recruiting more women has been put forward at times as an anticorruption measure (Hale, 2002).

The issue of recruiting women to reduce corruption is somewhat fraught. It does appear to be the case that, as women come into the ranks, more of them appear in the corruption profiles of departments, as they succumb to the same opportunities and pressures as men. Furthermore, survey research and analysis of complaint sources show mixed findings. While some ethical climate surveys find that women have higher ethical standards than men, this is not always the case, and women appear equally averse to reporting misconduct (Frank et al., 1995; Huon et al. 1995; Waugh, Ede & Alley, 1998). At the same time, Hunt's (1990) study, described in Chapter 1, is valuable for showing how women present as an alien culture that challenges and threatens a police culture that is corrupt, sexist, racist, and homophobic. Although women are not immune to misconduct, they appear to be highly resistant to it, and there is a good deal of evidence to show that women are subject to fewer complaints from the public, especially for excessive force and rudeness (Christopher, 1991, p. 84; Waugh et al., 1998; Wood, 1997, pp. 42-43). Women are also much better at de-escalating conflict through negotiation rather than threats or force (Braithwaite & Brewer, 1998). The National Center for Women and Policing in the United States, in its report, *Equality Denied: The Status of Women in Policing, 2000*, emphasized the relationship between male dominance and misconduct:

> The continued under-representation of women in policing is a significant contributing factor to the widespread excessive force and corruption scandals plaguing law enforcement today, scandals that are costing the US taxpayers tens of millions of dollars annually in liability lawsuit payouts for injuries and wrongful deaths of citizens (NCWP, 2001, p. 3).

The difficulty here is that recruiting women to reduce misconduct is somewhat exploitative. Fortunately, the imperatives of equity legislation mean that opening policing to women for reasons of fairness should also have beneficial effects in reducing corruption. Research evidence also shows that it is relatively easy to dramatically increase the representation of women by removing discriminatory barriers such as non-job-related physical tests, encouraging women to apply, and placing system controls—such as female representation on selection panels—in place against discrimination. (Prenzler & Hayes, 2000).

Polygraph Testing

The use of "lie detector" polygraph tests appears to be fairly widespread in American police departments (Cochrane et al., 2003). The LAPD Rampart Board of Inquiry recommended that

> Polygraph examinations should be administered routinely to *all* police officer candidates *prior* to conducting their background investigation with a particular emphasis on drug use and integrity issues. The cost associated with this effort will undoubtedly be offset by the reduced costs associated with disciplinary and litigation processes generated by problem officers (Parks, 2000, p 334).

However, polygraph tests are generally not accorded very much authority outside the United States. There is a basic division of opinion about whether they reliably register lies or simply emotional responses to questions (Thorne & Chantler, 2008). It is possible, nonetheless, that they have utility as part of a broad set of indicative measures, and as triggers for more detailed inquiries to verify or allay suspicions.

Illicit-Drug Testing

Drug testing has also been introduced into the battery of recruitment tests in a number of departments. The significant problem of drug corruption has led most of the more recent inquiries and reviews of police departments to recommend testing of both serving officers and all applicants (e.g., Cochrane et al., 2003; Ferguson, 2003; HMIC, 1999a, 1999b; Kennedy, 2004; Mollen, 1994). Drug tests are relatively simple to carry out and results are generally not disputed. Tests should cover steroids, as well as illicit drugs such as cocaine, amphetamines, and marijuana. The main problem with drug testing for recruits is that the more common tests, such as urinalysis, will only screen out those applicants who lack sufficient foresight to refrain from taking drugs within a few days of the test, although this can be as high as 3% of applicants, as reported in one study (Mieczkowski, 2002, p. 187). More intrusive and sophisticated tests, such as hair sample tests, can provide evidence of drug use up to several months prior to the test—approximately 7% of applicants were identified in this way in the same study. Multiple drug-testing modalities are also important to cover a range of drugs. For example, marijuana is more readily detected by urinalysis and cocaine by hair analysis (Mieczkowski, 2002, p. 189).

Home Visits

Some police departments use home visits in their recruit selection processes. The appearance of homes and home sharers is deemed to provide indications of the respectability of potential recruits. Home checks can include interviews with neighbors (PEAC, 1998, p. 68).

Intelligence Checks on Associates

Criminal history checks can be extended to include close associates, friends, and family, given concerns about potential personal links between police and organized crime groups or serious offenders. More general checks can be conducted through intelligence databases. Applicants should be required to disclose the names of close associates and any knowledge they may have of possible criminal activities (Ferguson, 2003, p. 20).

Character Checking in Recruit Training and Probationary Programs

Recruit training is structured in different ways. While many departments retain the basic academy system, others have adopted various shared systems with universities and colleges. Regardless of the location and length of training prior to trainees being sworn in, classroom observations, skills training, and simulated patrol exercises enable staff to assess the general conduct and character of potential recruits. These situations provide a crucial opportunity to identify unacceptable behavior such as cheating, sexism and racism, harassment, drunkenness, unjustifiable defiance, and other problem behaviors.

The use of probationary periods for new officers facilitates further checks on personal standards before achievement of the office of constable. Probationary periods are also variable, but a period of at least one year under close supervision and assessment is probably essential before an adequate level of confidence in the preparedness of probationers can be achieved (PEAC, 1998, p. 85). Drug testing should also be continued through the academy and probationary periods.

Higher Recruitment Age

Corruption inquiry reports have also frequently recommended raising the minimum recruitment age (e.g., Mollen, 1994, p. 116). Under a traditional policing model recruits often entered police forces directly from school and were sworn in when aged 18. Some departments provided cadetships in which boys as young as 15 or 16 could complete their schooling at the academy. These arrangements have fallen out of favor because of being breeding grounds for a negative conformist culture. Extended work experience outside the area of policing provides greater opportunity to test the character and conduct of potential recruits. Higher entry age requirements—in the vicinity of the mid-20s—also generally bring more maturity and resilience of character, and allow a greater period of time for criminal and traffic offense histories to come to light.

Personal Financial Checking

Checking the personal financial standing of potential recruits is undertaken on the grounds that weakness in this area would make recruits more vulnerable to forms of economically motivated corruption. Sources can include voluntary disclosures of bank records and checks with credit reporting agencies. Privacy laws might prevent employers from accessing data from credit rating agencies. However, employers can require applicants to supply a copy themselves. The ethical justification for this is summed up as follows:

- Police occupy a special position in the community and need to be subject to extra checks and balances compared to the rest of the community.
- There is a strong link between police facing financial difficulties and corrupt behavior—the public interest in preventing corruption outweighs the individual's interest in his or her privacy.
- The credit file will not be used to determine an application, but merely be placed before the integrity committee as relevant information (PEAC, 1998, p. 81).

Recruit Training and Education in Ethics

The terms "training" and "education" are sometimes used interchangeably and are sometimes used to denote different things. In the latter case, training often refers to the rote learning of practical skills, while education refers to a broader, more theoretical and critical development of knowledge and of independent learning skills. Ideally, a police officer's development of ethical competencies should involve both aspects.

Academy training should always entail comprehensive and systematic training in the department's code of conduct and in skills for the personal management of ethical issues (HMIC, 1999b; Kennedy, 2004; Parks, 2000). A separate ethics course, with a broader educational orientation, is also an essential part of the curriculum—distinct from a "pervasive method" of teaching—or "topic integration" in which ethics is covered across the curriculum in areas such as training in arrest law and procedures or interviewing suspects (Glenn et al., 2003, p. 127). A stand-alone approach should not exclude the pervasive method. In fact, the two should work together, with ethical principles discussed in the stand-alone course being reinforced and reapplied in the operational courses. A stand-alone course signals the department's commitment to ethical standards, and it allows for coverage of the complex field of police practice with ethics as a foreground issue (Kleinig, 1990).

In an academy ethics course it is essential that code positions be not simply asserted, but that their rationales are developed (see Chapter 3). For example, the prohibition on gratuities, a standard provision in police codes, needs to be explained in terms of the democratic principle of impartial policing. Police who accept gratuities enter a situation of obligation and create the appearance of potential bias. It is essential that recruits understand that the prohibition is not simply an expression of a miserly mentality, but is supported by democratic policing principles and by public opinion. It is also essential that police be trained in how to deflect offers of gratuities without causing offense (HMIC, 1999a, p. 43ff; Prenzler & Mackay, 1995).

Ethics education and training also need to be fully assessed. Most students will focus their efforts on assessable content (Gibbs, 2006). The content of assessment also clues in students to what teachers and the teaching institute consider valuable. Any gaps in assessment in relation to ethics will send a message that this area is not important.

Police ethical dilemmas, such as dealing with offers of gratuities, are predictable and standard responses need to be practiced in live simulations. Recruits also need to develop skills to independently negotiate more complex and ambiguous ethical dilemmas within the organization's mandated framework. This approach is further enhanced through the analysis and discussion of hypothetical and real-life ethical scenarios (Kleinig, 1990; Newburn, 1999; USDoJ, 2001, p. 14). The Mollen Commission report emphasized the need for ethics education to include case studies of major corruption scandals and of the biographies of corrupt officers. Inquires have also recommended the use of mixed police-civilian teaching teams to ensure that there is a counter to the tendency of instructors to tell "war stories" and support negative subcultural ethical practices (Kennedy, 2004; Wood, 1997).

The danger is that in a crowded academy curriculum, ethics is down-sized to make space for the imperatives of operational procedures, including the growing complexity of technology, such that ethics is seen not only as a minor issue, but a separate issue to "real" policing. This argument was made in a recent evaluation of police training in England and Wales. White (2006) alleged that training lacked "a moral compass because its methods have become separated from its purposes":

> The current vogue for "National Standards" and "Competence Frameworks" ... permit(s) a dislocation of training methods from the purposes of policing and support(s) unhelpful binaries such as theory/practice and fact/value. The unintended consequences or "hidden curriculum" of this approach is that police training reinforces traditional cultural prejudices and inhibits major change programs (e.g., problem-solving, diversity, community-focus). It is concluded that progress demands the development of an ethical foundation for a policing practice rather than a technical one (2006, p. 386).

One counter to this problem is to make police training facilities themselves learning facilities. That is, they should have a research and knowledge development function that feeds into all aspects of the training they deliver. One aspect of this should be a mission for "lessons learned" (Glenn et al., 2003). Academies should be concerned with constantly updating knowledge from academic research, from other police departments, and from the problems and issues within their own departments to ensure that the curriculum and teaching methods cover contemporary best practice in all aspects of police work. This should include all aspects of ethical issues and corruption prevention.

What is needed as part of such a program are properly controlled studies of the impacts of different types of ethics education and training on police officer attitudes, and even on their conduct. There is some evidence from outside police studies that ethics education can raise the level of moral reasoning and improve trainee confidence in handling ethical issues (Ede, 2000, pp. 228-229; Schlaefli, Rest & Thomas, 1985; Self, Baldwin & Olivarez, 1993). However, this appears to be an area in policing where significant research is needed (Ede, 2000, p. 228).

Higher Educational Standards

Advocates of police professionalization argue that tertiary education offers a broader awareness of the social context of policing and improved management skills, as well as leading to improvements in the basic operational skills of communication, negotiation, and problem solving (Dantzker, 1993; Potts,

1981). Other proposed advantages of tertiary education for police include the development of greater understanding and tolerance of minority groups and differing lifestyles, and more ethical decision making (Carter, Sapp & Stephens, 1989). A tertiary setting is also considered more appropriate for a critical assessment of ethical issues (Kleinig, 1990). The general conclusion from the research to date is that higher education has a favorable impact upon both integrity and performance, including complaint levels, use of force, sickness rates, and stress levels (Aamodt, 2004; Carter & Sapp, 1992; Paoline & Terrill, 2007; Sherman, 1978a). Education levels are, in fact, predictors of academy performance across all aspects of training (CJC, 1996b; PEAC, 1998, p. 41). And, contrary to some critics of police higher education, well-educated police are not necessarily more likely to leave policing early simply because they have transportable qualifications (Jones, Jones & Prenzler, 2005).

Tertiary education for police is a theme taken up by many modern commissions of inquiry. Reports frequently condemn traditional police training as part of the misconduct problem and recommend higher education, either pre-academy or in a cocurricular arrangement, as a means of improving the maturity and ethical sophistication of police (e.g., Mollen, 1994, p. 119ff; Wood, 1997, pp. 195, 281).

In-Service Training and Education

In-service training, or "professional development," is concerned with maintaining and updating knowledge and skills. It is designed to keep staff in step with best practice principles and new knowledge in their field. Maintenance, and indeed advancement, of police knowledge of ethics is essential given the deterioration of recruits' high personal standards as a result of experience on the job, including pressures from negative aspects of the police organizational culture (Catlin & Maupin, 2002; Kleinig, 1990). Despite this well-known problem, police frequently appear reluctant to place training to maintain and advance ethics on the same par as that of other skills. Hyams (1990) noted that,

> [i]n many organizations, the academy is the last time that employees are exposed to ethical standards. It is not the last time that they are exposed to officer safety training, nor is it the last time that training in technical skills occurs. Technical skill training occurs career long, and so should training in ethical standards (p. 78).

There is a strong obligation of police management to ensure that staff retain ethical competence and remain fully conversant with the ethical standards of the department. This is an area where "slippage" in the integrity system easily occurs simply due to the costs and the practical demand pressures of police work. Releasing officers from their regular jobs for training courses entails a reduction in frontline policing capabilities. In-service ethics education, like any in-service training and education, needs to be accessible and take into account work/family balance issues. Some kinds of incentives, such as pay point increases and time off for study, are probably essential to involve all or most staff.

As officers move into management positions, it is also essential that they become more competent in ethical leadership and corruption prevention, and that they understand that the ethical conduct of their staff forms a key part of their supervisory responsibilities (see Chapter 11). It has also been argued by at least one police department review that psychological assessments be required for all applicants for promotion and all applicants for "sensitive and high-risk units" (Ferguson, 2003, p. 24).

Conclusion

Recruitment and training present vital opportunities for police to select people predisposed to ethical policing, and then to develop and maintain ethical competencies in these people. In recruitment there is now a standard battery of tests that all departments should have in place, including criminal history checks, referee reports, psychological tests, drug tests, and panel interviews. Ethics training is unlikely to win popularity contests among police, but it is nonetheless essential to ensure, at a minimum, that police know what is expected of them in regard to professional conduct. Recruit academy training should entail detailed systematic training in the department's code of conduct, involving scenarios and simulations, delivered by mixed police-civilian staff. Integrity training should be both stand alone and integrated, with ethics seen as permeating all aspects of police work.

A great danger in police human resource development is that the good work of comprehensive recruit selection and training procedures will be undone by a negative police culture and the inherent strains of police work. The best antidote to this problem is to have a high-quality integrity system in place, including close supervision of frontline officers, a state-of-the-art complaints and discipline system, and consistent risk management and early intervention systems. Mandatory in-service ethics training and education is one essential component of this comprehensive system.

An Advanced Complaints and Discipline System

6

A robust and fair complaints and discipline system is essential to control misconduct, encourage public confidence in police integrity, and ensure the loyalty and confidence of honest police. Complaints (or "disclosures" or "reports") from the public and police about alleged or suspected misconduct remain the primary input component of a disciplinary system. Complaints provide the main trigger for investigations, and are also a key source of intelligence. It is therefore essential that a complaints system is easily accessible, highly responsive, comprehensive, and accountable. Major problems can easily arise when both the public and police feel unable to lodge a complaint, or when they are diverted from complaining by fear of reprisal. Problems also arise when the system is not all-inclusive, so that patterns of recorded allegations understate or skew the level of problems across a department. Care must also be taken to ensure that the response to reported misconduct is measured and proportionate. Significant disaffection is likely to be generated by both excessive and inadequate responses to complaints. Striking the right balance is not an easy task, with a basic divergence of options between

1. A retrospectively oriented system that is procedurally fair and methodical, oriented toward finding the truth, and applying a just response to misconduct, including measured forms of punishment;
2. A future-oriented system focused on behavioral improvements, primarily through efficient processing of complaints and dispositions centered on retraining or close supervision; and
3. Future-oriented "restorative" responses, centered on reconciling conflicts either through mediation between parties or efficient localized forms of communication, explanation, and apology.

A good complaints systems needs to be able to put in place an appropriate response both to concerns about justice—on the part of all parties involved with each allegation—and the need to maximize ethical standards across the organization. One way to get this balance right is through continuous quality assurance and auditing processes involving a range of measures and stakeholders.

Background

A recent Commonwealth Human Rights Initiative report on police accountability asserted that

> [p]erhaps the greatest public resentment over bad policing is reserved for
> impunity—the safety from punishment provided by authorities and supervi-
> sors to errant police and the lack of accountability. In addition, it includes a
> boundless tolerance for poor performance in delivering safety and security
> and protecting the rule of law (CHRI, 2005, p. 9).

The Christopher Commission into the LAPD observed that

> [n]o area of police operations received more adverse comment during the
> Commission's public hearings than the Department's handling of citizen
> complaints against LAPD officers, particularly allegations involving exces-
> sive use of force. Many community groups and members of the general pub-
> lic firmly believe that the Department is incapable of disciplining its officers
> (Christopher, 1991, p. 153).

Similarly, the Fitzgerald Inquiry into the Queensland Police found that

> [t]he Internal Investigations Section has been woefully ineffective, hampered
> by a lack of staff and resources and crude techniques. It has lacked commit-
> ment and will and demonstrated no initiative to detect serious crime. ... The
> Section has provided warm comfort to corrupt police. It has been a friendly,
> sympathetic, protective and inept overseer. It must be abolished (Fitzgerald,
> 1989, p. 289).

These two police departments operated under a simple minimalist model of
accountability (Prenzler & Ronken, 2001a). The model was almost universal
up to the 1970s, after developing with various permutations in the 19th century within a highly limited version of the "professional model" discussed in
Chapter 1. Improvements were made in policing as a result of the introduction of salaried employment, recruitment tests, training, and a hierarchical
system of authority and discipline. "Constabulary independence" was a key
principle: the idea that police should operate at arm's length from elected
officials. And in practice police commissioners and chiefs have enjoyed
much more autonomy than other heads of government departments (Bryett,
Harrison & Shaw, 1997). In terms of control of police conduct, this traditional system gave primary responsibility to police disciplinary command.
Interventions would occur at various levels in the hierarchy depending on
the gravity of allegations. In larger departments, audit functions and inves-

tigative and disciplinary responsibilities were assigned to inspectorates or internal affairs units.

Within this model, elected officials provided some external scrutiny and democratic accountability through various means such as questions in parliament. Governments could also resort to independent commissions of inquiry if they were dissatisfied with the treatment of allegations against police. However, the main source of standing external control was provided by the courts. This occurred through the occasional civil or criminal case against police, but on a more routine basis through the examination of police evidence in criminal prosecutions and the application of the exclusionary rule in court when police evidence was obtained illegally (Sarre, 1989).

The main elements of the minimalist model are

- Line management control for complaints investigations and discipline
- Judicial scrutiny of police conduct in the courts and use of the exclusionary rule
- Detached political oversight with resort to independent inquiries as a last resort

It is now apparent that this model is entirely inadequate to detect and prevent police misconduct in any systematic and reliable fashion. The interventions simply did not match the high intensity pattern of misconduct risks in policing. A related factor was a state of management disbelief or denial concerning the systemic nature of corruption. However, it is now well understood that a sophisticated complaints and discipline system—an advanced model—is a central plank in the fight against corruption, and also has a key role to play in promoting integrity and good conduct. A good deal of the work of such a department will involve provision of a quality response to the large numbers of complaints it can expect to receive.

The following sections describe some of the major characteristics of an advanced complaints and discipline system, the challenges such systems face, and some key principles behind the right mix of responses.

Complaints and Discipline

A "complaints and discipline system" is not confined to processing complaints and it is not confined to discipline in the sense of punishment. However, the term is useful because it captures a core operation within a larger integrity system. "Complaints" denotes the key role of complaints in providing the main source, or a major source, of demand pressure on the system. And while the word "discipline" has many negative connotations in a liberal society, it retains value in the broad sense of the word: not just punishment but a deliberative and measured approach to achieving an objective, forms of self-control in an organizational sense, and even the concept of a specialist area of knowledge. It should also be kept in mind that citizens are the ultimate authority and the ultimate recipients of a police discipline system. Some kind of punitive response—one that will be experienced as painful or undesirable by a police officer—will probably always need to be available for police integrity management to fulfill a social demand for retribution for more serious breaches of duty and to deter potential bad behavior by those officers less responsive to other measures designed to positively shape police behavior.

Chapter 4, "Measuring Misconduct and Integrity" discussed the highly problematic nature of complaints. Some points to note from that discussion are that

- Complaints are generally a poor source of forensic information suitable for prosecution in courts. Typical substantiation rates are around 10%, although they can go higher.
- Despite this, complaints need to be subject to careful preliminary assessment to test the quality of evidence.
- Some complaints are likely to lead to evidence of various types of misconduct, including serious misconduct, if investigated properly.
- Complaints systems need to take seriously what might be considered more "customer relations" issues, where problems need to be identified and "fixed" rather than individuals blamed.
- Complaints also need be taken seriously because they represent the "tip of the iceberg" of public dissatisfaction.
- Complaints also need to be carefully recorded, with as much detail as possible, to allow for trend analysis, diagnostics about conflict, and measurement of impacts of conflict reduction initiatives.

Additionally, because complaints represent police-citizen conflict and public dissatisfaction, reducing complaints will also be a key aim of any complaints and discipline system. However, as we have also seen, interpreting complaints can be difficult. Increases in complaints may be one effect of an improved system as the confidence of would-be complainants increases. A drop in complaints might show the system is working to deter misconduct and fix systematic problems, or it might reflect disenchantment with the system. As indicated, final outcomes in terms of punishments are also questionable. A disciplinary system may have high substantiation rates but fail to properly sanction misbehavior. Conversely, a system may be too harsh and insensitive to the difficulties and provocations of police work. Other research methods need to be used to help explain trends.

Key Elements of an Advanced Complaints and Discipline System

In the face of these complexities some basic principles about complaints processing need to be built into an integrity system. At a minimum, complaints need to be taken seriously and subjected to standard tests regarding the quality of evidence. Furthermore, there needs to be a consistent application of different response paths. An advanced complaints and discipline system is inevitably complex, involving diverse response options, and its effectiveness will be difficult to objectively evaluate. Nonetheless, the task of building a quality system cannot be avoided. A weak system will result in an out-of-control misconduct problem and high levels of public dissatisfaction. Overall, complaints need to be taken seriously, complainants provided with a fair hearing, and productive responses applied. The following subsections set out the main components of an optimal system for detecting misconduct, achieving public confidence, satisfying participants, and raising or maintaining the standard of police conduct.

A Professional Standards Unit

"Professional standards unit" or similar terms have now replaced the older term "internal affairs." "Internal" sounded too much like it excluded public interest matters and involved a cover up, and "affairs" had an unfortunate double meaning. The essential point, though, is that a distinct organizational element is needed that is dedicated to the investigation of complaints, the gathering of intelligence about corruption, as well as the detection and prevention of corruption. The advantage of a specialist unit is that it cannot be distracted by other tasks and is accountable, in theory at least, for failures in police conduct. Its operations should allow for the development of specialized skills and knowledge about corruption control, the selection of committed investigators, and the enforcement of common standards and procedures (Henry, 1994; Knapp, 1972). If complaints and misconduct are handled exclusively at the local level there is enormous scope for inconsistency, for the development of "safe havens," and for the entrenchment of long-term problems. Local area commanders may even be involved in corruption, further adding to the unlikelihood of any disclosures and repair. The structure and processes of a professional standards unit should therefore facilitate the collection of data about conduct across the whole department, and for the authoritative and consistent application of investigative standards and discipline.

Adequate resourcing of a professional standards unit is crucial to the success of a complaints and discipline system. Although resources are always subject to competing demands, and funding of a professional standards unit cuts into core service delivery, an adequate response to complaints is a major test of a police department's commitment to ethical standards. If investigators are overwhelmed with cases they will become stressed, be tempted to cut corners, and the time taken to finalize matters will blow out. Performance measures (see below), in association with assessment by the external watchdog agency, will be of significant value in assuring that resources are adequate.

There is now an ongoing debate about how much of the routine work of a professional standards unit, such as complaints investigations, should be done by an external oversight agency in order to prevent bias or the perception of bias. The focus of this chapter is on a large work profile for a professional standards department, as this is the most common arrangement, but it should be kept in mind that much of this work can, or should, be done by an outside watchdog agency (see Chapter 10).

Mandatory Police Reporting and Whistle-Blower Protection and Support

Given the long history of police cover-ups and nondisclosure, including by police who are not themselves corrupt, another crucial element of an advanced system is a legal requirement that all officers report any observed or suspected misconduct, including hearsay. Police should be prosecuted if undisclosed knowledge of corruption comes to light (USDoJ, 2001, pp. 7-8). Internal informants, when not ignored, have also frequently been ostracized, persecuted, and threatened. Many police informants have feared for their lives (Fitzgerald, 1989; Knapp, 1972). The potential for the intimidation of witnesses needs to be countered by strong whistle-blower protection legislation and an infrastructure that allows for practical protection of witnesses, including provision of safe houses and even new identities where necessary.

Empirical research on the impact of compulsory whistle-blowing and whistle-blower protection is sorely lacking. One attempt to measure effects in the post-Fitzgerald reform period in Queensland found very mixed results. Interviews with long-serving officers found that there was "fairly broad agreement among those interviewed that police were now more likely to report fellow officers for misconduct than they were in the pre-Fitzgerald era" (Brereton & Ede, 1996, p. 113; CJC, 1997). This was largely attributed to concerns regarding retribution if unreported misconduct came to light. However, ethical climate surveys showed very low levels of willingness to report a range of observed misconduct types—up to a third indicated they were willing to report more serious types of misconduct such as theft and process corruption, but this went down to approximately 5% for misconduct such as using the police database for personal enquiries. One study in the

U.S. state of Georgia, using a survey of police, found that willingness to disclose observed misconduct was moderately increased by the presence of a mandatory reporting policy (Rothwell & Baldwin, 2007).

At this point it would appear that compulsory whistle-blower legislation is one of those things that is necessary in principle, but its affects on behavior are unclear or likely to be weak. It should be noted, though, that part of getting the principle right is clear wording in legislation that requires police to report all suspected or rumored misconduct, so police cannot make the excuse that misconduct coming to their attention was not proven (Brereton & Ede, 1996, p. 110).

Reception

Under a minimalist model of complaints and discipline police were able to deploy a range of strategies for deflecting complaints (Christopher, 1991; Russell, 1978). Simply lodging a complaint was made difficult, with complicated paperwork, complainants made to wait for long periods, and failure to communicate in a timely fashion. In the Australian state of Victoria, for example, the Beach and Richardson reports emphasized how many complaints or potential complaints would not even get to "first base":

> In my opinion, the Board's inquiry established beyond any doubt that ... there was no satisfactory avenue through which a citizen could lodge a complaint against Police misbehavior in the expectation it would be thoroughly and impartially pursued. Regrettably, this is apparently due in no small measure to an attitude of the Police mind, which is affronted by the impertinence of the civilian in making a complaint at all, and which then in a defensive reflex, classifies him as a troublemaker, or as being anti-Police, or motivated by malice or ill-will (Beach, 1978, pp. 106-107).

> Many lawyers and members of the public had so little confidence in the present system of investigations by the Internal Investigations Department that many serious complaints about the police were not being lodged (Richardson, 1987, p. 17).

A good complaints and discipline system starts with a reception facility that makes it easy for complainants to lodge a complaint (USDoJ, 2001, pp. 7-8). This means that a variety of media need to be available, including post, telephone, and even the development of Web or e-mail based access, as well as interpreter services. A legal requirement should stipulate that all complaints (or information) are recorded, including anonymous and verbal complaints. Complainants should be made to feel safe and able to provide all information relevant to their complaint. Complainants should also be able to complain directly to the internal professional standards unit or to an external agency, as well as to local police.

Because one of the aims of a system will be to ultimately reduce complaints, there will be pressure within a complaints reception facility to deflect complainants. This is a difficult tension to reconcile, but tests of the system, such as with "integrity tests" on complaints reception, can be one counter to this (Finn, 2001, p. 124; Marx, 1992; Mollen, 1994, pp. 103-106). Another method is surveys of the public and victims of crime, with specific questions about the experience of complaining.

One difficult issue concerns the standard for accepting complaints. At one extreme is the acceptance of all complaints, including anonymous verbal complaints. At the other extreme is the requirement that complaints are submitted in writing, are signed, and include a contact address. The former arguably encourages trivial and vexatious complaints, while the latter arguably deters genuine complainants afraid of repercussions. One compromise is to encourage complainants to make their complaint in writing and provide personal details with the rationale that this aids investigations and communication, and allows for resolution options that include the complainant. At the same time, all complaints, regardless of format, should be recorded, subjected to preliminary assessment, and included in an intelligence database. One innovation introduced by the Police Ombudsman for Northern Ireland is to report the number of complaints investigations that were discontinued due to complainant "noncooperation" (PONI, 2007a, 2007c; see also 2006a). Doubts about the genuineness of this category should be assuaged by the fact that the Ombudsman is independent of police.

Case Assessment and Allocation

Complaints are normally sent from reception to a complaints officer, who checks details of the complaint and provides summary information in relation to probable categories of offenses and any efforts to check details with the complainant. The complaint then passes to a panel that meets on a regular basis. A team approach is essential here in order to prevent any one individual from having too much personal influence, and also to ensure that a range of opinions is canvassed. Chapter 10 on external oversight of police argues that assessment panels should consist of a majority of "civilian" members from the oversight agency to counteract any tendency toward bias or the appearance of bias, by police. A standard set of options should then be considered, depending on the nature and gravity of the allegations and the quality of initial evidence provided by the complainant. Complaints are best assessed as:

1. Having insufficient information for further action other than communication with the complainant regarding the reasons for this decision;
2. Belonging to another agency or section and referred on to that agency (e.g., a complaint about a local government parking inspector mistakenly identified as a police officer);
3. Suitable for immediate mediation (see Chapter 7);
4. Suitable for managerial resolution at the local level (see Chapter 7);
5. Constituting a "flagged" complaint under an early warning system and suitable for separate profiling and possible early intervention or further investigation (Chapter 8);
6. Suitable for investigation; and
7. Possibly vexatious—investigate and consider options including prosecution of the complainant.

A standard agenda item for a complaints assessment panel should be to consider feedback on the outcomes of previous decisions at points 1 through 7 to ensure that referred matters are not being "buried" or inappropriately managed by other sections and departments, and to inform future decisions about the best response to current complaints on the agenda. For example, if the panel has evidence that local resolution is not being done well then they should avoid that option while making their concerns known to senior management. The panel will also normally consider complaints that come back to it from earlier referrals. These might be cases where mediation has been unsuccessful or where a complainant has volunteered more information after their matter was deemed unable to be substantiated.

The same panel, or a separate panel, should also consider the outcomes of investigations once the investigative component has been closed. Options here include those listed at points 1 through 5 and 7 above, as well as referral to a disciplinary panel, misconduct tribunal, or the public prosecutor.

Quality Investigations

Inquiries that uncover widespread or serious misconduct in police departments inevitably are harshly critical of how complaints are investigated. The 1997 report of the Royal Commission into the NSW Police Service identified "[a]n inherent bias in investigations as the result of which the Service failed to carry out impartial investigations or pursue allegations with the same rigour or approach seen in ordinary criminal inquiries" (Wood, 1997, p. 201).

Assessments of police investigations of complaints in the United States have found that officers' accounts were often readily accepted and evidence to the contrary dismissed, while complainants were frequently interrogated and "evidence to incriminate [them was] … scrupulously sought" (USCCR, 1981,

p. 68; see also Parks, 2000, pp. 336-337). Virtually every significant review or commission of inquiry has condemned the record of police investigations in similar terms. Unfortunately, problems of poor investigative quality often continue even after major inquiries and reform. For example, the first review by the New South Wales Police Integrity Commission of the post-reform operations of the Police Internal Affairs section provoked it to make a special report to parliament highly critical of investigations. The report provided a detailed catalogue of weaknesses in police processes, including (PIC, 2000, pp. i-iv):

- Lack of proper planning of investigations,
- Failure to engage in background checks—for example, on officers' complaints histories—before conducting an investigation,
- Inadequate use of electronic surveillance,
- Insufficient encouragement to officers to make admissions,
- Insufficient encouragement to officers to disclose misconduct by colleagues,
- Investigators involved in conflicts of interest, such as investigating a colleague in their work area,
- Officers investigating other officers superior in rank,
- A general lack of rigor,
- Less rigor applied than in comparable cases in which the suspect was a member of the public,
- Internal Affairs being under-resourced,
- 43% of cases where the police decided not to investigate should have been investigated,
- 22% of cases where police decided to take no further action should have been pursued.

One of the effects of these problems is high levels of complainant dissatisfaction. In a typical survey result from a study in the 1990s, of people who made complaints against the Metropolitan Toronto Police, over 70% did not feel confident with police investigating their complaint. At the end of the process, only 14% felt their complaint had been dealt with fairly, while 35% believed police were biased in their handling of the complaint investigation, and 15% claimed police did not look at all of the evidence (Landau, 1996; see also Chapters 7 and 10).

A major challenge, therefore, for any modern complaints and discipline system is to follow the proper recording of complaints with a systematic and productive process. A first step is to approach complainants in a way that makes them feel they can "tell their story" without repercussions and with a fair response (USDoJ, 2001, pp. 7-8). As indicated above, the level of investigative rigor applied should be at least the same as that applied by police to crime reports. One implication of this is that independence is a critical criterion. If police are to undertake the investigation, then the investigating officer should at a minimum be at a higher rank to the subject officer, not a friend or close colleague of the officer, and from outside the subject officer's station or squad. Any conflicts of interest, real or apparent, should be declared, and in most cases the designated officer should be absented from the investigation. Any hint or appearance of a conflict of interest is likely to lead to a perception of bias. The professional standards unit should also be managed by a senior officer, generally a deputy commissioner or deputy chief, and staff should be independent from the normal chain of command in order to prevent interference in investigations.

More generally, investigators should receive specialist training in the area, and be highly experienced and successful in investigations in other areas prior to transferring to the professional standards unit. In Britain, one Inspectorate report recommended that specialization be recognized and facilitated by the creation of national standards and accreditation for internal investigators (HMIC, 1999b, p. 10). Recruitment also needs to pay attention to the psychological resilience of investigators, both in managing stress and resisting pressure from colleagues.

Given that internal affairs can carry a stigma, incentives in pay and status might need to be utilized. One option is to make a period in internal investigations a requirement for investigator training (under supervision) and accreditation or promotion. This may, however, mean that inappropriate persons work in the area. Consequently, senior management needs to match responses to conditions to obtain the best investigative capacity. For example, the Rampart Inquiry report recommended that the LAPD's Internal Affairs Group halt the system of open application to investigator positions and, instead, "hand pick" the best detectives: "[T]hose selected for these assignments must be guaranteed retention of their advanced pay grade position and given preference of assignment upon completion of their IAG assignment" (Parks, 2000, p. 337).

A major problem identified in police internal investigations is a tendency for investigating officers to give the subject officer the benefit of the doubt, suggest excuses or alibis, and disclose information at an early stage that encourages them to deny the allegations. The reverse of this approach is the intimidation or badgering of officers under investigation—often associated with the term "interrogation." Although this approach entails a breach of procedural fairness and human rights, it is also a technique that has not been shown on balance to be effective (Baldwin, 1992). It is also a technique well known to police and is therefore unlikely to be effective. A middle-ground approach needs to be taken that is focused on objective fact finding, without any signs of camaraderie or sympathy for the accused. This involves not discouraging officers from making admissions. "Cognitive interviewing" techniques that encourage witness recall should also be used where appropriate.

A number of other controls need to be placed on investigations, including prohibiting subject officers and investigators from discussing the matter with colleagues, recording all interviews, copying (where applicable) and securing all forms of evidence, and recording all file access by name, date, and purpose. This is particularly important to facilitate quality audits (see below). Investigators should also be required to consider procedural and cultural issues within a squad or station, not just confine their inquiries to the possible culpability of an individual officer.

Final Outcomes

Even where police investigations are of a high quality and result in high substantiation rates, the effects on police integrity are undermined by low level final outcomes, such as reprimands and small fines (Dugan & Bread, 1991; Griswold, 1994). Reinforcement of misconduct occurs when breaches of the rules are not detected or not substantiated, but it also occurs when substantiated breaches receive minor penalties and also when there are no additional penalties for repeat breaches. In the words of a recent U.S. National Institute of Justice study, *Enhancing Police Integrity*: "Officers learned to gauge the seriousness of various types of misconduct by observing their department's diligence in detecting and disciplining those who engaged in police misconduct" (NIJ, 2005, p. 3).

The usual complaint about police disciplinary outcomes made by reviews and inquiries is that, like the investigation process itself, favoritism is shown to police. In this case, bias is evident in light penalties. For example, in the mid-1990s the Queensland Criminal Justice Commission initiated a special review of police disciplinary decisions. The review was undertaken by a former magistrate. Of 30 charges recommended by the CJC against 19 officers, only four were accepted as substantiated by police and two of these resulted in "manifestly inadequate" penalties. The auditor conceded that some charges had weak evidence but concluded with confidence that there were 12 charges involving eight officers where "justice had not been done" (CJC, 1996c, p. 15). These findings, and public disquiet over prominent cases in which police received light sentences for serious misconduct, compelled the Commission to seek authority to appeal to a tribunal against police disciplinary decisions.

At the same time that police internal discipline has historically often been considered weak, it can at times also be excessive and biased. Following the Ramparts scandal in Los Angeles, the independent panel charged with evaluating reform in the LAPD found that internal discipline was perceived by officers to be generally weak, but it was also described as arbitrary, unfair, erratic, and often overly harsh (RIRP, 2000. pp. 16, 21). A complaints and discipline system needs to be seen as fair, with appropriate penalties, if it is to have the confidence of rank-and-file officers.

The lack of information about outcomes has also been a common problem in public reporting on the operations of complaints and discipline systems. Lack of communication directly to complainants about outcomes can also be a problem, and a good complaints system needs to include a mechanism by which complainants and police can appeal against the disposition of their cases.

Inquisitorial Methods and Administrative Authority

Numerous corruption inquiries have emphasized how police felt immune from prosecution because of their ability to escape convictions under the high standards of proof of the adversarial system in criminal courts. Even where internal investigations are thorough and there is a will to prosecute, the best intentions can be destroyed on the floor of the courtroom. This is often due to the increased standard of proof in criminal proceedings when compared to that of civil proceedings (ALRC, 1995; Fitzgerald, 1989). Consequently, a complaints and discipline system can easily fall into the ironic situation where less serious charges against police are substantiated on a lower standard of proof, and more serious charges are acquitted on the higher standard (Lersch, 1998). A study of the outcome of charges against police in Queensland found that 35% of criminal charges resulted in an officer being found guilty or resigning; for matters treated as "official misconduct" the figure was 50%; for "misconduct" it was 74%; and for "breach of discipline" it was 78% (CJC, 1997, pp. 66-67). The study also found that officers who face criminal charges were much more likely to plead not guilty because of the greater potential penalties. The obvious effect of this is that officers who the Commission believed were guilty of serious offenses were being acquitted at a much higher rate than those the Commission believed were guilty of minor

Sidebar 6.1: The Pinkenba Six

"On a cold night in 1994, six police officers in an inner city area of Brisbane picked up three Aboriginal boys aged 12, 13, and 14. The boys had criminal histories, but on this occasion no charges were laid against them and there was no evidence of a crime being committed. The police left the area without authorization [and took] the boys in three patrol cars 14 km to Pinkenba, an industrial suburb with an area of waste land on the outskirts of the city. The boys were abandoned after their shoes were removed and thrown into a lake. Following disclosure and investigation by the CJC, the Public Prosecutor laid criminal charges against the police of deprivation of liberty, thereby putting the very young boys through the rigors of the adversarial system. Eades' (1995) analysis of the withering cross-examination show[ed] the cultural insensitivity of the entire committal process. The Magistrate dismissed the case, alleging the boys were unreliable witnesses. The police defense counsel cynically exploited the trait of 'gratuitous concurrence' in which Indigenous People's concern with politeness requires they agree with a proposition despite their true opinion. After the committal failed, the CJC referred the matter to the police. Deputy Commissioner Aldrich dismissed three officers and demoted four (including the Supervisor). He then suspended the sentences, effectively absolving all seven" (Prenzler, 2000, pp. 669-670).

offenses. An example of this problem is provided in Sidebar 6.1 from a case of alleged abduction by police of Aboriginal children.

An inquisitorial system in relation to police discipline (involving "administrative law" or "public law") applies lower penalties than those available in the criminal courts. Most importantly, imprisonment is not an option. The system also operates on a lower civil standard of proof—"the balance of probability"—as opposed to the criminal standard—"beyond reasonable doubt." The system trades off lower penalties against traditional rights that apply in an adversarial criminal court and favor the defendant, especially the right to silence. Officers found guilty cannot be sent to jail, but they must answer questions or face contempt proceedings, and they can be demoted or dismissed as well as fined. Of course this has been the bread and butter work of police disciplinary hearings for many decades, but it is usually confined to lower level matters, with the power vested in a disciplinary board, a single senior officer, or the police chief.

With the introduction of misconduct tribunals, consisting of one or more magistrates or judges sitting on the tribunal, a greater degree of judicial rigor can be brought into the process, and more intermediate and serious offenses can be brought into the inquisitorial process. In fact it could be argued that all charges should be automatically dealt with within an inquisitorial system. Once that process is complete, then matters can be referred to the public prosecutor. For example, an officer might be found guilty of serious assault by a tribunal and be dismissed from employment. The same officer might then be charged criminally. This is sometimes carried out in reverse—when a failed criminal prosecution is followed up with a disciplinary action—often attracting the ire of police unions with a charge of "double jeopardy." It is essential that the judicial officers sitting on tribunals are properly trained in the principles of an inquisitorial system and understand that they should adopt an active truth-seeking role, not serve merely as umpires of a contest between advocates, as in an adversarial criminal court (Prenzler, 2000).

At the core of the inquisitorial approach is the capacity to respond flexibly to evidence of probable misconduct. A key component of this is the capacity to remove officers considered unsuitable. Another component is the capacity to deter misconduct. The threat of jail is not a significant loss in this regard. Because most police are committed to a police career, and have families and mortgages, they have a strong stake in conformity, and are therefore likely to be responsive to perceptions of a high probability of detection and intermediate sanctions, especially dismissal. The flexibility of the system also allows for referral to a range of complaints resolution and behavior modification techniques that have significant potential to restore public confidence and realign officer behavior with organizational standards (see below).

Officer Rights

Inquisitorial processes abrogate defendant rights that are part of an adversarial system of justice. However, the process should never entail abrogation of a set of due process rights associated with the concept of "natural justice," such as the right of the accused to be present at a hearing, the right of reply, the right of appeal, the right to legal advice, and the right to legal support at the hearing. For police to have faith in the system there must be avenues of review or appeal to a higher authority or court (so long as the same standards of inquiry and proof are applied).

Police officers should also be fully informed of the structure of the system (as a component of training), the types of offenses and range of penalties that apply, and their rights and responsibilities within the system. The system also needs to be time efficient, as officers are likely to be highly stressed when under investigation or while there are outstanding complaints against them. Confidence must also be built through the communication of case outcomes to individuals and through a process of general reporting that allows transparency in all nonconfidential matters.

A Disciplinary Matrix

Readers might assume that all police departments have highly calibrated hierarchies of offenses with matched penalties. In fact, some research suggests that such tables are often vague and unwieldy, and wide open to misuse (Walker, 2003b). The more a system allows discretionary decision making without adequate guidelines, the more decisions can be biased and arbitrary.

Hence, police disciplinary decisions can be highly inconsistent, alternatively too lenient and too harsh (RIRP, 2000), depending on the officer making the decision. This problem can be countered with a detailed disciplinary matrix that is widely available to officers and the public.

Alternative Responses

Many jurisdictions over the last few decades have been involved in a move away from a simplistic investigate-prosecute-punish model of police account-ability toward more creative and effective strategies. The two main strategies of relevance here are alternative dispute resolution and early intervention systems. These are described in detail in subsequent chapters. While formal investigations and sanctions should remain as a mainstay of a complaints and discipline system, consideration should always been given at all stages to the greater utility of other responses.

Advanced Techniques

Successful judicial inquiries into police corruption have provided crucial les-sons about practical strategies to reveal misconduct, especially in the area of covert techniques. These include the use of undercover agents and infor-mants (including "turned" police informants), covert recording devices, and integrity tests. Drug and alcohol tests have also been successfully applied in reform programs. A simple or traditional set of investigative techniques, based on interviewing witnesses and collecting available forensic data, will generally be incapable of revealing secretive police corruption. Advanced techniques need to be included in the repertoire of investigative processes triggered by complaints, as well as operating as parallel proactive integrity strategies (see Chapter 9).

Responding to Vexatious Complaints

Just as some officers receive many complaints, some citizens complain on a frequent basis or make complaints that are vindictive. Some of these may be justifiable, but others may be harassing or malicious (NSW Ombudsman, 2002). There is a positive trend for oversight agencies to prosecute malicious complainants as a way of deterring this abuse of the complaints system and as a way of reassuring police that their interests are being protected (NSW Ombudsman, 2002).

Another counter to vexatious complaints is the use of handheld tape recorders by police. Some officers carry their own as a form of self-protection against baseless allegations. The Royal Commission on Criminal Justice that followed the English miscarriages of justice cases encouraged their use. They can provide a deterrent to police misconduct, protect officers against false complaints, and assist in resolving allegations (RCCJ, 1993).

Technical innovations now also allow for practical deployment of body-worn video (BWV), usually head-mounted around an ear (Home Office, 2007). A pilot project in Plymouth (England) involving 300 officers found that BWVs "significantly improve the quality of the evidence provided by police officers at incidents" (p. 6). Their use led to increased numbers of guilty pleas, and

> BWV recordings have also been shown to those wishing to make complaints about police actions at the scene of or en route to incidents. In a number of cases the complainants have reconsidered their complaint after this review, thus reducing investigation time for unwarranted complaints (p. 7).

Complaints in the pilot area declined between comparable time periods by 14%, from an already low number of 28 down to 24. This was insufficient to support an inference of causality. Only 5% of recorded policing incidents were attended by police wearing the cameras. However, as indicated, there were reports that some offenders who threatened to make complaints changed their minds after being shown the video evidence. In addition, "significantly there were no complaints against officers wearing head cameras" (p. 47). With all the equipment patrol officers are now required to carry, research and development is being carried out with new utility vests that can also house recording devices (Dibben, 2008).

Quality Control

System maintenance and research related to improvement are crucial to ensure that complaints and discipline systems do not deteriorate, and that they take advantage of new technologies and innovations. One important method is regular surveys of complainants and police. Although the two groups have potentially irreconcilable interests over the outcomes of investigations, survey research shows they both want the same thing in terms of process, including swift resolution, being kept informed, and having an opportunity to have their say. Three-year intervals probably provide for a reasonable schedule for such surveys. Survey instruments need to ask probing questions about how the investigation was conducted, including types of questions asked, the attitude of the investigators, timeliness, and the adequacy of communication (CJC, 1994; Landau, 1994, 1996; Maguire & Corbett, 1991). Public opinion surveys are important for gauging awareness of the complaints and discipline system, and perceptions of its effectiveness.

Auditing of case files is another important process that should cover assessment, investigations, and disciplinary decisions, and be carried out by an independent panel of experienced lawyers and investigators. Benchmarks should also be set, through experience and consultation with other agencies, in regard to targets for completion of cases (e.g., 30 days for nonserious matters, 3 months for investigations) and for convictions (such as 90% of tribunal cases). Appeal outcomes provide another measure of performance. Successful appeals constitute a negative, but should feed into procedural improvements. The quality of whistle-blower support should be a standing item in reviews and audits by external oversight agencies (CJC, 1997). Feedback from whistle-blowers will be a key source of information about the strength and impartiality of the integrity system.

Conclusion

Police departments need to establish professional standards units with adequate powers and resources to identify and prevent corruption. The unit should operate to ensure consistency in complaints processing and independence from police loyalties. It should build a central repository of intelligence data to inform proactive prevention strategies. The system for receiving complaints needs to be made easy for complainants, and complainants should be made to feel safe and able to provide all information relevant to their matter. Complaints systems need to be strengthened by internal compulsory reporting legislation and enforcement, as well as strong whistle-blower support mechanisms.

Professional standards units should be run by a top-level commander with a focus on employing quality investigators operating under strict quality standards. The system should also be inquisitorial, focused on finding the truth and achieving the best resolution of a matter, and removing officers who commit repeat breaches or serious offenses. Punitive responses need to be balanced against remedial and restorative responses. Independent quality measures are essential to prevent backsliding into weak, biased, and ineffective processes.

Alternative Dispute Resolution

7

The book so far has emphasized the need to "get tough" on police misconduct, in part through a discipline system that is seen to thoroughly investigate complaints and apply firm punishments where misconduct is identified. Punishment should serve as a deterrent but also as an expression of society's disapproval of misconduct. At the same time, punishment is generally considered most appropriate in cases of more serious or repeat breaches of standards, and as a type of "last resort" option. A variety of other responses have been alluded to that may be more appropriate—that is, fair or productive—in differing circumstances. One of these options is the removal of unsuitable officers from police work, as the behavior of serving officers, rather than retribution, should be the focus of any complaints and discipline system. Another appropriate response might be some form of remediation—through retraining, for example (see Chapter 8)—also oriented to improving behavior. Informal resolution and complaints mediation are other options that can serve a variety of productive purposes (including remediation).

This chapter reviews the research evidence about alternative dispute resolution (ADR), which shows it has a great deal of potential value in improving complainant and police satisfaction with the complaints process. It also, therefore, has a great deal to contribute to another of the key aims of a complaints and discipline system: improving public confidence in the police. It is also cheaper and faster than formal investigation and adjudication. There is a risk, however, that it allows management interest in the efficient disposition of complaints to dominate over proper misconduct prevention and more personal forms of mediation. Consequently, a number of quality control mechanisms need to be in place to ensure ADR is working consistently with the broader purposes of an integrity system.

The ADR Movement

Informal resolution and mediation of complaints against police are applications of the wider philosophy and practice of alternative dispute resolution. Mediation normally involves parties to a dispute sitting down with a neutral coordinator who facilitates an understanding of the facts and causes of the disagreement on both sides and works toward an amicable resolution. The term "mediation" is sometimes applied in a strict sense to parties being treated as equals and without an assumption of guilt. In other forums it is used more widely to refer to any reconciliation or problem-solving process involving an intermediary. Mediation is one form of alternative dispute resolution. Other forms of resolution may not require all parties to a dispute being together in a meeting. For example, a consumer complaint might be resolved by an apology or an offer of restitution by a company representative or manager. "Hybrid" forms of these approaches can also operate (Walker, Archbold & Herbst, 2002, p. 1).

ADR is an alternative to "adversarial" dispute resolution procedures embodied in the traditional civil and criminal courts. These forums usually involve a contest between parties, with a winner-takes-all result. Generally speaking, stakeholders in these processes, including litigants and plaintiffs as well as witnesses and victims of crime, are dissatisfied with the hostile, expensive, time-consuming, and impersonal nature of the process. In fact, in the standard adversarial system, accused persons are usually "rendered mute" by legal representation, and victims are downgraded to the status of witnesses who can only answer set questions (PONI, 2005, p. 13). Voluntary mediation was first introduced into civil courts in many countries in the 1970s, where it proved to be popular as a cheaper, more efficient, and more satisfactory way of resolving conflicts (Walker et al., 2002). Compulsory mediation has also been introduced in some courts, such as family courts, as an initial first step to try to broker matters early and preempt a legal battle. Forms of mediation or conferencing have also been introduced in criminal law, mainly for minor juvenile offenses but increasingly for adult and more serious offenses (Hayes, 2007).

Alternative dispute resolution is consistent with the philosophy of restorative justice. This approach to criminal justice attempts to put the needs of victims back at the center stage of the justice process, and to focus on reconciliation between victim and offender rather than an adjudication and punishment process administered by an abstract state. Restorative justice was also founded on research showing that many victims are less interested in punishment than explaining to the offender what happened to them, hearing the offender's side, and having input into the outcome of the case. Victim-offender mediation or "conferencing" involves victims and offenders sitting down with a third party who manages a discussion about the effects of the crime and the reasons why the perpetrator committed the offense (Walker et al., 2002). The formal process usually results in an agreement, including an apology or a contract regarding restitution.

There is mixed evidence about the role of victim-offender mediation in crime prevention. There are numerous intervening variables that will affect whether or not an offender commits more offenses. These factors, such as family circumstances or peer pressure, are likely to be much more powerful than a 2-hour mediation session. However, surveys of victims and offenders generally show very high levels of satisfaction with the process and the outcomes, and there is some evidence that offenders can develop empathy and remorse in a way that will help them desist from further offending (Cunningham, 2008; Hayes, 2007). Given that mediation generally does not increase crime, and may even reduce crime, overall it seems to be a very positive option that can significantly contribute to victim healing and recovery and a sense of justice.

ADR for Complaints Against Police

The success of alternative dispute resolution in other fields logically led to its application to the large volume of complaints against police. As we know, a model focused on investigation of complaints, prosecution, and punishment has generally poor outcomes. Complainants are usually dissatisfied for a variety of reasons beyond the low substantiation rates. These reasons include perceptions of bias, the length of time involved, and lack of communication (see also Chapter 10). Police also find the process stressful, alienating, and too lengthy.

The philosophy of restorative justice is particularly resonant with the aims of most complainants. Surveys indicate that the majority is not looking for revenge, a punitive outcome, or financial compensation, although some certainly are (CJC, 1994; Corbett, 1991). Most want to have their complaint recognized by the department and the subject officer, be able to communicate their feelings about the incident to the officer, and stop the alleged behavior from happening to other people. Other aims include obtaining an explanation or an apology (Maguire & Corbett, 1991; Sviridoff & McElroy, 1989; Walker, 2001).

Informal resolution for police complaints was introduced in England and Wales in 1985 in the wake of the various scandals described in Chapter 1, and efforts to improve the management of complaints (Corbett, 1991). The most recent review of programs in the United States (Walker et al., 2002) identified only 14 active programs. Implementation dates were not identified, with the exception of a model program in Minneapolis, which began in 1990. In Australia, an alternative dispute resolution program was introduced into the Queensland Police in 1993. The Queensland system involved three types of strategies: mediation, informal resolution, and managerial resolution. These are described below, including the advantages and disadvantages of each approach, as outlined by Ede and Barnes (2002).

Mediation

Mediation is also sometimes referred to as conferencing. It involves trained neutral mediators who "assist the parties to discuss the events and resolve the matter in a way that is mutually satisfactory" (Ede and Barnes, 2002, pp. 118-119). The agreement is usually written down and signed. Under mediation, a sanction is not usually an option. However, mediation can result in an admission of culpability and/or an apology from the accused officer, or the accused officer may accept that the complainant had genuine reasons for feeling aggrieved. The officer may also agree to change their behavior without necessarily agreeing it was wrong. The parties may also "agree to disagree" and be satisfied simply with having had their say. Mediation has a number of positives and negatives in relation to complaints against police:

> Mediation may help complainants convey their personal perspectives of the incident to the subject officers and may even result in the officers becoming more self-aware and consequently improving their behavior. But it will provide little or no information that the police service can use to determine whether any monitoring of the subject officers or their supervisors is warranted, nor where any changes to work practices are necessary to avoid complaint-generating behavior in the future (p. 124).

Mediation is most appropriate for minor or intermediate allegations about rudeness or inaction, but it can also apply to more serious allegations, especially of excessive force, harassment, or false arrest, especially if corroborating evidence is lacking.

Informal Resolution

Informal resolution, or "conciliation," involves a third party who acts on behalf of the police department to resolve the allegation. The third party is usually an authorized member—an officer coordinating the process—who is usually senior to the subject officer and who communicates directly with the complainant to seek a resolution. Again, the process is not oriented toward punishment or blame. The authorized officer may provide an explanation for what happened or make an apology on behalf of the department. The officer may also convince the subject officer to make a personal apology. Informal resolution "may provide simple and speedy relief to complainants in minor matters, but there must be doubt about its positive impact on the behavior of subject officers, let alone its ability to deal with systemic issues" (Ede and Barnes, 2002, p. 124). Informal resolution is considered suitable for "minor complaints that raise no concern about the subject officer's ongoing behavior" (p. 127). It is particularly good for complainants who "just want to be heard and acknowledged" (p. 127) and do not necessarily want to meet with the subject officer.

Managerial Resolution

Managerial resolution or "local resolution" gives officers in charge of stations, or local area supervisors, authority to respond to both the concerns of the complainant and to the associated conduct or competence issues involving the subject officer. The process can involve similar responses to those undertaken with informal resolution, but with the important added dimension of possible remedial interventions with the officer concerned, such as counseling, guidance, retraining, or close supervision. The response can also address systemic issues in the workplace. These actions should be communicated to the complainant. Managers usually have considerable discretion in this process. They are not required to officially substantiate a complaint and punitive actions are generally excluded. Consequently,

> [a] danger with managerial resolution is that supervisors will try to minimize the seriousness of allegations or cover up evidence they discover in order to avoid negative implications for their management evaluations. They may also try to dissuade complainants from persisting with a complaint or appealing against an unsatisfactory outcome (Ede and Barnes, 2002, p. 125).

Again, this type of response is best suited to minor and intermediate complaints, but can include serious allegations.

Evaluations of ADR for Complaints Against Police

The introduction of alternative dispute resolution to complaints against police has generally been considered very successful in addressing many of the problems associated with the investigative model. For example, Table 7.1 shows results from the introduction of informal resolution in the Queensland Police in 1993. The informal resolution procedure was compared with similar cases subject to formal investigations on criteria such as complainant and subject officer satisfaction, time taken, and cost. Most of these cases involved lower level breach-of-discipline complaints related to allegations such as rudeness, bad language, inaction, and harassment, but they also involved some allegations of improper arrest, minor assault, consumption of liquor, and damage to property. The outcomes of the process included "explanation accepted by complainant" in 39% of cases, "agreed to differ" in 32%, and an apology in 26% (CJC, 1994).

The data in Table 7.1 indicate that on all measures, informal resolution appeared to be the better option. Additionally, there were similar positive effects for complainants who underwent informal resolution in regard to the perceived effort of the authorized member, in the opportunity to express their

Table 7.1 Summary Results From Informal Resolution in the Queensland Police Service

Complainant satisfaction with outcomes	Formal investigation N = 144	Informal resolution N = 241
Satisfied	28%	60%
Dissatisfied	72%	40%
Complainant satisfaction with process	Formal investigation N = 148	Informal resolution N = 243
Satisfied	40%	76%
Dissatisfied	60%	24%
Complainant perception of time taken	Formal investigation N = 148	Informal resolution N = 243
Very quick/reasonable	43%	72%
Too long	57%	28%
Police satisfaction with outcomes	Formal investigation N = 185	Informal resolution N = 256
Satisfied	68%	76%
Dissatisfied	32%	24%
Police satisfaction with process	Formal investigation N = 188	Informal resolution N = 254
Satisfied	76%	83%
Dissatisfied	24%	17%
Police perception of time taken	Formal investigation N = 189	Informal resolution N = 259
Very quick/reasonable	35%	75%
Too long	65%	24%
Time taken	Formal investigation N = 3,416	Informal resolution N = 452
Average number of days	142	55
Financial cost	Formal investigation N = 107	Informal resolution N = 77
Average cost	AU$500	AU$138

Sources: Adapted from *Informal Complaint Resolution in the Queensland Police Service: An Evaluation,* by CJC, 1994, Brisbane: Criminal Justice Commission. Copyright 1994 by Crime and Misconduct Commission, adapted with permission. "Alternative Strategies for Resolving Complaints" by A. Ede & M. Barnes, 2002, in T. Prenzler & J. Ransley (Eds.), *Police Reform: Building Integrity* (pp. 115-130), Sydney: Federation Press. Copyright 1994. Adapted with permission.

view during the process, in the degree to which they were kept informed, in the achievement of their aims, and in an improved view of the police service. Similar results were found in the Queensland project for complainant satisfaction involving managerial resolution (Ede & Barnes, 2002, p. 122). However, a follow-up study of the informal resolution system found some slippage in lower complainant satisfaction levels and a sense that the authorized officers were not making sufficient effort (CJC, 1996a).

These findings have been mirrored on the whole in studies in other jurisdictions (Bartels & Silverman, 2005; CCRC, 1999; Sviridoff & McElroy, 1989). For example, Maguire and Corbett's (1991) assessment of the British system found that when complainants' matters were investigated, 10% were satisfied and 90% were dissatisfied. When their matter was informally resolved, 57% were satisfied and 43% were dissatisfied (p. 59).

One negative finding from the Queensland Police informal resolution evaluation concerned the lack of opportunity for the realization of a key goal of many complainants: to meet with the officer. Police themselves were also denied the opportunity to meet with complainants:

> Of the complainants who did not have a meeting with the officer, 50.5 per cent in the first study and 60 per cent in the follow up survey said they would have liked a meeting. In both studies, around 20 per cent of the officers said they would have preferred it if the IR [informal resolution] had included a meeting. ... However, the complainant and officer surveys indicate that meetings were actually held in only about five per cent of cases in the first survey and about two per cent in the follow up survey (CJC, 1996a, pp. 20, 32).

The same finding was obtained in the British study. The large minority of complainants who were dissatisfied with the informal resolution process (43%) were disappointed for several reasons. Responses indicated that one reason was the foreclosure of mediation:

> In only one of the 30 cases did a meeting take place between the complainant, the AO [authorized officer] and the officer involved ... yet when asked over a half said they would have liked such a meeting, many of these wanting either to talk through the incident, express how they felt about it or get the officer's explanation or views on the matter (Corbett, 1991, p. 55).

The study also found that, although subject officers tended to think mediation was a waste of time, four in ten were willing to meet with the complainant. Additional problems identified included the coordinating officer appearing to favor the police officer, lack of follow-up communication about the final outcome, and confusion among subject officers about whether or not participation implied an admission of responsibility. The researchers also found that many of the authorized officers essentially missed the point about restorative justice and treated the process as an informal investigation in which they took verbal evidence and came to a summary conclusion about who was telling the truth (Corbett, 1991, p. 55; Maguire & Corbett, 1991, pp. 85-90). The study also found considerable variation in the uptake of informal resolution. While almost one-quarter of complaints against police in England and Wales were subject to informal resolution, this varied from 12% to 48% between police forces (Maguire & Corbett, 1991, pp. 75-76).

Similar problems were identified in the Queensland study, and both studies found there was considerable scope for improvement. Some of this potential can be seen from case study examples described by Corbett, some of which are included in Sidebar 7.1. It can be seen from these cases that the coordinating officer plays a pivotal role and needs to be consistent in procedural fairness and promptness. There also needs to be pressure on subject officers for prompt responses to the process, and the system also needs to include all police employees.

Sidebar 7.1: Problematic Cases of Informal Resolution from the Complainants' Perspective

1. "A man was asked to accompany his brother, a juvenile, to the station so he could answer some questions. Instead, once there his brother was immediately charged and then questioned. The complainant wanted to get a solicitor for his brother and told him several times that he didn't have to say anything if he didn't wish. The officer conducting the questioning lost his temper and, according to the complainant, told him to 'shut up, get out, I've had enough of you' while pushing him to the door. The complainant was unhappy with the officer's manner, feeling he should have specified the complainant's role and the boundaries of it. As to the resolution itself, the format in this case was similar to many others we came across. The AO [authorized officer] asked if the complainant was prepared to meet the officer concerned, although he could not guarantee that the officer would apologize as the complainant wished. In the event, the AO telephoned the next day, having spoken to the officer, but did not mention a meeting. Describing himself as 'a bit dissatisfied' with the end result, the complainant said, 'He didn't mention that the officer was not prepared to apologize but instead apologized on behalf of the force for how I'd been dealt with. So, although I was kept abreast of the process, I was prepared to meet the officer again but that didn't happen. I wasn't informed of what he had said exactly

and whether the Chief Inspector told him to adopt a less aggressive attitude towards the public.'"

2. "A man muttering obscenities exposed himself to the complainant in the street. Although used to such things in her job as a psychiatric nurse, she felt frightened and later telephoned the police who promised but failed to visit. Several weeks later she recognized the man, who had been arrested for a major offense, on television. At this point she complained about the police failure to follow up her information. On being told that the failure to pass on the information was down to a new civilian telephonist, and thus a person not subject to the police disciplinary procedures, the complainant reluctantly accepted there was little more the police could do."

3. "In one case, following a robbery in which the complainant's son was an initial suspect, the police telephoned the son's place of employment and told his manager they wanted to speak to him as he was suspected of a robbery. The son had in fact been at work at the time of the robbery, and the mother complained about the disclosure of information. According to the complainant, five or six meetings took place between herself and different senior officers before she was eventually given a written apology, the only outcome she wanted."

(Corbett, 1991, pp. 53-54)

Sidebar 7.2 highlights some problems that can occur with informal resolution from the subject officer's point of view. In these cases the officers felt they were not allowed to have their say and that they were pressured to appear as if they accepted the accusations against them. These cases demonstrate the need for informal resolution to be fair and objective. Caution has to be exercised so that equity is not sacrificed to a police department public relations exercise.

Sidebar 7.2: Problematic Cases of Informal Resolution from the Police Perspective

1. "The IO [investigating officer] agreed the complainant was obnoxious but I wasn't given any option about it. It was a fait accompli—he said, 'Don't say anything. I've got to advise you informally that this is not the way to talk to the public. Sign here.' But I hadn't insulted him. I was told off for something I hadn't done. *He* annoyed me, not the complainant, not being able to say anything. I wasn't even able to say

I didn't want the advice because I wasn't guilty. I had no chance to explain my reaction and whether I accepted what had been said. I've got several over the years, and the points add up on my file, and I'm cross."

2. "[Informal resolution] has its advantages for C and D [complaints and discipline] because it saves them time, but the disadvantage for us is that it's not properly looked into. I wasn't asked if I wanted to accept it. I was shown this long statement and I agreed with every word of it except at the bottom where it said I was rude. I was not asked if I had been. If it was a full-blown complaint I'd have shown I'd done my job right."

(Maguire & Corbett, 1991, p. 83)

It is possible that the dissatisfaction expressed by both sides in these cases would be reduced by mediation. In a recent evaluation of informal resolution in Northern Ireland, 58% of complainants expressed the view that they "expected to be able to meet with the Police Officer(s) who [they] complained about" (PONI, 2005, p. 27). This, and the previous reports on complainant support for mediation, stands in contrast to a study in Calgary, which found that "[t]he majority of complainants offered mediation refused it and cited perceptions that a formal complaint investigation would be more suitable and a lack of faith that mediation would result in a positive outcome for them" (CCRC, 1999, p. 93). However, "78% of officers who were offered mediation, accepted it and of these, 83% were satisfied with the outcome" (p. 92). What is important here, nonetheless, is that complainants were at least offered a choice. Not all complainants want to meet the subject officer (Bartels & Silverman, 2005), so informal or managerial resolution can work for this group. The Northern Ireland study, in fact, recommended that "in normal circumstances it should be for the complainant to decide to engage in either the mediation or informal resolution process" (PONI, 2005, pp. 27, 33).

The Northern Ireland study concerned a police-led informal resolution system. An additional finding from the complainant survey was that 73% thought that "the informal resolution process should be handled by people who are independent of the police" (PONI, 2005, pp. 27-28). It is likely that this view would extend to the management of mediation. A New York City study of complainant satisfaction that compared cases mediated independently by the Civilian Complaint Review Board (CCRB) with those subject to full investigation found that very high levels of satisfaction were possible for cases independently mediated. For example, 81% of those who experienced mediation felt that "real issues of the complaint [were] brought out in mediation/interview," compared to 32% whose complaints were investigated. In terms of conciliation, 73% who experienced mediation felt they "understood the officer's point of view" compared to 6% whose complaint was investigated (Bartels & Silverman, 2005, p. 625). Overall, 69% of complainants who experienced mediation felt that the "final disposition was fair and appropriate," and 75% were satisfied with the "overall CCRB experience" (p. 625).

One role for citizen oversight bodies (Chapter 10) is in conciliation between police and complainants in the role of the independent mediator (Finn, 2001; Quinn, 2006). Another source of mediators is professional staff from mediation units attached to the courts (Ede & Barnes, 2002). A positive example of independent mediation is provided in Sidebar 7.3. However, there might also be a case for the availability of police mediators for those complainants who are happy with an internal mediator.

Sidebar 7.3: An Example of Successful Independent Mediation

"An officer was ticketing a car parked on the wrong side of the street when the owner came out of her house to complain. The officer ran the woman's name through the computer and found that a person matching her description had an outstanding warrant. The officer (a female) pat searched the woman and asked her to wait in the back of the cruiser. The officer then received more information indicating the woman was not the same person, so she released her. The woman filed a complaint because she felt the officer had embarrassed her in front of her children. The officer, in turn, was angry she had to mediate the issue because she felt that, having done nothing wrong, the department should have told the woman the case was closed. At the session, the mediator sat between them and asked them to decide who would talk first. The officer did, asking, 'Was I rude?'

'No.'

'Did I act professionally?'

'Yes.'

The officer then explained why she had asked the woman to sit in the car, showing her the printout that indicated a person fitting her description—approximate age, race, gender, and same last name—had a warrant out for her arrest. The officer said, 'I can understand why you were embarrassed, but if I was going to have you sit in the back of my cruiser, I needed to make sure you weren't carrying a gun that you could shoot me with in the back of the head.' The woman became less frustrated and ended up satisfied with the officer's explanation."

(Finn, 2001, p. 78)

Quality Control, Intelligence, and Behavioral Change

Alternative dispute resolution involves a number of risks that need to be controlled. One risk, as we have seen, is that it is used as a cheap and convenient bureaucratic means for dealing with the problem of complaints. In that regard the idea of "desktop informal resolution" sounds particularly ominous (CJC, 1994, p. viii). Even if complainants are satisfied, the process may conceal genuine misconduct and repeat breaches of standards. For example, the Queensland study cited above found that in a 27-month period there were 118 police officers with three or more complaints against them that were dealt with by informal resolution procedures (including 23 with five or more complaints) (CJC, 1996a, p. 28). Early intervention to deal with repeat complaints should be a first option in many cases, and this is facilitated by recording and retaining as much information as possible about all complaints, including the outcomes of informal resolution (CJC, 1996a; Corbett, 1991). In terms of improving officer behavior, it would appear that managerial resolution is a better option, followed by mediation, rather than simple informal resolution procedures. But hybrid forms of management resolution and mediation might also be best. What is also needed is good research that compares the possible effects of different dispositions on overall complaint patterns and on repeat complaints against individual officers.

In theory, mediation should lead to improved conduct as subject officers learn about citizen reactions to their actions. A U.S. Department of Justice publication, *Mediating Citizen Complaints Against Police Officers: A Guide for Police and Community Leaders* (Walker et al., 2002), focused on mediation as the best form of alternative dispute resolution for improving community relations. Sidebar 7.4 sets out the theoretical arguments in favor of mediation—many of these are supported by the research evidence cited in this chapter.

Sidebar 7.4: "Potential Benefits of Mediation"

"Benefits for police officers:
   1. Better understanding of interactions with citizens
   2. Opportunity to explain actions to citizens
   3. Greater satisfaction with complaint process
   4. Empowerment
   5. Chance to learn from mistakes

Benefits for citizen complainants:
   1. Greater opportunity to meet goals

2. Greater satisfaction with complaint process
3. Better understanding of policing
4. Empowerment

Benefits for police accountability:
1. Greater responsibility for one's actions
2. Positive changes in police subculture

Benefits for community policing:
1. Goals consistent with those of community policing
2. Problem-solving process
3. An opportunity for dialogue

Benefits for complaint process:
1. More efficient complaint processing
2. Cost savings
3. Higher success rate

Benefits for the criminal justice system:
1. More trust in justice system
2. Lower crime rate"

(Walker et al., 2002, p. 5)

Ede and Barnes (2002) provide a useful set of guidelines for matching the most appropriate type of response to different types of complaints. Sidebar 7.5 sets out questions that complaint assessment officers should make in determining the best course of action between (a) formal investigation, (b) informal resolution, (c) managerial resolution, and (d) mediation.

Sidebar 7.5: Questions to Guide Complaints Disposition Decisions

1. **"How serious is the complaint?** As the seriousness of the allegation is an important determinant, this must be ascertained as soon as possible. Initial inquiries probably need to be made by a complaints officer who is a lawyer or trained detective well versed in precedents and prevailing standards.

2. What is the complainant's objective? As complainant satisfaction is an important outcome, it is necessary to find out what complainants want to see happen as a result of making the complaint. Usually complainants will have little knowledge of the various responses available, and so these need to be explained in a manner that enables them to understand that there are other options apart from a formal investigation that can satisfy their concerns. This can be done face to face or via telephone. Care must be taken not to influence complainants to accept a 'soft option.'

3. What is the subject officer's complaints history? To avoid repeated use of ineffective responses it is essential to review the subject officer's complaints history to see if there is a pattern of complaints and remedial responses that have already been tried. ...

4. What is the subject officer's version of events? Traditionally, the subject officer is not officially spoken to about a complaint until all of the evidence available from other sources has been gathered. It may well be that if spoken to immediately the incident comes to notice the officer will make concessions that will help decide how the matter should be dealt with. Concerns about induced confessions have no application in circumstances where officers can be directed to answer questions. Officers can be reinterviewed if the matter proceeds to investigation."

(Ede & Barnes, 2002, pp. 128-129)

To reiterate, as part of quality control in ADR it is essential that all aspects of the complaints process and different dispositions are recorded and analyzed for trends. This can allow for identification of, and informed responses to, questionable trends, such as divergence between complainant perspectives on outcomes and police department records, or increasing exclusion of complainants from the process. Inconsistencies in the use of different options between police divisions can also be identified by this process. Regular surveys of complainants and police about their experience of the process should be part of the monitoring and improvement process (CJC, 1996a). Some examples of useful statements linked to positive and negative indicators are cited below from Bartels and Silverman's study focused on comparing mediation and investigations (2005, p. 624):

- Real issues of complaint brought out in mediation/interview
- Had a "say" in complaint disposition
- Listened to by the mediator/investigator
- Rights were respected by the mediator/investigator
- Level of trust in the mediator/investigator
- Feel complaint was fully resolved
- Understood officer's point of view
- Complaint's final disposition was fair and appropriate
- Satisfaction with overall experience

Another important way of ensuring that informal resolution is operating optimally is to systematize the steps involved so that the coordinating officer is required to ensure proper consultation regarding all options (CJC, 1996a). There should therefore be a printed form that lists steps and includes a checklist that requires officers to attest to the fact that mediation has been offered to both parties. There is also a case to be made for the compulsory participation of officers in mediation where it is requested by complainants. A printed procedures form should also require records of time involved between steps and a signed agreement between parties as to the outcome. Outcomes from managerial resolution that can include behavioral modification options for officers also need to be recorded. An ideal time standard should also be established and included as a benchmark on the checklist. Both parties should also receive written notification of the final outcome of the process and a summary record of the process.

Coordinating officers also need to be thoroughly trained in all aspects of informal resolution, especially in the research findings and types of issues discussed in this chapter. This should not just be an administrative role. Police officers who manage and administer alternative dispute resolution systems should be experts on the topic and maintain their knowledge through in-service training sessions and group debriefs with academic and other experts in the field.

Despite the higher cost and general negativity associated with formal investigations, this option needs to be retained as a first option for more serious complaints, with mediation as a fallback option if evidence is not forthcoming. Formal investigations should also be considered as part of an officer profiling process, triggered as an automatic response to multiple minor and intermediate complaints above a threshold level, such as three or more per year or a lower average over a longer period (CJC, 1996a; see also Chapter 8 on early intervention systems). In addition, consistent efforts need to be put into addressing the factors that are identified as causing dissatisfaction with the investigation process, including communication, perceptions of bias, and lengthy time periods. Investigations should not be allowed to run down simply because informal resolution is available.

One difficult issue concerns confidentiality. Some police mediation systems require confidentiality, which can be waived if the parties agree (Ede & Barnes, 2002). Confidentiality may encourage officers to be cooperative and even make admissions, but it reduces any intelligence value in the process and can serve to hide misconduct. However, at a minimum the details of the allegations and the outcomes of the resolution process must be recorded.

Informal resolution of complaints can also be used where the initial response to a complaint is a formal investigation. Unsubstantiated complaints can be mediated, but even if a complaint is sustained, mediation and apology might be better responses than various punitive responses. The Oppal Commission in British Columbia recommended that the use of informal resolution strategies be available "as early in the complaint process as possible and throughout all stages of the process" (Oppal, 1994, p. 1-10).

Conclusion

Informal resolution of complaints against police offers considerable scope for dealing positively with the large volume of minor and intermediate complaints that lack corroborating evidence or which are unlikely to be resolved to the satisfaction of all parties through an expensive and time-consuming investigative process. The primary purposes are to improve complainant satisfaction and public confidence in police. ADR should also provide a learning opportunity for individual police officers, and for police departments committed to improving behavior. Despite the very positive findings from many evaluations of alternative dispute resolution procedures, a number of areas in reported practice appear amenable to improvement. Informal resolution systems tend to underutilize face-to-face mediation, and there is also a wider problem of the inconsistent uptake of informal resolution options across departments. Better training of coordinating officers and a more systematic approach to working through options, including a detailed paper trail, should allow for better deployment of options. Although forms of alternative dispute resolution are limited in their preventive effects, there is also scope through an intelligence-led approach to identify officers with complaint histories that require remedial intervention.

System Controls and Risk Management

8

This chapter deals with a relatively new area of police integrity management, which can be described in terms of system controls, risk management, or intelligence management, including early warning or early intervention systems, integrity profiling, and complaints profiling. The main aim of this approach is to preempt misconduct and associated operational errors by conducting risk assessments of police actions and putting in place as many controls as possible to limit the chances of unethical and damaging behaviors from occurring. A drug raid is a good example. This is a high-risk operation, both for mistakes and corruption. Chemicals can be spilled and explode, or large quantities of cash can be pocketed by police. Consequently, strict procedures need to be put in place to ensure that adverse events cannot occur.

Risk management also entails collecting and analyzing as much information as possible about police behavior in a way that will allow for the identification of early or potential signs of misconduct. These risk indicators can then be used to design, implement, and assess prevention strategies. Research to date suggests that wide data collection and analysis, and targeted interventions can be highly effective in reducing complaints and improving police-citizen relations. This then limits the need to resort to complex investigations and punitive responses "downstream." At the same time, risk management data can also be used to inform investigations that lead to convictions and disciplinary responses where necessary.

Background

In the type of traditional or "minimal" model of police accountability described in Chapter 6, complaints and other information about alleged or suspected misconduct are investigated by interviewing witnesses or seeking other sources of corroboration. If the evidence appears adequate, a prosecution will be initiated, either in a disciplinary hearing or a court of law. The complaint is either then substantiated and a penalty is imposed, or it is not substantiated and the matter is dropped. Because of the common problem of finding evidence, this approach can mean that a great deal of misconduct is not brought to light.

This problem follows from the fact that policing is an occupation characterized by a high degree of independent action by front-line operatives. What is really happening out there in the field? As we have seen in chapter

4 on measuring misconduct and integrity, this can be a difficult question to answer. Managers concerned with monitoring police behavior need to mobilize as many sources of information as possible. Advances in information technology now make this possible on a large scale. Consequently, computer-based intelligence gathering and complaints profiling are essential for any state-of-the-art police integrity system. Although this is recognized as an emerging imperative in policing, its emergence appears to be fairly slow and limited. A 2001 survey in the United States (Archbold, 2005) found that only 14 out of 354 police departments identified risk management as a strategy they had adopted to reduce police liabilities.

Strategic Intelligence

Chapter 4 described a number of sources of information about police in the form of "de-identified" statistics from surveys and from aggregated complaints and prosecutions data. Information that relates to specific individuals, or even police work units, is often referred to as "intelligence." Where it is used to inform interdictions, especially in terms of arrests, it is often referred to as "tactical intelligence" or "strategic intelligence." The use of intelligence about police misconduct follows the same principles as those applied to police management of "criminal intelligence" (Brown, 2001; Ratcliffe, 2008). Criminal intelligence is focused on information that assists in the identification of offenders, although it can also relate to other aspects of police work such as locating victims or locating the proceeds of crime. Sources include eyewitness accounts of the appearance of a suspect, as well as trace evidence such as fingerprints and DNA, or a document trail. Criminal intelligence can also refer to information that may be used to make predictions about likely reoffending, such as prior convictions and employment status, or assist in a clearer understanding of the possible motivations of an offender, such as an anger management problem or drug habit. Intelligence includes incomplete fragments or isolated pieces of information that might be used to inform suspicions about a person but which on their own do not constitute legally admissible evidence, such as the mere presence at a crime scene of a known person's fingerprint or an adverse psychological test result. A great deal of intelligence data is therefore provisional, indicative, and exploratory.

The ability to cross-reference or "match" these types of data with fresh case information and findings from ongoing investigations is a crucial means of casting the information net as widely as possible. Special risk assessment or intelligence units that manage this type of computer-based information management are now vital to modern law enforcement:

> Information is the life blood of law enforcement. ... Police administrators and planners are finding it more and more necessary to collate seemingly unrelated bits of information into some kind of understandable whole so that they can use their already strained resources as effectively as possible. The need for accurate and timely information about criminal activity has led to the creation of criminal intelligence units to gather, analyze and disseminate information in support of operational units (Brown, 2001, p. 64).

A related area of strategic crime analysis that can be applied to integrity management is crime mapping, which focuses on the clustering of crimes in particular geographical locations or around particular times of day (Eck & Weisburd, 2002).

Information about possible police officer misconduct comes from a variety of sources, including supervisor reports, drug and alcohol test results, or compulsory incident reports (on events such as use of force or discharge of weapon). Considered in isolation, none of these sources may appear to say anything of significance about an officer's conduct. However, added together over time they may provide a quite different picture, indicating patterns of behavior that need to be addressed. This view is summed up in the findings of a large-scale review of the police integrity system in the United Kingdom performed by the Home Office:

> Her Majesty's Inspector considers it good practice to maintain a central repository for suspicions—internally or externally generated—to allow collation, analysis and appropriate action to be taken. Currently, there could be information or intelligence held about potentially dishonest officers in different locations within a force, such as the complaints and discipline department, informant contact reports, divisional discipline books or grievance procedure reports. The Inspection Team found little evidence these threads were being pulled together to provide a comprehensive picture of suspected staff (HMIC, 1999a, p. 59).

Complaints

As we have seen, complaints are a major quantitative source of information about possible police misconduct. Although many complaints contain little of substance in terms of legally admissible evidence, they need to be taken seriously in any formal system of police accountability. Their significance receives added weight from the fact that many people who have a grievance against police will not complain, and making a complaint can be an intimidating experience.

Traditional mechanisms for dealing with complaints limit investigations to the immediate circumstances of the complaint or related allegations in order to ensure that the investigation is not tainted by assumptions based on previous conduct. While this process is procedurally fair, it does not contribute to the identification of complaint patterns and profiles of risk. For example, police officers may have substantiated complaints against them with penalties that have not led to dismissal. Over the years the number of substantiated complaints may accumulate without supervisors or disciplinary boards being aware of the situation. The same can occur with unsubstantiated complaints, where the frequency should arouse suspicion. An example is sexual harassment of female motorists by a male traffic officer. The officer may make suggestive comments to a woman pulled over for a misdemeanor offense. When she complains and the matter is investigated, the case is unsubstantiated because there are no witnesses and the officer denies the allegation. When the officer does it again the same process occurs. This can go on indefinitely unless a record of all complaints is kept and checked on a periodic basis.

As noted in the chapter on complaints and discipline, reinforcement of misconduct occurs when breaches of the rules are not detected or not substantiated. But it can also occur when substantiated breaches receive minor penalties and there are no additional penalties for repeat breaches. Over time, under these circumstances, a small number of officers can attract a large number of complaints, while suffering only minor penalties. Sidebar 8.1 lists findings from studies of police handling of complaints and incident reports. They all highlight the same diagnostic, that a small number of officers are usually responsible for a disproportionately large number of complaints. This is similar to criminological findings regarding crime statistics that indicate overall crime figures are pushed up by repeat offenders. This fact carries important implications for crime prevention. If the repeat offenders can be stopped, then large reductions can be made in the overall rate of victimization. The same applies in theory to police complaints. In that regard, the idea of early intervention also has strong theoretical support from criminological research on criminal careers and the onset, persistence, and desistence of offending. Risk factors can be used to identify potential criminal offenders, and early intervention (through remedial programs for exam-

Sidebar 8.1 Examples of Findings About Patterns in Complaints Against Officers

The Christopher Commission on the Los Angeles Police Department Complaints. "Of approximately 1,800 officers against whom an allegation of excessive force or improper tactics was made from 1986 through 1990, over 1,400 officers had only one or two allegations. But 183 officers had four or more allegations, 44 had six or more, 16 had eight or more, and one had 16 allegations.

Use of Force Reports. Of nearly 6,000 officers identified as involved in use of force reports from January 1987 through March 1991, more than 4,000 had fewer than five reports each. But 63 officers had 20 or more reports each. The top 5% of officers ranked by number of reports accounted for more than 20% of all reports, and the top 10% accounted for 33%." (Christopher, 1991, p. 36)

The Kolts Commission on the Los Angeles Sheriff's Department

"Research by the Kolts Commission found that of approximately 8,000 sworn officers in the LASD, a group of 62 officers was subject to a total of just under 500 'Force/Harassment investigations' (including numerous shootings). This was under a system where there was no compulsory recording of use of force cases. These officers accounted for five or more investigations each in a 5-year period. Many had seven or more reports. One had 17, one 25, and one 27. Seventeen of the deputies were responsible for 22 lawsuits resulting in nearly $3.2 million in jury awards or settlements paid out by the county." (Kolts, 1992, p. 160)

The New South Wales Ombudsman

"Preliminary research by my office suggests in excess of 200 police officers have complaint histories which indicate they may present a significant risk to the police service and community. Some of these officers have very serious substantiated complaints against them, including criminal matters. Others have between 20 and 40 complaints of varying degrees of seriousness." (NSW Ombudsman, 2002, p. 8)

The Queensland Crime and Misconduct Commission

The Crime and Misconduct Commission has been monitoring conduct issues associated with a cohort of police recruits from 1997 to 1998. After 7 years of service the 1,062 officers had drawn 1,669 complaints, with 62.5% attracting one complaint or more and 37.5% attracting no complaints. However, 7% (75) of the officers had drawn one third of the complaints (555). (Legosz, 2007; for an almost identical finding see Lersch & Mieczkowski, 1996) ple) can reduce the frequency and seriousness of later offending (Farrington & Welsh, 2007).

Another common finding regarding "problem officers" (Kolts, 1992, p. 157) is that they are frequently rewarded by their department. In relation to the 62 LASD deputies discussed in Sidebar 8.1, the Kolts Commission found that

> [o]verall, the evaluations in personnel files of the illustrative group were extremely laudatory. Many files were filled with documentation of formal and informal compliments and commendations, no matter how trivial. In sharp contrast, there was near silence about investigations for excessive force. ... In addition, a history of Force/Harassment investigations did not stand in the way of promotion to field training officer or highly-coveted assignments. ... Nearly all of these officers continue to patrol the streets of Los Angeles (pp. 160, 161, 158).

The Commission selected a number of cases for detailed examination. One of these is included in Sidebar 8.2.

Sidebar 8.2: "Deputy B"

"Since joining the LASD, deputy B has been the subject of 17 Force/harassment investigations, 3 of which related to shootings. In 1984, the Department proposed to fire deputy B for writing a false police report that resulted in a failed prosecution. Although not explained in deputy B's personnel file, deputy B was permitted to resign in lieu of being fired. Deputy B's personnel file also does not explain why deputy B was reinstated just over eight months later.

"One 1990 investigation of deputy B concerned a citizen's allegation that deputy B struck the citizen in the mouth with a metal flashlight, knocking out four front teeth. The allegation was deemed 'Unsubstantiated,' although the investigation confirmed that a blow from deputy B caused two caps on the complainant's teeth to come loose, and a document in the IAB investigative file expressed concern with deputy B's 'extensive record of prior investigations for similar allegations.'

"In a 1989 complaint, a motorcycle rider alleged that, after a short chase, deputy B beat him with a flashlight. A number of independent witnesses corroborated the complainant's story. The matter was referred to the D.A.'s office for prosecution, but was ultimately rejected. After subsequent IAB investigation, the complaint was deemed 'Unsubstantiated.'

"A 1987 investigation concerned allegations that deputy B put a suspect in a patrol car, ostensibly to question him, and then punched and struck the suspect with his flashlight. The department referred the matter to the D.A.'s office for criminal prosecution. A prosecution of deputy B was initiated, but was later dismissed for prosecutorial misconduct. The Department then withdrew its initially proposed 10-day suspension and entered a finding of 'Unsubstantiated.'

"Although deputy B has a history of use of excessive force—he was twice referred to the D.A.'s office for possible criminal prosecution—and was once fired for writing a false police report, he is viewed by his superiors as a 'hardcharger' and a good deputy. Deputy B's evaluations over the time period are consistently 'very good.' In his 1991 evaluation, the only criticism was that deputy B was too willing to make arrests without calling for backup. His 1989 evaluation states that deputy B 'seldom generated citizen complaints.' Throughout the above time period, deputy B's 'meeting and handling the public' skills were also consistently rated 'very good'" (Kolts, 1992, pp. 162-163).

Principles of Complaint Profiling and Early Intervention

Gradual recognition of the phenomenon of repeat complaints against police led to calls for remedial interventions. The 1981 U.S. Commission on Civil Rights recommended that all police departments should develop systems for identifying problem officers (USCCR, 1981, 2000). The main technique that has been adopted is complaint profiling, or integrity profiling, using a variety of indicators. In a "point and flag" system, a warning flag is raised when a specific number of points is accumulated from weighted indicators in a given time frame—typically two or more in a 12-month period (Bassett & Prenzler, 2002). While quantitative indictors are usually used to trigger profiles, a profiling system should be flexible and include qualitative sources, such as supervisor performance appraisals. The following types of indicators are usually included in a warning/intervention system (Berkow, 1996; Walker, Alpert & Kenney, 2001):

- Citizen complaints
- Internal complaints/disclosures
- Discharge of firearm
- Unusual absenteeism/sick leave
- High-speed pursuits
- Vehicle collisions
- Injury to arrestee
- Failure to attend court

- Use of force incidents
- Adverse work performance reports
- Suspensions, fines, or other disciplinary outcomes
- Litigation
- Failed prosecution briefs

Misconduct indicators need to be considered in context and thresholds adjusted for different work units. Police in high crime and high arrest areas will attract more complaints than those in other areas (Lersch, Bazley & Mieczkowski, 2006). Consequently, an understanding of the different task environments needs to be built into the early warning system. Indicators also need to be weighted according to different levels of seriousness, so that a flag might be raised after two complaints of a serious matter vis-à-vis four complaints of a minor nature.

Another important aspect of a comprehensive early warning system is that all complaints should be included and used to trigger alerts, including cases that are not substantiated. According to Berkow,

> [t]he key to a successful system is to include as much data as possible. The blending of a wide range of indicators may well bring an officer to the top of the list where a review of a single aspect would not (1996, p. 24).

Even withdrawn complaints should be included because they may suggest intimidation of complainants. Data about outcomes of complaints should also go into the mix when building a profile. If a thorough investigation identified the officer as exonerated of the complaint, this should also be recognized. Intelligence gathering can be further enhanced by the provision of secure internal and external "confidential reporting lines," widely promoted, with specially trained call center staff to handle approaches (HMIC, 1999b, pp. 125-126).

At the same time that all these often inconclusive pieces of information are being drawn together, it is extremely important that officers understand that profiling is an objective process conducted "without prejudice and with a presumption of innocence" (Ede et al., 2002a, p. 9; see also Coble, 1997, on legal issues). Officers will feel threatened by the prospect of disciplinary action. They will also be concerned that having a record, even if they have been cleared of wrongdoing, will prejudice their career prospects or affect people's view of their character. It is therefore vital from the point of view of both organizational morale and ethical practice that officers subject to profiling are allowed to give their side of the issue at stake, and that their responses form part of the record. It has also been argued that officers should, in most cases, know what their complaint history is, and how it is being used in performance assessments. Officers should also "have the right to have noted on their complaint history matters which are disputed" (NSW Ombudsman, 2002, p. 15).

"Early warning systems" or "early intervention systems" are generic terms. Within a police department an official name for the system might be something like Professional Performance Enhancement Program (PPEP) (Walker et al., 2001, p. 4). A program of this type typically involves the following steps. Once a profile has been prepared, the officer is called to a meeting where the indicators are discussed. Meetings can be conducted by professional standards officers, but it is normal for the officer's supervisor to be included. One of the most important aspects of a meeting is simply to alert the officer to the fact that close monitoring is in place. Meetings are not disciplinary hearings, but a degree of cooperation by the officer is usually required. Various outcomes are possible. It is possible that an officer's explanation for the adverse indicators is accepted and no further action is taken. More typically, without the officer necessarily making explicit admissions, a remedial plan is developed that can include counseling, assistance with lifestyle issues such as gambling or alcoholism, retraining, or close supervision. Close supervision can include the supervisor observing the officer on the job interacting with citizens (Walker et al., 2001). The action plan will include a time frame, with progress reports and a final sign-off date. Figure 8.1 outlines the theoretical progression of an individual profile and intervention that leads to the reduction or elimination of complaints. The model includes a complaints trajectory without intervention, and also a relapse and second intervention process.

Individual Profiling: Some Case Studies

One of the earliest accounts of early intervention within policing comes from the famous Oakland Police Department Violence Reduction Project of the early-1970s (Toch & Grant, 2005). The project was an example of a form of problem-oriented policing and action research, focused on the problem of physical conflict between police and citizens. A distinctive feature of the Oakland project was that the new system was developed through close consultation with police officers. A Violence Reduction Unit generated a peer-based early intervention system. Officers who passed a threshold for involvement in violent incidents were required to attend a peer review panel where they discussed the incidents with their colleagues, identified factors in their behavior and attitudes that may have contributed to the conflict, and made commitments to a changed approach to suspects. The system produced marked reductions in violent encounters between police and citizens (pp. 235-239).

There was little available on the topic in the main criminology literature until 2001, when the U.S. National Institute of Justice (NIJ) published

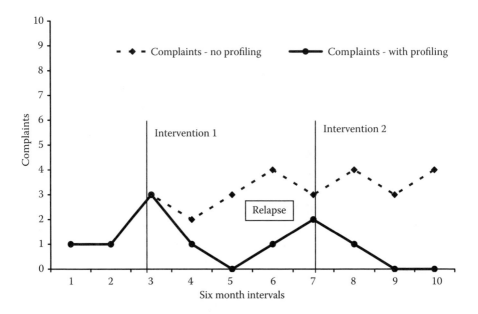

Figure 8.1 Theoretical model of the effect of early intervention on an individual police officer. Note. Adapted from "Complaint Profiling and Early Warning Systems" (p. 141), by M. Bassett and T. Prenzler in Police Reform: Building Integrity, T. Prenzler and J. Ransley (Eds.), 2002, Sydney: Federation Press.

a report *Early Warning Systems: Responding to the Problem Officer* (Walker et al., 2001). The national survey found that 27% of a large sample of departments had an early warning system in place. The report included three case studies that demonstrated the potential of early warning systems to reduce complaints. The departments were Minneapolis, New Orleans, and Miami-Dade. The study concluded that introducing the systems had a "dramatic effect" on reducing poor performance records and complaints. In summary, the following results were reported (Walker et al., 2001, p. 3):

- In Minneapolis, the average number of citizen complaints received by officers subject to early intervention dropped by 67% one year after the intervention.
- In New Orleans, that number dropped by 62% one year after intervention.
- In Miami-Dade, only 4% of the early-warning cohort had zero use-of-force reports prior to intervention; following intervention, 50% had zero use-of force reports.

In Miami-Dade, an earlier evaluation (Charette, 1993) showed that in the first year of operation, in 1981, the Early Identification System flagged an average of 37.5 staff per quarter. In the following 11 years the average was 7.6 per quarter—in a period when staff numbers increased by 90%.

Interviews conducted for the NIJ study showed that police officers involved in the intervention programs were generally positive about their experiences. Early intervention can save careers that are on the slide. Supervisors benefited from the fact they were compelled to take action against officers with questionable records and had evidence on hand about officer behavior.

In a related program focused on tackling rising payouts associated with civil litigation, the Los Angeles Sheriff's Department in 2003 implemented a Strategic Risk Management program to reduce litigation and the costs of litigation. The program (a) expedited cases with merit in favor of the litigant, (b) thoroughly investigated and challenged cases deemed to be without merit (especially those with high costs attached), and (c) addressed systematic behavioral and procedural issues identified from analyses of litigation cases. The results "surpassed even LASD's most optimistic expectations": "The fiscal year 2003-4 statistics, when compared to the previous fiscal year, revealed that the active caseload decreased 17.8 percent, that new lawsuits decreased 26.9 percent, and that judgment and settlement costs decreased more then 55 percent" (Jones & Mathers, 2006, p. 126).

The Victoria Police Early Intervention System

In Australia, the Victoria Police were pioneers in trialing an early intervention system (Macintyre, Prenzler & Chapman, 2008). All complaints are entered on the Ethical Standards Department's (ESD) computerized database ROCSID (Register of Complaints, Serious Incidents and Discipline). When a member receives two or more complaints in a 12-month period the database automatically flags the member. Staff from the Research and Risk Unit (RRU) generates a "member profile." The profile elaborates on the complaints history of the officer and includes information on sick leave, use of force reports, supervisor assessment reports, and other data that might help inform a management response.

Depending on the seriousness of possible misconduct shown in a profile, a member may be charged criminally or be prosecuted by a disciplinary tribunal. In other cases, a remedial action plan will be developed. The plan is negotiated between various groups, including the RRU, regional Ethics and Professional Standards Officers (EPSOs), and Area Management. The area managers normally meet with the member to discuss the profile. The meeting covers the dimensions of the problem behaviors and recommendations for improving them. A remedial plan is finalized that includes periodic review and an end date when measures should have been implemented.

A study of the impact of individual profiles and interventions in the Victorian system was conducted for the period 1997 to 2004 (Macintyre et al., 2008). Counts were taken of the number of complaints recorded against a sample of 44 officers for the 16 quarters prior to profiling and intervention, and eight quarters after. The data included seven members who resigned within the post-intervention window, and the resignations were attributed to the spotlight being placed on these members' behavior. The complaints mainly related to behavioral issues such as duty failure and minor assault. In the 16 quarters prior to being profiled the whole sample received an average of 15.1 complaints per quarter. For the eight quarters after profiling there was a 71% reduction to 4.3 complaints per quarter. It was projected that the sample would have received at least a further 121 complaints over two years (15.1 per quarter) had they not been profiled. Instead, they received only 35 complaints over the eight quarters following interventions. Hence, it was asserted that 86 complaints were prevented, with a savings of several millions of dollars in reduced complaints processing costs.

Of additional interest is the fact that complaints in the sample group were increasing in frequency before intervention and then began to decline following intervention. This is shown in Figure 8.2, with the inclusion of trend lines. The trend line for the pre-intervention complaints demonstrates that they would have been expected to continue to increase without intervention. Conversely, the number of complaints post-intervention continued to decline.

Early Intervention: Unit Profiles

While the focus of profiling is generally on individual officers, it should also be used to examine work units or locations. Complaints are not normally spread evenly across a police department but can cluster in certain units, including more intense "hot spots." In one of the few studies on this topic, Ede et al. (2002a) used Queensland Police data to demonstrate the potential for analyzing complaints at the level of police operational units (primarily stations). Drawing on the criminological concept of crime mapping, analysis of complaints was conducted at a more specific level than previously attempted. The study also attempted to control for the effects of different task environments—by comparing units of similar size and similar duties—and by comparing complaint patterns in terms of concentration and prevalence. A high concentration of complaints was related to a problem with small numbers of individuals attracting a large number of complaints. A high prevalence, or wider spread of complaints, was related to a more diffuse problem of workplace culture. Of 436 units, 38 had no complaints and 79 had either a high concentration or a high prevalence. Five units had a high concentration and high prevalence.

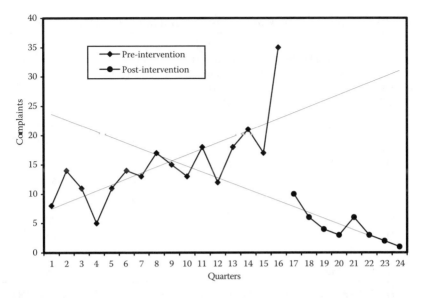

Figure 8.2 Victoria Police Early Intervention System: complaints for sample before and after profiling and intervention. N = 44. Note. Adapted from "Early Intervention to Reduce Complaints: An Australian Victoria Police Initiative," by S. Macintyre, T. Prenzler, and J. Chapman, 2008, International Journal of Police Science and Management, 10(2), p. 246. Copyright 2008 by Valthek Publishing. Adapted with permission.

This approach was put into action by the Victoria Police, who introduced unit profiling along with individual profiling. In the Victorian system, unit, or location, profiles rely largely on complaints data, rather than other indicators that are more relevant in the assessment of individual members (Macintyre et al., 2008). Profiles were conducted for nine locations—five were "uniform" and four were "CIB" (detective branch). Location risk assessments identified issues that were addressed with retraining programs, modified management styles and policies, or by moving individual members away from areas where problem behavior appeared to have become ingrained. Table 8.1 shows the number of complaints recorded before the profile, the expected number of complaints without profiling, the number of complaints after profiling, and the percentage change. The table shows that the number of complaints decreased at every location for the four quarters after profiles were conducted, with one exception (I) where no change was recorded. On a per-quarter basis, there was a 58% decline from an average of 15 complaints before intervention to an average of 6. As with the individual profiles, a time-series version of the data showed that complaints were increasing before the location interventions and then continued to decrease after the interventions.

Table 8.1   Victoria Police: Work Location Complaints Before and After

Location	Complaints before profile (16 quarters)	Expected complaints without profile (4 quarters)	Complaints after profile (4 quarters)	Change (%)
A	60	15	2	-86.7
B	43	10.75	8	-25.6
C	32	8	4	-50.0
D	32	8	4	-50.0
E	20	5	2	-60.0
F	16	4	0	-100.0
G	16	4	2	-50.0
H	15	3.75	1	-73.3
I	8	2	2	0.0
Total	**242**	**60.5**	**25**	**-58.6**

Note. From "Early Intervention to Reduce Complaints: An Australian Victoria Police Initiative," by S. Macintyre, T. Prenzler, and J. Chapman, 2008, *International Journal of Police Science and Management, 10*(2), p. 247. Copyright 2008 by Valthek Publishing. Adapted with permission.

Broader Risk Management and Threat Assessments

As we have seen, policing is a high-risk occupation for misconduct, but risk is not spread evenly. Particular officers or stations may be more prone to misconduct than others. Furthermore, particular types of police work, or aspects of police operations, also carry specific risks. Examples include:

- Detectives and process corruption
- Traffic patrol and opportunistic bribes
- Watchhouses and assaults or deaths in custody
- Motor vehicle patrols and dangerous high-speed pursuits
- Special tactics units and excessive force in raids and sieges
- Drug squads and on-selling of drugs or shakedowns of dealers
- Illicit access to and misuse of confidential information

These are areas that require strict controls, regular risk assessments, and close monitoring to ensure that abuses do not creep in. Risk assessments of this type utilize a variety of sources, including complaints and other data listed above, but they can also use social science methods such as surveys and interviews, analyses of incident data, participant debriefs, and follow-up inquiries on media reports. An associated area of risk management is more in the domain of strategic risk assessments, which have been used in Britain on an annual basis to forecast emerging and potential threats, such as attempted criminal infiltration of police ranks (HMIC, 1999b, p. 9). The following sections outline some key examples of risk management protocols. Although they are not all about corruption in the classic sense, they do provide good examples of cases that straddle both ethical and technical issues. The protocols are designed to preempt the kind of "ambiguous cases" discussed in Chapter 1, where a small series of misjudgments can lead to disaster.

High-Speed Pursuits

Police work may call for high-speed vehicle pursuits at times, but research clearly shows that most of the initial violations that trigger pursuits, such as traffic infringements, are not sufficiently serious to justify the resulting deaths and injuries among officers, offenders, and the public. Contemporary best practice standards now place severe limits on officer discretion in pursuits (Hoffman, 2003; Rix, Walker & Brown, 1997). Controls include:

- A high threshold of grounds for high-speed pursuits (e.g., probable crimes above relatively minor traffic violations)
- A low threshold of grounds for terminating a pursuit (e.g., bystanders)
- Absolute speed limits of 30% to 40% above the posted limit
- Radio supervision of drivers by a senior officer
- Regular refresher training that includes research findings that contradict myths about the value of pursuits

Data Access Controls and Data Trails

Electronic storage and access systems now make data access controls and tracking relatively simple, using procedures commonplace in information technology security. Controls include (HMIC, 1999b, pp. 128-129):

- Sequestering of highly sensitive databases, such as informant registers and Professional Standards data
- Password access on a strict "need-to-know" basis
- Regular automated password change requirements
- Entry questions about access purposes
- Automatic timeouts to prevent secondary access
- Regular audits to identify illicit access
- Automatic alerts about attempted unauthorized access or unusual activity

- Passwords connected to building security swipe cards so that an alert can be triggered if a staff member has left the building but appears to be on the computer system

Informant Management

The use of informants as an anticorruption strategy is discussed in the following chapter on covert tactics. Informants have often had a corrupting influence on police. The following points have emerged from corruption inquiries and reviews as key mechanisms for minimizing hazards in this area (HMIC, 1999b; ICAC, 1994; Parks, 2000, p. 352):

- Informants must be named in documentation, including all aliases.
- Access to the identities of informants must be limited to a very small circle, with strict electronic database access protocols (see above).
- All police-informant relations must be supervised by a "third party" senior police officer.
- The supervisor must have personally met the informant.
- The supervisor must have regular meetings with the police officer.
- All payments must be recorded.
- The value of information must be continuously assessed and the relationship terminated if the information is not of demonstrable forensic value.
- Oversight agencies should routinely scrutinize informant management systems.

Due Process in Investigations and Prosecutions

A number of procedural safeguards have been developed over time in legal systems to limit the capacity for corruption in investigations and prosecutions. These are often referred to as the "legal regulation of policing" (Dixon, 2006). It is essential to maintain these traditional procedures, despite the fact they have been shown to be far from foolproof in preventing process corruption. These procedures include the following:

- Police informing suspects of their rights
- More serious cases being taken over by lawyers in a public prosecutors office
- Application of the "exclusionary rule" in the courts to exclude evidence obtained illegally

- Application of "laws of evidence" governing standards of "proof" (e.g., excluding hearsay)
- Access to independent legal counsel for accused persons, including free access for low-income defendants

There are a number of other more contemporary innovations that are now considered essential to a more finely tuned criminal justice system with built-in counterweights to prevent deliberate or accidental errors. The additions are particularly vital given pressure on police to produce "results" in the post-9/11 counterterrorism environment.

- The introduction of audio taping (and audiovisual recording) of police interviews has been an important innovation in deterring process corruption and improving transparency in investigative processes. Dixon's (2006) research—involving analysis of tapes and surveys of police, prosecutors, defense lawyers, and judges—concluded that audiovisual recording of police interviews did not provide 100% protection against manipulation. However, overall, it … has been successful in putting an end to the long dispute about verballing, and is perceived by many criminal justice professionals to have increased guilty pleas, reduced trial length, reduced challenges to the admission of confessional evidence and increased public confidence in the justice process (p. 330).
- Police investigative techniques and the quality of prosecution briefs of evidence can be audited by reviewing tapes, surveying charged persons, surveying public prosecutors, using expert panels to assess the quality of investigation files and briefs, and by inspecting facilities for securing evidence (e.g., CMC, 2004b).
- Preventing process corruption also requires a robust criminal justice system that (a) gives low weight to confessional evidence and eyewitness testimony and requires corroboration of these sources, (b) limits the capacity to hold suspects without charge to a few days, and (c) takes a more inquisitorial approach to hearings, including judges and magistrates who actively challenge the prosecution and quality of evidence (Langdon & Wilson, 2005; Stevens, 2008).
- To remedy miscarriages of justice it is also essential for convicted persons to have access to a well-resourced and powerful standing body whose sole task is to review questionable cases without the traditional high threshold tests applied by appeal courts. The lead government agency in the field has been the English Criminal Cases Review Commission, created in the wake of the Runciman Commission into the English miscarriages of justice cases discussed in Chapter 1. The Commission has shown itself to be an agency with

teeth. Despite the many limitations under which it operates, about 65% of the convictions it has challenged have been quashed (Scher & Weathered, 2004).

Corruption Hazards and Rotation of Personnel

One classic aspect of police corruption is the tendency for corruption to be concentrated in squads where it becomes entrenched over time, with new entrants being socialized into a squad's particular "scam." One recommendation made to counter this problem is the rotation of personnel through high-risk areas (HMIC, 1999b, p. 36; Knapp, 1972). The idea is that corrupt networks will be disrupted through transfers, and that new arrivals will pose a threat to any ongoing scams, especially if there is a well-advertised system of compulsory disclosures and even of covert informants.

The risk with a rotation policy is that vital specialist knowledge can be lost and staff morale can be affected by compulsory relocation. Some kind of balance is needed. Limits of between 5 and 7 years in one position have been recommended (Kennedy, 2004, p. 175; Mollen, 1994, p. 124). However, it is important that a rotational system is properly planned, explained, and monitored to ensure it works to optimal effect with as few negative impacts as possible. Moving one officer often means moving a whole family, including children in school and a spouse with a job. Rotation should therefore also be based on good risk assessments. If there is no evidence of corruption it might be best to leave things as they are. It should also be kept in mind that staff movements can be generated without compulsion, through incentives such as pre-promotion experience, remote area allowances, discount housing, and other benefits.

Miscellaneous Areas of High Risk

There are a number of additional high-risk areas of policing where specific controls and close monitoring are required. Three examples follow.

Raids

Strict protocols need to be in place to manage police raids (Prenzler, 2006). Checking mechanisms are essential to ensure that the right location has been selected and there are minimal risks to innocent parties such as children. A clear plan of action is required, with a clear division of labor and chain of command, including close supervision by senior staff. Video recording, where feasible, will provide a deterrent to misconduct and a source of evidence if disputes arise. Follow-up debriefs should be part of a cycle of monitoring and improvement.

Public Order Policing

A set of international best practice principles has been developed in the area of public order policing to prevent over-policing and under-policing of protests. Wherever possible, police need to engage in early formal negotiations with protestors; demonstrate support for the right to protest; and draw up an agreement about acceptable behaviors, start and finish times, and march routes. They should also encourage protest organizers to appoint their own crowd marshals, clearly communicate a commitment to act on breaches, and provide an adequate physical force capability in reserve if required (Baker, 2005).

Theft of Property

Strict procedures are also required to prevent opportunistic theft of police property, including the property of detainees held by police and trial exhibits (including drugs held in storage). "Situational prevention" measures are particularly applicable here, including property marking, sign-in and sign-out requirements, limited access, minimum target hardening standards (including locks and safes), frequent banking ("target removal") and devices to facilitate compliance (such as user-friendly forms and the availability of financial consultants) (Ede, Homel & Prenzler, 2002b).

Intelligence Gathering for Investigations and Covert Operations

The type of data described so far can be used for profiling with a view to summary disciplinary interventions or remedial interventions. The data can also be used to inform two other forms of follow-up—either more traditional investigative processes of the "fact finding" kind (Chapter 6), or testing of the probity of suspect officers through the use of undercover operations including integrity testing and covert surveillance (Chapter 9). The outcomes of these follow-up processes may result in a finding that suspicions were unfounded or lacked sufficient evidence, or they may result in a range of responses including warnings, retraining, dispute resolution, disciplinary sanctions, or criminal prosecutions. The key point is that suspicions developed from the intelligence-gathering processes need to be pursued by all reasonable and legal means so that, as far as possible, the department can have confidence that officers are not engaged in misconduct. All data collected in follow-up investigations, even if they appear to exonerate officers, need to be kept on the record for future risk assessments (Parks, 2000).

Maintaining Momentum and Maximizing Yields

The U.S. NIJ study of early warning systems found that systems had a tendency to evolve over time (Walker et al., 2001). While some improved, others went through periods of decline and neglect. Two of the most important criteria for success of systems are therefore (a) maintenance and (b) improvement-oriented research and evaluation. Early intervention is an internal application of problem-oriented policing and intelligence-led policing strategies, considered most likely to be effective in police-led crime reduction efforts. In *Intelligence-Led Policing*, Jerry Ratcliffe sets out 10 "structural and cultural standards" considered essential to maintain and get the most from strategic criminal intelligence systems. These standards are directly applicable to risk management systems in integrity management, and are listed in summary form in Sidebar 8.3. Two qualifiers that apply in relation to integrity systems are (a) that the approach is one part of a wider system, and (b) that minor and intermediate offenses should not be ignored.

Sidebar 8.3: Ten Yardsticks for Intelligence-Led Policing

"1. There is a supportive and informed command structure.
2. Intelligence-led policing is the heart of an organization-wide approach.
3. Crime and criminal analysis are integrated.
4. The focus is on prolific and serious offenders.
5. Analytical and executive training are available.
6. Both strategic and tactical tasking meetings take place.
7. Much routine investigation is screened out.
8. Data are sufficiently complete, reliable, and available to support quality products that influence decision making.
9. Management structures exist to action intelligence products.
10. There is appropriate use of prevention, disruption, and enforcement."

(Ratcliffe, 2008, pp. 235-236).

Conclusion

Integrity risk management, early intervention, and procedural controls are imperfect techniques. They involve a number of limitations and problems that need to be acknowledged. These include the difficulty of identifying genuine misconduct from unsubstantiated complaints and other indicators, as well as the fact that complaints may be vexatious and that some misconduct (such as consensual corruption) might not lead to complaints. Despite these limitations, evidence suggests that an information-rich, intelligence-based, risk management system is an essential component of a larger advanced integrity system.

Advanced Techniques 9

Many modern inquiries, such as the Knapp Inquiry in New York City, have observed that previous inquiries had often failed to uncover significant corruption. This was despite strong suspicions about police misconduct among prosecutors, lawyers, politicians, activists, some police, and members of the public. Major reasons for the success of more recent inquiries include the application of nontraditional investigative techniques and extra legal powers, such as the ability to turn witnesses, or the ability to compel answers to questions. Innovative or advanced techniques include the use of undercover operatives and integrity tests or "stings," as well as telephone taps, listening devices, and video surveillance. Other, more supportive strategies include internal witness support systems.

Inquiries have also found that reform agendas set by previous inquiries usually failed to last. Corruption that had been suppressed for a time had resurfaced. Again, another reason for this has been the failure of professional standards units and oversight agencies to make use of all the available technical developments as part of a permanent and growing toolkit against corruption (e.g., Mollen, 1994). What is now apparent is that anticorruption agencies need to have this full repertoire of techniques at their disposal if they are to stay ahead of corrupt police. This repertoire now also includes drug and alcohol testing and personal financial audits. This chapter discusses these techniques, as well as several others, including the use of informants and spies.

Background

Advanced techniques are designed to identify and deter corruption in a highly systematic or targeted fashion. In combination they provide a net of surveillance that should be difficult to elude. A large part of the premise for the adoption of these intrusive and sometimes controversial techniques is that police corruption can be highly secretive, and that police are in a unique position to learn skills for eluding detection. Advanced techniques are normally oriented to confirming or dispelling suspicions about individuals or small groups. But it has also been argued that, without giving away any specifics of particular operations, they should be widely communicated to police as a primary deterrent mechanism (Homel, 2002). If every encounter police have with citizens, or every operation they perform, is potentially an encounter with an undercover informant or is potentially being covertly recorded, this provides a powerful disincentive to act corruptly. This is particularly important given the alleged strength of police solidarity and the power of socialization and coercive techniques for enmeshing officers in corruption webs. The possibility that colleagues are "spies," or that situations are recorded simulations, creates a potentially powerful "functional divisiveness" (Henry, 1994, p. 167).

Covert operations depend on secrecy and therefore require low-profile facilities located away from normal police offices (HMIC, 1999b, p. 112). The extent to which these techniques are deployed depends on need assessments and is likely to vary from department to department. They are, of course, controversial and pose a variety of risks, including physical risks to participants and risks to privacy and due process. They require high-level skills and careful planning, and are generally recommended as "tactics of last resort" (Girodo, 1998; Marx, 1992, p. 170). Nonetheless, their routine use—or at least their availability—is widely endorsed. The LAPD Rampart Board of Inquiry, for example, recommended that

[a] Public Integrity or Professional Standards Unit ... continually conduct sting operations and other investigative strategies (such as financial checks) to find and root out corruption. ... The single most important lesson learned from other police departments' corruption scandals is the need for an aggressive anti-corruption program (Parks, 2000, p. 337).

Integrity Testing

Integrity tests involve simulated misconduct opportunities that are monitored to record the responses of subjects. An early use of integrity testing was in New York City during the Knapp Inquiry of 1970 to 1972 (Knapp, 1972). The Commission initially made limited progress with traditional investigative techniques. However, breakthroughs occurred when "turned" officers were placed in undercover sting operations. Corruption opportunities, such as cash baits at fake drug pads, were organized in situations where there were strong suspicions that officers were taking money. The tape-recorded responses of officers provided crucial evidence of misconduct (Daley, 1978).

Tests of this type have since become a vital strategy in investigations of corruption. Australian jurisdictions have introduced tests with some success. Particularly dramatic results were achieved in the Royal Commission into the New South Wales Police Service with hidden cameras in stings using turned officers (Padraic, 2006; Wood, 1997). Integrity testing then became part of the array of anticorruption strategies in the post-inquiry period. A testing program was introduced by both police Internal Affairs and by the major oversight body, the Police Integrity Commission. A 1999 survey found that Victoria and Queensland had also introduced integrity tests. In the most detailed data made available from the New South Wales Police, of 90 operations, 37% revealed misconduct, 27% showed no misconduct, 12% were forwarded for further investigation, and 24% were inconclusive or were discontinued. A total of 51 criminal charges followed from the "failed" tests. Of these, 54% were against police, 23% were against staff, and 23% were against civilians (Prenzler & Ronken, 2001b).

Targeted and Random Tests

Integrity tests can be divided into targeted and random types. Targeted tests are directed at specific individuals or small groups in response to intelligence or complaints indicating a corruption problem, but where adequate proof for successful criminal or departmental prosecution is lacking. Examples are provided in Sidebar 9.1. Random testing implies that simulations are not directed at any specific officers or sections, but are assigned on a systematically random basis. Systematic random testing has been advocated as a more reliable method for both assessing corruption levels and deterring corruption, operating as a kind of audit system similar to the highly successful deployment of random breath testing to detect and deter drunk driving (Homel, 2002). However, targeted testing has been strongly favored in practice over random testing.

Sidebar 9.1: Sample Integrity Tests

"The largest New York City corruption investigation since the Knapp Commission in the early 1970s ... was in Brooklyn's 77th Precinct. Thirteen officers were suspended following an investigation. The officers were alleged to have taken cash and drugs from addicts and dealers. A drug dealer who complained was wired and he gathered evidence against two officers. In the 'domino' process common to undercover investigations, under threat of prison the two officers were then wired and gathered evidence against their colleagues" (Marx, 1992, p. 160).

"In Los Angeles a tip from an FBI informer passed on to the police led to the setting of a trap that caught two members of a special burglary unit. After an initial investigation, a fake burglary situation was created and the suspects took the bait and were arrested. They were part of a special burglar alarm response unit. After responding to the alarms, the officers would then pilfer the stores themselves. They were believed to trip the alarms of stores specializing in expensive electronic equipment and then respond to the alarms. Investigators turned the tables and set off the alarm at one such store. They then watched as the two made several trips carrying out cash and expensive goods, which had been treated to leave an indelible, invisible mark on anyone who touched them. In later searches of their homes and those of several other suspects, authorities seized almost a truckload worth of electronic equipment" (Marx, 1992, p. 160).

"Gregory Joseph Sweeney thought he'd landed a handy $270 bonus to brighten the graveyard shift. But at the end of the night the senior constable had succumbed to one of the [New South Wales] Police Service's first stings on its own brethren. The sting, known formally as an integrity test, had involved more than a dozen police, including two female police who had masqueraded as night-clubbers. The test began when a Nissan sedan was reported stolen to Senior Constable Sweeney from Taree police. He was told also a vanity bag in the missing car contained a sum of cash. The stolen car was recovered by Senior Constable Sweeney, who was then videotaped removing $270 cash from the vanity bag and placing it in his pocket. Nearing the end of his shift a plain clothes detective stopped and searched Sweeney. The $270 was recovered and the constable admitted the theft. Sweeney was charged with stealing and convicted, and placed on a two-year good behavior bond. Sweeney is one of at least 20 officers who have failed integrity tests since the integrity testing unit was established in February by Deputy Commissioner Mal Brammer. As with other targets, Sweeney was on the integrity testing unit hit-list of suspects, based on intelligence sent to the command by local area commanders and internal affairs spies" ("Anatomy," 1997, p. 4).

Random tests are more likely to be directed toward police in operational positions exposed to corruption opportunities. The most famous examples are from post-Knapp New York when wallets were left where police could find them, complaints against police were made to monitor responses by officers, or valuables were left at crime scenes (Henry, 1990; Marx, 1992). A revived program of random testing, introduced after the 1994 Mollen Inquiry, involved the random assignment of tests within specific precincts where there was a suspected corruption problem (KPMG, 1996). In Britain, the Metropolitan Police have run a type of random testing program that operates more in terms of quality assurance checks aimed at problems other than corruption narrowly defined, such as racism, sexism, and neglect of crime victims (HMIC, 1999b).

Legal and Ethical Issues

Integrity testing raises a set of ethical and legal issues around concepts of privacy, deception, entrapment, and provocation. The most challenging ethical issue concerns the step from discovering already existing misconduct to testing "corruptibility" (Marx, 1992). Critics claim that the focus on potential crimes, rather than existing crimes, entails unfair or unjustifiable temptation. The NSW Royal Commission concluded that policing "is so filled with operational and ethical dilemmas that temptation should not be placed in the way of an officer, unless reasonable cause exists to test that person's integrity" (Wood, 1997, pp. 511-512). Acceptance of the need for targeted testing is therefore based on the persistence of suspicions about specific officers, which have either not been allayed by conventional investigative methods or it is felt that conventional techniques will alert the suspect officer who will then desist. To be consistent in the application of this rationale it has been argued that integrity tests should resemble the suspected corruption as much as possible (Wood, 1997). These qualifiers appear to greatly reduce the strength of the entrapment accusation (Sherman, 1983). However, a pejorative judgment regarding entrapment depends, to a considerable extent, on the degree to which an officer was influenced to act corruptly as a result of pressures entailed in the test. Specific circumstances are therefore crucial in judging the fairness of tests. The utilitarian argument in favor of targeted testing has been strengthened by the success of tests and subsequent confessions by targets of previous corrupt conduct (Daley, 1978; Prenzler & Ronken, 2001b).

Random tests, in contrast, are considered more difficult to justify, given lower levels of suspicion or the absence of suspicions, particularly in relation to individuals. Covert surveillance associated with random testing is also said to de-professionalize policing and creates an inhibiting climate of fear and mistrust (Kleinig, 1996). In contrast, others have argued that random testing and covert surveillance follow logically from an employer's responsibility to assess employee work performance and honesty (HMIC, 1999b; Marx, 1992), as in eavesdropping on telephone communications with customers and using dummy customers to monitor the response of service personnel (Bylinsky, 1991).

Police views on the issue are divergent. Police unions have opposed tests on grounds of entrapment, damage to morale, inhibiting effects on police work, misdirection of scarce resources, and potential hazards. They have also argued that testing of police is unfair unless it is extended to other occupations (KPMG, 1996). Henry (1990) noted that random testing in the NYPD was initially greeted with outrage from officers, but that it was eventually accepted as a necessary evil to protect police reputation. In New South Wales, a statewide education program was conducted prior to implementation of targeted tests. Marketing emphasized the slogan, "honest police have nothing to fear from integrity testing." Despite some opposition, it quickly became accepted as a standard anticorruption tool. The union added its support, arguing it provided a means to remove officers who betrayed their colleagues and as a mechanism for addressing public distrust of police (Newton, 1997).

Surveys of police have shown support for targeted corruption in serious cases and opposition to random testing. A recent survey of inspector level police in Australia found very high levels of support for targeted integrity tests, on the order of 86% to 91% for scenarios involving suspected bribery in drug lab raids, opportunistic bribes at random breath tests, and thefts from a police station. Support for targeted tests for suspected racism and inappropriate responses to domestic violence calls were much lower at 41% and 36%, respectively. Support was also lower for random tests involving similar scenarios—50% for the drug lab bribes scenario, 46% for opportunistic bribes, 58% for theft from police stations, 29% for racism, and 27% for domestic violence responses (Prenzler, 2006). A U.S. survey of middle and upper-middle police managers found similar high levels of support—approximately 87%—for launching stings against police in a drug shakedown scenario and a scenario involving sexual harassment of offenders (Girodo, 1998).

The legality of integrity testing and related covert practices has been upheld in the courts as part of the contractual rights of employers, within certain bounds of privacy and within the area of an employee's responsibilities (Cozzetto & Pedeliski, 1997). In common-law countries, entrapment can only be used as a defense where clearly there is coercion involved. Consequently, it is important that sting scenarios merely provide an opportunity for a crime to be committed without undue pressure. The fact that the situation is a simulation, e.g., the participants are actors or the alleged drugs are powder, also does not provide a defense in law (Prenzler & Ronken, 2001b). However, variations in law between jurisdictions mean that agencies planning integrity tests should obtain legal advice as a routine part of planning. It is also necessary to introduce special legislation to facilitate tests, particularly with a view to protecting undercover agents who perform illegal actions in the course of running tests (such as possessing drugs and offering them for sale). Enabling and protective legislation generally now go under terms such as "controlled operations" and "assumed identities" (Prenzler & Ronken, 2001b).

Associated Issues

A number of other objections have been raised against integrity testing. Cost is an obvious one, with diversion of resources away from the primary law enforcement and crime prevention functions of police. A review of the NYPD program by KPMG in 1996 also suggested that it was difficult to create realistic scenarios for random tests, and officers were often able to detect test situations. Targeted testing, however, produced a much higher detection rate because of the capacity to tailor scenarios to the profile of suspected officers (KPMG, 1996). Marx (1992) provides examples of expensive and embarrassing "keystone cops" fiascos, with overlapping operations between different agencies. He also warns that integrity tests and other covert tactics can be misused to harass and discredit rivals within an organization.

A further issue concerns what to do with officers who fail tests. It could be argued that the simulated nature of the circumstances in which the offenses were committed would serve as a mitigating factor in any disciplinary or sentencing judgment. The limited evidence available on this issue is that professional standards units dispense the same punishment to those who failed tests as to those caught in real corruption (Prenzler & Ronken, 2001b).

Drug and Alcohol Testing

Drug and alcohol testing is a developing area of quality assurance and duty of care in many occupations, especially where there are major safety concerns (Mieczkowski & Lersch, 2002). In Britain in 1999, the Inspectorate recommended that the threat posed to policing from drug misuse meant that "forces should now be treating the area of drug testing as a professional standards priority" (HMIC, 1999b, p. 19). In policing, drug and alcohol testing has been introduced in various forms. It can be used on a mandatory basis in recruitment, and on both a random and targeted basis for operational police (Prenzler & Ronken, 2001b).

In New South Wales, alcohol testing of police was introduced in 1997 and drug testing in 1998 after the Royal Commission found widespread abuse of alcohol and drugs by police (Wood, 1997). Alcohol tests were conducted on a random basis, with targets selected by computer and without regard to rank. Drug tests were introduced on a targeted basis based on reports by supervisors and other sources. Subject officers were not forced to provide the urine samples required, but officers who refused to take a test were liable to be dismissed. Initial findings produced results that were open to interpretation, but nonetheless were seen as demonstrating the value of a testing regime (Prenzler & Ronken, 2001b). Of the 5,473 random alcohol tests conducted in 1998 and 1999, 13 officers returned positive tests. Of 44 targeted drug tests conducted in 1998 and 1999, nine resulted in a positive finding. In 1998 the NSW Police also introduced a parallel program of compulsory drug and alcohol tests following all incidents involving death or serious injury. Up to the end of the 1998 to 1999 period, 125 officers had been tested in relation to 42 incidents. Two officers returned positive tests for illicit drugs, with no positive results for alcohol. Overall, the relatively low rate of "positive" results—or failed tests—indicated that the tests had a deterrent effect, given the extensive problems identified by the Wood Commission, and as an audit mechanism they indicated a very high level of sobriety among on-duty officers.

In drug and alcohol testing, a "fail" result appears to draw more diverse responses than integrity test results, including treatment options, despite the fact that drug and alcohol tests are not simulations (Mieczkowski & Lersch, 2002). In the case of random alcohol tests in New South Wales, "all officers who tested positive were offered and accepted rehabilitation counseling" (NSWPS, 1999, p. 34). A much tougher line was taken on positive drug results, with the expectation of dismissal and criminal charges. In some cases officers could be maintained on a probationary system if they participated in rehabilitation and accepted random tests for 5 years. In introducing drug and alcohol testing, the approach of the NSW Police combined the perspectives of employee health, workplace health and safety, and corruption prevention. This was in line with the Wood Commission analysis, which recommended that testing occur in consideration of the following:

- The interests of rehabilitation in the circumstances of a job that is at times dangerous and stressful;
- The incompatibility between resort to criminal behavior and the holding of an office in law enforcement; and
- The dangers of handling motor vehicles and firearms, and dealing with the public when affected by alcohol and drugs (Wood, 1996, p. 15).

The rationale for police drug testing in New South Wales took cognizance of the particular risks for corruption when police use drugs. The survey of Australian police inspectors cited above (Prenzler, 2006) found that 97% believed targeted testing for drug use was justified, with 77% supporting random drug testing. Targeted testing for alcohol was supported by 97%, with 75% supporting random alcohol tests.

In the United States, research has suggested that police drug-users can escape detection. A study in two police departments found that

[t]here is an identifiable group of people in policing which appears to be drug-involved. It also appears that, at least in some situations, and for rapidly excreted drugs like cocaine, the use of urine may be producing underestimates

of these groups. The data support the idea that policing agencies may want to consider using multiple drug-testing modalities in order to maximize the identification of different drugs (Mieczkowski & Lersch, 2002, p. 581).

Research in New South Wales has also examined the level at which random drug testing needs to be undertaken in order for it to function as an effective deterrent. A 2005 study by the Police Integrity Commission, code-named Operation Abelia, found that

> NSW Police ... currently tests between 500 and 600 (or 3% to 4%) of its 15,000 officers each year. The overall impression from the information collected as part of Operation Abelia was that, in its current form, the NSW Police random drug testing program was not a highly visible deterrent. Nine of the 80 local area commands were not visited at all by a drug testing team during the first three years of random drug testing. On average, each local area command was visited only 1.5 times during this initial three-year period. A fundamental limitation of the current testing program was that some officers did not know that NSW Police conducts random drug testing. Officers disposed to using illegal drugs are not going to be deterred by a program of which they are unaware. In addition, some officers and former officers told the PIC that although they knew about random drug testing, they became less concerned about their illegal drug use being detected as time elapsed because they did not see any random drug testing happening. In order to increase the perceived risk of being caught, the PIC has recommended that NSW Police increases the number of officers tested as part of the random drug testing process to the equivalent rate of not less than 15 out of every 100 officers (or approximately 2,250 random drug tests conducted annually) for a trial period of five years (PIC, 2005, p. s-25).

Covert Surveillance

Again, the use of covert tactics, especially covert surveillance, has been influenced in the United States by the Knapp Inquiry and, in Australia, by the New South Wales Wood Commission. Covert strategies and the display of selected results in the media were considered key elements of the success of the Wood Commission, including the garnering of public support. Their continued use has been part of the gradual adoption of "standing commission" powers and strategies for maintaining the fight against corruption. The post-Wood Police Integrity Commission adopted telecommunications interception as "an essential and cost effective strategy" in large part because "the Royal Commission found its use of electronic surveillance was the single most important factor in achieving breakthroughs in its investigations" (PIC, 1998, p. 24). Wood (1997) emphasized that there needed to be a shift in anticorruption methods away from reliance on confessions and informants to greater use of physical evidence and surveillance. He also recommended continuous monitoring of technology to ensure that the best use was made of all available technologies against police corruption. A current example of this is the availability of Skype—telephone-like computer-based Internet communications—which corrupt police can use instead of standard landline telephones or mobile phones.

Surveillance is a particularly important strategy in police corruption investigations because of police knowledge of how to defeat standard investigative methods. A traditional form of investigation limited to witness testimony and interviews with suspects is likely to "give the game away" to corrupt police who can halt their activities or go further underground. A U.K. example of surveillance is provided in Sidebar 9.2. Once suspects are presented with irrefutable video evidence from surveillance they are likely to fold and make admissions and further disclosures that can shut down a corrupt network and bring associates to justice (Padraic, 2006). A further example, this time of a fixed covert camera operation, is included in Sidebar 9.3.

Sidebar 9.2: Covert Surveillance Against Suspected Corruption

"An experienced and well respected detective in a large metropolitan police force was renowned for achieving excellent results. His arrest and conviction rate was second to none. It was, however, well known that he had become disillusioned with senior officers, who he felt knew or cared little about investigating serious crime, and that he would often pay scant regard to the ethics and values of the organization. Despite this, he was very much left to his own devices, with little intrusive supervision. Following information from a source, a covert investigation was mounted. It was established that, during unauthorized and unrecorded meetings with an informant, the detective was passing sensitive information about police operations to a major, level 2 criminal. The relationship between the informant and the detective had become very close and wholly inappropriate. During the course of the investigation it transpired that the detective's level of rule breaking was extensive; for example, he was using the police vehicle as his own, making regular shopping trips and social visits and even teaching a member of his family to drive in it. The investigation resulted in the detective's conviction and a term of imprisonment" (HMIC, 1999b, p. 107).

Sidebar 9.3: Covert Fixed Camera Surveillance Against Suspected Corruption

In October 2005 the Office of Police Integrity (OPI) in Victoria, Australia, received a complaint from a criminal alleging he had been seriously assaulted by members of the elite Armed Offenders Squad. The allegations were consistent with others received from criminals, and an analysis of complaints showed the Squad received a disproportionately high number of complaints. Although some medical evidence was available, sufficient evidence of abuses was unobtainable. The OPI launched an investigation that included installation of a hidden camera in the ceiling of the Squad's interview room. In September 2006 the OPI began public hearings into the allegations. Three members of the Squad were asked questions about possible involvement in assaults, which they denied. The following day they were shown video footage from the hidden camera. The footage showed the detectives questioning a suspect about the location of jewelry and a gun used in a robbery. As the suspect was brought into the room he was asked, "You going to be all friendly and cooperative and tell us everything ... or are we going to do it the hard way?" When he didn't reply he was knocked to the floor and told, "Welcome to the armed robbery squad." The man was repeatedly slapped around the face while being questioned. One detective shouted, "Don't shake your f---ing head at me because when I get up you're going to be in f---ing agony." At one point the suspect's ear was bleeding and while being hit he was told, "That ear's coming off at the end of the day." He was also repeatedly struck in rhythm to the words, "F---ing ... armed ... robbery ... squad." At another point the suspect was tackled to the ground and held down while being kicked. When he asked to make a phone call he was hit with a telephone and told, "Want a phone call? Here it is. Here's ya f---ing phone call. Want to make another one?" During the video showing, one of the officers involved collapsed in the witness box and had to be carried from the hearing. The three detectives later pleaded guilty to assault and were also charged with lying to the OPI hearing (Berry, 2006; Collins, 2008; McKenzie & Berry, 2006).

Undercover Agents

The use of stings and covert surveillance is usually enmeshed with the use of undercover operatives—the shadowy players in covert operations. Undercover agents can be specially selected officers, often from outside the target officers' jurisdiction to ensure anonymity, or even civilian actors, or they can be corrupt officers who have agreed to cooperate with investigators. Usually these agents are used in operations that have a specific target and they work within a limited time frame.

One unusual variant of undercover operations was the famous case of "field associates" or spies in the NYPD in the post-Knapp period. These agents were recruited from the academy or from in-service training programs. They worked as regular police officers but with a duty to report suspicious behavior to control agents from Internal Affairs. Officers assigned to engage in follow-up investigations of reports were not given the agent's name. Internal informants were also used in the Oakland Police Department, and were apparently hand picked by the police chief and reported directly to him (Sherman, 1978b, p. 157). In New York City, agents were widely deployed, including to patrol units, but with a concentration of agents in high-risk squads:

> The reform commander of the newly centralized vice and narcotics enforcement unit was the first to use 'field associates'. ... The vice commander recruited field associates from among the graduates of the in-service training course that prepared selected uniformed patrol officers for their new assignments to vice and narcotics work. By early 1972, 70 of the 400 officers newly assigned to that 925-officer bureau had agreed to serve as field associates. Of course, the 330 new officers who were interviewed but not picked for the additional assignment as a field associate immediately spread the word that 'spies' were about (Sherman, 1978b, pp. 157-158).

Although strict control was placed on their identities, the program was publicized as a deterrent measure:

> Field associates were quietly infiltrated through every precinct and specialized unit in the agency, until they reached a rumored strength of one per ten officers in the department, and one in eight in gambling and narcotics enforcement units. The actual number of field associates deployed has never been revealed by the NYCPD, but it has also never attempted to quash rumors about their proportion within the force. Whether field associates actually account for ten percent of the department or that figure is the result of subtle disinformation, their effect upon corrupt activities within the police subculture is undeniable. This institutionalized program of controlled internal whistleblowing spread throughout the agency, creating a tremendous amount of functional anxiety and corruption consciousness. ... One never knew if his partner or another officer nearby was a field associate, secretly reporting his activities to IAD (Henry, 1990, p. 50; see also Barker, 1996, pp. 74-75).

Although the impacts were never apparently quantified, Henry (1990) argued that the program "shattered the implicit subcultural expectation of trust (if not tacit complicity) upon which corrupt officers depended" (p. 50). Internal informants were of little direct value as prosecution witnesses because of the need to protect their anonymity. Nonetheless, the program created a "functional divisiveness" across the organization that was crucial to stopping blatant corruption (p. 51). Furthermore, the identities of field agents were so well protected, and the program was so well managed, that experienced police had to abandon the system of initiating rookies into corruption through participation in minor infringements.

Undercover operations can involve considerable risks, for example, in drug buys where weapons are present. Operations can take extended periods of time, with agents needing to build relationships of trust with criminals and corrupt police. These long-term operations entail the same risks as occur with regular police undercover operations (Marx, 1988), including

- Deceiving people and infringing on their privacy, especially innocent third parties
- Participation in unethical and unlawful activities to ensure credibility, such as theft, and consuming and selling drugs
- Exposure to harm from drug use and the risk of addiction
- Physical risks from assault, kidnap, torture, and murder
- The risk of the Stockholm syndrome—when agents shift loyalties to the opposition
- A related problem where agents become attached to a wealthy and criminal lifestyle

Consequently, a thorough risk management system is essential both for safety and confidentiality. Agents need to be closely vetted for resilience, with systematic training and close supervision. There also needs to be limits set for permissible behavior by agents, such as prohibitions on murder or serious assaults.

Given the highly intrusive nature of undercover operations and the high risks, their use should be limited to targeted operations against persons reasonably suspected of misconduct (Girodo, 1998). It has been argued that, "the invasion of privacy represented by an undercover officer is much greater than that of an electronic bug or telephone intercept" (Gill, 2000, p. 205). Despite its apparent success, NYPD-style field associate programs do not appear to have been taken up elsewhere to any extent, and the 1994 Mollen Commission in New York did not recommend the program's reinstatement in its original form. However, it did require the creation of an undercover squad to engage in a form of hybrid random/targeted operations against particular organizational elements:

Internal Affairs must recruit and operate a cadre of undercover officers in the most corruption-prone precincts and commands. Their role should be to gather information on corruption within their commands and provide the basis for integrity tests, electronic surveillance, and other pro-active investigative measures (Mollen, 1994, p. 139).

Financial Audits and Indirect Incapacitation Strategies

Perhaps the most famous case in which an organized crime boss was brought to justice is that of Al Capone. Capone operated bootlegging, prostitution, extortion, and murder rackets in Chicago during the 1920s. He appeared to be immune from prosecution, partly because of police corruption and partly because he structured his operations in ways that forensically separated him from his henchmen. Eventually Capone's criminal career and reign of terror were brought to a halt when he was imprisoned on federal tax-evasion charges (Hilmer, 1998).

A similar process ended the career of Sydney's most notorious police officer, Roger "the Dodger" Rogerson. Rogerson appeared untouchable after failed attempts to prove strong suspicions against him of murder, conspiracy to commit murder, bribery, fabricating evidence, and "green-lighting" armed robberies and heroin trafficking. He was eventually dismissed from the force by a disciplinary tribunal over bank accounts he held under false names, which contained AU$110,000. He was also charged departmentally and later received criminal convictions and jail sentences for criminal associations and for conspiracy to pervert the course of justice. The sequence of events was triggered by a person making disclosures after overhearing discussions about the secret accounts. Rogerson was then identified by covert surveillance footage and bank staff witnesses. The conspiracy related to a plan to explain the money as the product of a cash sale. The conspirators were covertly taped (Whitton, 1990).

Cases like those described above have led to the acceptance of financial and asset audits as standard anticorruption tools. Forensic accounting can combine with tax laws as a powerful means to identify sequestered funds and bring suspect police to justice. Although the officers might not be convicted for the primary corruption offenses of which they are suspected, they can be dismissed from the service, effectively incapacitated, even jailed, and some recoveries can be made of illicit profits.

Financial audits can be operationalized on a random basis as a routine deterrence and audit method or, as is more likely the case, they can be targeted against suspect officers. One obvious trigger is an unaffordable lifestyle, including expenditures on gambling. While police may have legitimate sources of income above their salary, a proper risk management system will see a lavish lifestyle as a legitimate trigger for a financial probe. This normally requires special powers that override privacy laws. The LAPD Rampart Scandal involved police spending large amounts of money from drug sales and armed robbery without their finances being investigated by authorities. The Board of Inquiry stated,

> State laws must be changed to allow examination of an officer's financial record, particularly when that officer is in a highly sensitive assignment or there are indications that the officer may be living above his or her apparent means. Officers driving a very expensive automobile who boldly display a license plate taunting the IAG surveillance team or who display wealth far above their apparent means should expect to be asked about the source of their income. Restricting a law enforcement agency's access to this critical information only facilitates corrupt activities (Parks, 2000, p. 337).

The Ferguson report into the Toronto Police Service recommended automatic financial checks for promotions and certain assignments. It noted that

> [t]he Service does not today employ a consistent practice of thorough background and financial checks on persons being promoted and on persons being transferred to sensitive or high-risk units. This is particularly troubling since it is well known that personal debt and so-called high living are major contributors to police dishonesty (Ferguson, 2003, p. 24).

One notable aspect of the Roger Rogerson case outlined above was that the source of funds in his secret accounts was never confirmed, although it was suspected to be the proceeds of drug trafficking. Nonetheless, he was removed from the police force on a range of charges related to the false accounts, including conspiracy. This situation provides crucial insight into the value of using lesser charges as a method of removing officers strongly suspected of more serious offenses, but where sustainable evidence appears impossible to obtain. Lesser charges can include lying to investigators, refusing to answer questions (contempt), associating with criminals, or laundering money. At one level this is an unsatisfactory resolution of a matter. Nonetheless, if the convictions are based on objective evidence then there is a victory of sorts for anticorruption efforts.

Witness Protection Programs

Witness statements are a mainstay of the justice system and police integrity systems, despite the growth in other sources of evidence such as physical forensic evidence and audiovisual recordings from surveillance devices. Witnesses—both police and non-police—have been crucial in exposing corruption and bringing it to a stop. Unfortunately, they typically face numerous hazards of ostracism, and even at times have faced direct threats to their health and even their lives and the lives of their families. Witness support, as outlined in Chapter 6, therefore requires legislative prohibitions and severe penalties for any attempts to influence or threaten witnesses. Witnesses also need counseling and financial support. Even witnesses deemed to be at low risk from direct threats need to be managed carefully because they can be at risk of nonappearance in court due to drug usage, personal disorganization, or family issues.

In some cases, witnesses will also need support that involves covert operations in the form of safe houses, alternative identities, secure transport, and bodyguard-style protection from attempted assaults or attempted murder. Again, what is essential here is a technical capacity that can be rapidly brought into deployment, as well as a risk assessment procedure to ensure that protection levels are matched to risk levels, based on detailed assessments of available evidence. Some witnesses might need to be kept in protective custody against their will until a trial is over. Protections must extend to all aspects of operations, including the types of database security measures described in Chapter 8. This type of high-level protection is extremely resource intensive. Adequate cost-benefit analyses need to be undertaken, but the safety and well-being of witnesses should remain a crucial criterion.

Conclusion

Advanced techniques are essential tools against misconduct, especially in large police departments with a high-risk profile for corruption. This does not mean that high-risk strategies, such as integrity testing, need to be continuously deployed, but the legal capacity and knowledge need to be in place to ensure that they can be applied when needed. There is a strong case, however, for deploying other strategies, such as drug and alcohol testing, on a routine basis as a means of ensuring ongoing compliance with professional standards, along with targeted testing where suspicions are aroused or following critical incidents. There is also a strong case for the use of randomized or partially randomized "quality assurance" tests in areas such as police responses to crime reports, responses to domestic violence calls, and responses to social minorities, given that policing has been so fraught with allegations of bias in these areas.

The evidence also suggests that traditional investigative techniques are greatly assisted by covert technologies, including audio and video surveillance and phone taps, as well as more traditional forms of undercover policing. Financial investigations are also potentially useful in exposing and stopping corruption. The importance of these methods needs to be emphasized in police training programs so officers understand why they are being used.

External Oversight

10

This chapter examines the issue of independent investigation and adjudication of complaints against police, and the external oversight of police integrity management. The case for independent review is well established, based on the generally poor to dreadful record of in-house investigations, as well as the wider problem of perceptions of bias and an intrinsic conflict of interest in relation to internal processes. David Bayley formulated a first principle of modern police accountability as follows: "Police cannot be trusted to police themselves. Exclusive reliance on internal investigations and discipline is foolhardy. Civilian review is essential" (1991, p. iv).

In general, then, the debate has moved beyond this point to questions about the extent of direct external involvement and control, particularly in investigations and disciplinary decisions. External anticorruption bodies are frequently described as "watchdogs without teeth" (Burger & Adonis, 2008), so what is required to give them "teeth" is a crucial question. The position adopted here does not seek to prescribe an exact division of labor between police and an external agency. Considerable variation in the relationship is feasible based on differing conditions. At the same time, the chapter promotes a large operational role for an external agency in the complaints and discipline system, with a minimum reserve power of direct involvement and control on a discretionary basis. It also advocates an essential role for external agencies in auditing the quality of police discipline processes and prevention strategies, and it advocates complainant choice about who processes their complaint.

Background

External—sometimes called civilian or citizen—oversight was initially developed as a counter to the charge that police internal investigations were compromised by the natural tendency (apparent in most organizations) to close ranks and cover up misconduct. The creation of police internal affairs departments did little to mitigate this problem in many cases. Greater external control also received support from criminological theory, specifically the concepts of "relational distance," a factor in the willingness to prosecute crimes (Black, 1980; Grabosky & Braithwaite, 1986), and of "regulatory capture," when regulated organizations obtain undue influence over the regulator (Prenzler, 2000). Police departments that do not have adequate accountability systems to prevent managerial disorganization and administrative breakdown—often products of entrenched corruption—eventually have external oversight forced upon them, including through court decrees (Dias & Vaughn, 2006; Mollen, 1994). The repeated failure of police to properly investigate and discipline their own has driven the evolution, mainly beginnning in the 1950s, away from police control toward civilian control (Finn, 2001). The powers and functions of these oversight agencies can vary significantly (Finn, 2001), but two fundamentally different models are apparent (Prenzler & Ronken, 2001a):

A "minimal review model" in which agency staff

- Respond to appeals from dissatisfied complainants;
- Audit selected files; and
- Recommend changes to police procedures or disciplinary decisions.

A "civilian control model" in which agency staff

- Conduct independent investigations into complaints or any matters that come to their attention;
- Deploy a variety of advanced investigative tools, including the power to compel answers to questions and conduct covert surveillance;
- Make disciplinary decisions or initiate prosecutions; and
- Evaluate police internal corruption prevention strategies.

Stakeholder Perspectives

The remainder of this chapter summarizes some of the background positions behind Bayley's claim regarding the need for external review and examines in more depth the debate around a substantive or controlling role for oversight agencies in police accountability. The debate is organized around the experiences and perspectives of key actors and stakeholder groups. These are, primarily, commissions of inquiry, oversight agencies, complainants, police, the public, civil liberties groups, and government review bodies. This is followed by a brief review of the performance of oversight agencies as reported in the literature to date and a description of a model agency structure.

Inquiries

Public or judicial inquiries have frequently revealed the gross failure of police departments to act zealously against corruption (see Chapter 1). Inquiry reports have repeatedly emphasized the fundamental need for independence

in investigations and discipline. In the United States, one of the earliest
national inquiries to call for civilian review of police was the federal Kerner
Commission, which followed the race riots of 1967 (Kerner, 1968). But one
of the most influential inquiries has been the Knapp Commission in New
York City. A critical element of the success of Knapp was its ability to instill
confidence in police witnesses to testify in the belief that they would be protected from reprisals and that the disclosures they provided would be put to
good effect. Consequently, independent control of intelligence about police
conduct was a core recommendation, as reported in Sidebar 10.1.

**Sidebar 10.1: Knapp Commission Findings on Internal Versus
External Investigations**

"A basic weakness in the present approaches to the problem of police
corruption is that all agencies regularly involved with the problem rely
primarily on policemen to do their investigative work. The Department
relies exclusively on its own members. The District Attorneys ...
although they have a few non-police investigators, depend primarily on
policemen. ...

"At the present time a citizen wishing to make a complaint about
a policeman knows that his complaint will ultimately be investigated
by other policemen. This discourages complaints, because many New
Yorkers just don't trust policemen to investigate each other. ...

"This distrust is not confined to members of the public. Many
policemen came to us with valuable information, which they consented
to give us only upon our assurance that we would not disclose their
identity to the Department or to any District Attorney.

"Any proposal for dealing with corruption must therefore provide
a place where policemen as well as the public can come with confidence
and without fear of retaliation. Any office designed to achieve this must
be staffed by persons wholly unconnected with the Police Department"
(Knapp, 1972, pp. 13-14).

The words "wholly unconnected" were used in the Knapp Report because
of the tendency for protective solidarity to extend beyond one agency to
another agency that works cooperatively with it. Hence, Knapp argued that
district attorneys did not provide a suitable office for processing complaints
because "they work so closely with policemen that the public tends to look
upon them—and indeed they seem to look upon themselves—as allies of the
[Police] Department" (1972, p. 14).

Despite these strong statements supporting external investigations, post-Knapp reforms were focused on revamping the Internal Affairs department (Henry, 1994), and the need for independent control was subsequently restated by the later Mollen Commission. The Mollen Report stated that, unless external review agencies were able to continually monitor and investigate police, reforms would only be temporary and police would inevitably revert back to corruption. The revival of serious corruption in the NYPD prompted the Mollen Commission to recommend a more powerful independent commission to perform continuing audits of police internal disciplinary processes. It also needed to be

> ... empowered to conduct its own intelligence gathering operations, self-initiated investigations, and integrity tests ... [with] unrestricted access to the Department's records and personnel ... powers to subpoena witnesses ... take testimony in private and public hearings, and the power to grant immunity (1994, pp. 153, 154).

In Britain, the 1981 Scarman Report into the policing of race riots led to the establishment in 1985 of the Police Complaints Authority (PCA), charged with supervising investigations of serious matters and reviewing investigations conducted by police from outside the subject officer's force (Maguire & Corbett, 1991). The original Scarman Report recommended independent investigation in principle, but suggested there were too many practical obstacles to full implementation. Subsequently, however, Scarman (1986) argued that operationalization of the principle was possible, especially in light of Police Federation (union) support:

> Many will continue to criticize [the complaint system] so long as the investigation of complaints remains in police hands. ... Only the establishment of an independent service for the investigation of all complaints against the police will silence their criticisms (pp. 182-183).

The PCA was dogged by allegations that it was a "toothless tiger." The high profile Stephen Lawrence Inquiry was critical of the PCA's reliance on police investigators, and weaknesses in the disciplinary process greatly exacerbated problems of ethnic minority dissatisfaction with police. The report observed that "investigation of police officers by their own or another Police Service is widely regarded as unjust, and does not inspire public confidence" (MacPherson, 1999, p. 333). In response to these and other criticisms, the Home Office created the Independent Police Complaints Commission (IPCC) in 2004. The IPCC has a regional presence and is obliged to carry out independent investigations of serious incidents, such as deaths or serious injuries inflicted by police. It also investigates all allegations involving senior police and all serious allegations, such as those involving organized or process corruption (IPCC, 2008). The Commission, however, remains a mixed model, with substantial reliance on police for investigations and limitations on disciplinary decisions (Seneviratne, 2004).

In Australia, the landmark Fitzgerald Inquiry in Queensland exposed a total failure in police management to control corruption (Fitzgerald, 1989). In addition, the report condemned political interference in investigations and neglect by a complacent state government. To create a safe haven for police whistle-blowers and to insulate the accountability process from politicization, Fitzgerald recommended the creation of the Criminal Justice Commission (CJC)—later the Crime and Misconduct Commission (CMC)—cited as among the most powerful oversight agencies in the world (Harrison & Cunneen, 2000). However, the CJC/CMC's independence has been marred by the fact that it lacks a disciplinary function and is reliant on seconded police investigators, exposing the organization to regulatory capture (Prenzler, 2000). At the same time, the CMC emphasizes its "own motion" capacity to investigate any matter for any reason, using non-police investigators on a discretionary basis (CMC, 2004a).

The New South Wales Wood Commission recommended the creation of a new Police Integrity Commission (PIC) with responsibility for the investigation or review of serious misconduct and oversight of all police conduct issues, including training and management (Wood, 1997). The PIC, established in 1996, cannot employ any present or past member of the NSW Police Force (PIC, 2004, p. 2). The Wood Commission, however, also argued that the Police Service needed to retain primary responsibility for controlling corruption, 'otherwise there was a risk that it might abandon all responsibility and interest in maintaining high standards of integrity' (1997, p. 524). Consequently, the PIC can only recommend action against an officer, either by the Police Service or the public prosecutor.

Oversight Agencies

Civilian review agencies are frequently the products of inquiries, and often function as standing or permanent commissions of inquiry. At the same time, they frequently support the view that police should have primary responsibility for discipline and should deal with the bulk of complaints (e.g., ALRC, 1995). However, the frustration entailed in supervising or auditing police frequently drives these agencies to seek greater powers and resources (e.g., PIC, 2000). Expanded powers are not always confined to those used potentially against police, but can include powers to protect police, such as prosecution of vexatious complainants. A common experience also relates to the lack of prevention-oriented research or strategies adopted by police (Landau, 1996;

PIC, 2000). The types of enlarged powers sought by oversight agencies, and the reasons, are listed in Table 10.1 (see also CHRI, 2005, Chapter 6).

Complainants

Complainants have a strong personal and emotional stake in police account-ability, and they provide the main source of routine work for complaints and discipline systems. One of the most extensive studies of complainant satis-faction was performed as part of an evaluation of the complaints system for England and Wales, operating after the establishment of the PCA. The major-ity of complainants surveyed felt that the PCA's independence and effective-ness were compromised, either because the investigations were carried out by the police or because of perceived close links between the PCA and the police (Maguire & Corbett, 1991). A decade later Waters and Brown (2000) found similar complaints about the PCA: 80% of complainants surveyed felt their complaint had not received fair treatment and 67% strongly agreed that "complaints should be investigated by an independent body" (2000, pp. 631-632). The findings from other studies of complainants all show similar out-comes, with satisfaction generally in the range of 5% to 30% (Brown, 1987; CCRC, 1999; CJC, 1994; Hayes, 1997). When asked what they felt they had achieved under a police-dominated system, typical statements made by com-plainants in Maguire and Corbett's study were (1991, pp. 168-169):

- "Nothing achieved, a wasted two years of heartache to myself and my family, waste of money."
- "I achieved the knowledge that police investigating police is a farce."

The Maguire and Corbett study did find slightly higher rates of satisfaction among citizens whose complaints were investigated by police under civilian supervision. Although only 4% of both groups were satisfied with the out-come, 26% with supervised cases were satisfied with the whole experience, compared to 17% with unsupervised cases (1991, pp. 162, 164).

The presence of an external agency can create a misleading expectation of independence, followed by disillusion when the agency's involvement in the process proves to be marginal. Interviews with complainants regarding their experiences with the Ontario Police Complaints Commissioner (PCC) showed that the presence of the PCC created a false impression of a fully independent process (Landau, 1994, 1996). Many complainants were disap-pointed and upset when their complaints were investigated by police. About 75% of interviewees felt the Commissioner was "not at all, or not very involved in their case," and this underlay the "considerable dissatisfaction with the internal nature of the investigation" (1996, pp. 305, 307). Interviewees also felt that police were too legalistic about admissible evidence and tended to

Table 10.1   Types of Increased Capacity Sought by Oversight Agencies

Capacity sought	Reason
Authority to appeal police disciplinary decisions contrary to agency recommendations	Strong sense that police decisions were too lenient
Representation on disciplinary panels	Police decisions considered too lenient or open to perception of bias
Complainant right to appeal to agency against police decisions	Police not responsive to complainant dissatisfaction
Use of the civil standard of proof ("balance of probabilities")	Difficulty in substantiating complaints using the criminal standard ("beyond reasonable doubt")
More resources	Insufficient staff to conduct adequate audits or investigations
Expanded supervision of police investigations	Complainant and public perceptions of police bias
Serious cases investigated directly by the agency	Public trust demanding independent investigation in high-profile cases or extremely serious matters
"Own motion" power to investigate any matters	Evidence of misconduct not reported in formal complaints. Dissatisfaction with the rigor of police investigations
Public inquiry	Occasional need to hold an open inquisitorial forum, especially with high public interest and trust at stake
Receive complaints	Police deflection of complainants
Order police to reinvestigate cases	Audit findings of unsatisfactory investigative rigor or premature closure
Conduct integrity tests	Continued suspicions regarding corruption not exposed by conventional investigations
Apply wiretaps and receive transcripts of intercepts from other law enforcement agencies	Need for independent sources of intelligence
Apply for a search warrant	Need to circumvent police lack of cooperation in supplying documents
Compel answers to questions	Suspect police hiding behind right to silence
Direct police to notify complainants of mediation option	Police not informing complainants of the availability of mediation

Table 10.1   Types of Increased Capacity Sought by Oversight Agencies
(continued)

Capacity sought	Reason
Issue protection orders for whistle-blowers	Threats to internal witnesses
Proactive prevention capacity	Lack of action by police to conduct research on misconduct and develop prevention plans

Note. Adapted from "Stakeholder Perspectives on Police Complaints and Discipline: Toward a Civilian Control Model," by T. Prenzler, 2004, *Australian and New Zealand Journal of Criminology*, 37(1), p. 94. Copyright 2004 by Australian Academic Press. Adapted with permission.

give the subject police officer the benefit of the doubt. Landau noted that "perhaps the most salient feature in the minds of complainants remains the fact that the police investigate the police" (1996, p. 310). The following comments by survey respondents typify this view (p. 304):

- "It was the greatest shock—as soon as I phoned them, they passed all the information to the police."
- "If they really were an independent body, they would do their own investigations from the start."

Furthermore, as noted in Chapter 7, recent research by the Northern Ireland Police Ombudsman found that complainants wanted mediation to be conducted by an independent agency with the subject officer present.

Police Perspectives

Police obviously have a lot at stake in the complaints process, with potential for career-damaging impacts and, at its most extreme, losing their jobs and going to jail. In many jurisdictions police have been stridently opposed to external oversight and have at times mobilized successfully to block its introduction, curtail agency powers, or even close down agencies (Finnane, 2008). However, studies also show that many police officers see value in independent investigations (Finn, 2001, p. 118; Liberty, 2000, p. 5). Reiner (1991), who interviewed chief constables in England and Wales, found that

- 52% rejected the proposition of a fully independent system
- 18% felt there were strong arguments for both systems
- 30% were supportive

Those in favor did not necessarily believe that an independent system would be more effective in identifying and preventing misconduct, but felt it was essential to ensure public confidence and remove perceptions of bias.

As part of their study of the British police complaints system, Maguire and Corbett (1991) interviewed officers who had complaints against them. Just over half were concerned that external investigators would not understand the pressures on police. However, just under half felt civilian investigators could "'weed out' trivial or malicious complaints at an early stage without being suspected of doing so unfairly" and would improve the credibility of the complaints process as a whole (p. 70). Somewhat similar findings were made in Adams' (1997) survey of police in Britain:

- 50% supported the existing system of investigations by police
- 33% preferred investigation by an independent body
- 20% expressed equal confidence in both
- 85% supported the view that independent investigations would improve public confidence

More recently, a survey by the Northern Ireland Ombudsman found that 58% of police officers surveyed felt that complaints should be independently investigated (PONI, 2004).

Public perceptions can be important to more progressive police unions and they can be willing to accept external control when scandals involve large-scale discrediting of police integrity. During the Wood Commission in NSW, the Police Association developed a policy of complete externalization of investigations as a way of removing any doubt about bias and cover-ups (Prenzler, 2004). Similarly, following the Rampart Scandal in Los Angeles, the Los Angeles Police Protective League asserted that independent investigation and adjudication of complaints was necessary for public confidence (Barry, 2000).

Public Opinion

Public confidence is a frequently cited criterion for evaluating police accountability systems (Walker, 2001). The British Social Attitudes Survey has on occasion included a question on police complaints processing, with the question restricted to serious complaints. In the 1996 survey, 89% of respondents supported the proposition that serious complaints "should be investigated by an independent body, not by the police themselves" (Tarling & Dowds, 1997, p. 206). Other public opinion surveys also show very high levels of public support for independent processing of complaints (Jenkins, 1997; McGuire Research Services, 2000, p. 11). In 1999, a regular public survey sponsored by the Queensland CMC introduced more detail into the questions. The study found that 88% of respondents agreed with the statement that "complaints against the police should be investigated by an independent body, not the police themselves" (CJC, 2000b, p. 4). However, levels of support also varied with the type of complaint:

- For rudeness, 59% supported police handling the complaint and 30% supported an external body or person.
- For an assault complaint, 39% favored police and 47% favored an external investigation.
- For bribery, 23% favored police and 70% preferred an external investigation (CJC, 2000b, p. 4; for similar results from a British study see IPCC, 2007b, p. 21).

Civil Liberties Groups

Civil liberties lawyers have a prominent role in defending falsely accused persons and victims of police violence, and their experiences tend to make them mistrust police internal accountability processes. In the United States, the 1998 Human Rights Watch report analyzed excessive force cases and concluded that the problem was at epidemic levels. Case studies of 14 large cities led to a damning critique of internal affairs as largely ineffective to identify, punish, or deter misconduct. The American Civil Liberties Union (ACLU) has been at the forefront of the campaign against police control of discipline. The Union has argued that weak oversight is better than no oversight, but also claims that weak external review "emboldens police officers with a propensity to abuse their power, and gives false assurance to civilians who file a complaint" (NYCLU, 1998, pp. 5, 12). The NYCLU has also alleged that external review agencies

- Have insufficient staff to effectively manage the volume of complaints, especially those that involve legal complexity
- Have insufficient staff to carry out research on complaint and incident patterns
- Frequently lack powers to conduct hearings, obtain documents, compel answers to questions, or conduct covert operations
- At times fail to attract public support because of lack of community representation on their management boards (see also www.aclu.org/police/civoversight/index.html).

The most significant opportunity for police subversion occurs in the practice of restricting review boards to recommending disciplinary actions, which can then be overturned at the discretion of the Police Chief (ACLU,

1992). For example, the San Francisco Office of Citizen Complaints has been a stand-out agency in the United States because it investigates all complaints against police. At the same time, final disciplinary decisions remain within the province of the police (Finn, 2001). These intrinsic faults in the structure of police oversight have meant that many victims of police abuses resort to civil action. Despite the obstacles to litigation, police in the United States pay out many millions of dollars each year through the civil courts. The NYPD, for example, has been subject to numerous successful lawsuits. In the period 1994 to 1997 the city paid almost US$97 million in claims against police (NYCLU, 1998, p. 8).

One of the sources behind the new IPCC in the United Kingdom was a report by the National Council for Civil Liberties (Liberty, 2000). Researchers visited oversight agencies overseas, reviewed the literature, and consulted with stakeholders and experts. The report noted the growing convergence of opinion supporting independent processing of complaints and addressed a number of concerns about practical obstacles to implementation. It challenged the view that only police have the skills necessary to investigate police by citing the range of occupations that require generalist and specialist investigative skills. The report also observed that external agencies can progressively recruit and train non-police investigators. At the same time, police experience was recognized as an invaluable resource. Liberty therefore made the following recommendations to balance these competing principles:

- The investigative staff of the IPCC should comprise at least 75% civilians with no more than 25% seconded or ex-police officers.
- The investigations should take place in a team structure reflecting the above proportions.
- The IPCC should have the decision as to who are selected as seconded police officers.
- Investigative teams should always be headed by a civilian team leader.
- The creation of disciplinary panels comprising an assistant chief constable and two non-police members (2000, pp. 40, 49).

Government Reviews

The issue of independent investigation and adjudication of complaints has also been the subject of numerous reviews by law reform commissions and parliamentary committees. The 1981 U.S. Commission on Civil Rights study, *Who Is Guarding the Guardians? A Report on Police Practices*, criticized the limited powers of review boards and analyzed the way police investigators deflected and intimidated complainants (USCCR, 1981). A follow-up report argued that police misconduct and public mistrust had increased in the two decades after the first report, highlighting the need for review boards to exercise subpoena power and "disciplinary authority over investigations of police abuse incidents" (USCCR, 2000, p. 12). The LAPD has been a major focus for this issue. Following the Rampart Scandal, a government panel charged with evaluating reform comprehensively censured self-regulation, including specific reference to the police chief's abuse of his statutory authority to reject external disciplinary recommendations (RIRP, 2000).

In Canada, the expansion of civilian oversight has been driven less by serious corruption than by breakdowns in police-community relations and dissatisfaction with police handling of complaints, chronicled by various government-sponsored reviews (Landau, 1994; McDonald, 1981; Oppal, 1994). The Office of the Public Complaints Commissioner was set up in Toronto in 1981. It was restructured, with its jurisdiction enlarged to the whole of Ontario in 1990, and an independent Special Investigations Unit was created to deal with serious incidents (see www. occps.ca/).

In Northern Ireland, efforts to reform the Royal Ulster Constabulary included an influential review of the complaints process. The 1997 Hayes Report went straight to the heart of the issue:

> The overwhelming message I got from nearly all sides and from all political parties was the need for the investigation [of police] to be independent and to be seen to be independent. ... The present arrangements ... lacked credibility because ... it was the Chief Constable who decided what was a complaint, because there was no power of initiative, and because the complaints were investigated by police officers. ... The main value which was impressed upon me was independence, independence, independence (Hayes, 1997, p. v).

The Hayes recommendations were endorsed by the larger Patten Inquiry into policing in Northern Ireland (ICPNI, 1999), and in 2000 a powerful Police Ombudsman for Northern Ireland was created. The Ombudsman may refer less serious matters to the Chief Constable for formal investigation, but in practice it investigates all public complaints using civilian investigation teams. There is also a capacity to appeal police decisions to an independent tribunal or direct the Chief Constable to take disciplinary action (Seneviratne, 2004).

The Performance of External Agencies

Evaluating the impact of external oversight agencies (or police integrity agencies) is difficult because of the same problems of interpretation of activity measures of police complaints and discipline systems described in Chapter 6. A significant problem, noted above, is that external agencies often only have powers to recommend disciplinary actions. It is therefore difficult to properly evaluate the impact of an agency whose power is truncated at the final point in the process. Despite these methodological difficulties, there has been some research addressing performance questions. The limited evidence suggests that the more interventionist an agency is, and the more it engages in independent investigations or close supervision of police investigators, the more likely it is to score on positive indicators than preceding police-dominated systems (CJC, 1997; Herzog, 2002; Maguire & Corbett, 1991; PONI, 2002a, 2002b). One of the most comprehensive attempts to evaluate the impact of external oversight and an externally driven reform agenda was carried out in Queensland in the mid-1990s by the police watchdog body the Criminal Justice Commission, covering the first 5 years of reform (CJC, 1997). The study found that

- Survey data showed a strong improvement in public confidence in police integrity and in the complaints process.
- There was a significant increase in public complaints, indicating improved public confidence.
- Although there was a continuing high volume of complaints there were promising declines in allegations of duty failure, fabrication of evidence, and serious assaults, despite increased police arrest rates.
- The rate of substantiation of investigated complaints rose from around 14% per year under the preceding system (prior to the Fitzgerald Inquiry) to an average of 27% per year in the 4 years following the first year of establishment of the new system.
- There was a much greater acceptance by police of disciplinary recommendations.
- Auditing indicated that police were more willing to implement recommendations to improve integrity systems, such as introducing informal resolution procedures and ethics training.
- There was evidence of a weakening in the code of silence from interviews with middle ranking and senior police, from ethical climate surveys, and from complaints by police.
- Confidential interviews with police also indicated significant improvements in police conduct and in the likelihood of misconduct being detected.

At the same time, the CJC acknowledged areas where reform had been considerably less than optimal. These included gaps in ethics education across ranks, a weakening of disciplinary recommendations by police in practice, and gaps in whistle-blower protection.

In the United States, the 1998 Human Rights Watch report on police brutality noted that the quality of complaints disposition data held by internal affairs departments in the 14 cities studied was so poor that comparisons were impossible (Human Rights Watch, 1998, p. 60). In an earlier attempt to address the performance of different agencies, Luna (1994) made approximate matches between 10 police departments that lacked external oversight and seven with oversight. Over a 3-year period the sustained rate by internal affairs without oversight for use of force allegations was 12%, compared to a sustained rate by oversight agencies of 19%. Strangely perhaps, the sustained rate for all allegations without oversight was 22%, compared to 9% for the oversight agencies. Luna discovered that oversight agencies with independent investigative authority received six times as many complaints as internal affairs units. She also identified a decline in use of force complaints made to external agencies, which she attributed to a deterrent effect on both police and false complaints. For example,

> In Berkeley during the years 1974 to 1977 (the first three years of the Review Board's existence) the number of complaints regarding the use of force dropped 67%. In San Diego County the percentage of complaints alleging the improper use of force dropped from 22% to 17% during the first year of operation of the Review Board, and the number of death cases dropped by 46%. ... These figures suggest that the existence of a formal external review mechanism engenders officer restraint. They might also suggest that public awareness of the agencies' vigorous investigative process dissuades bogus filings (Luna, 1994, p. 6).

Public opinion is usually strongly supportive of external agencies, with a positive view of their effectiveness in making police more accountable. Support for the work of these agencies and their contribution to improved police conduct is generally in the range above 70% (e.g., ACLUT, 2000; ICAC, 2000; IPCC, 2006; Seneviratne, 2004). At the same time, however, it is often apparent that survey respondents are probably not fully informed of the precise division of labor between police and the external agency. In other words, they do not know whether the agency is substantively independent or reliant on police for much of the operational work.

Complainant satisfaction would appear to be a key criterion for the success of external agencies, given the major problem of complainant dissatisfaction with police investigating police. However, some attempts to measure possible improvements in complainant satisfaction have been confounded by continuing police, or ex-police, involvement in these agencies, under the rubric of independent processing (de Guzman, 2007; Herzog, 2002; Thomassen, 2002). The Minneapolis Civilian Review Authority (CRA) is unusual in that "former police" conduct investigations, the police chief has the final say on discipline, but "civilians with no professional experience as sworn officers conduct the hearings" (Finn, 2001, pp. 34, 36). In one evaluation of the CRA, Walker & Herbst (1999, p. 4) found that 76% of complainants felt "they had a chance to tell their side of the story," 79% felt that "the CRA staff member listened to them," and 55% felt the outcome was fair.

The Northern Ireland Ombudsman presents as one of the most independent external agencies. Its surveys of complainants have shown mixed results, but they are generally fairly positive and are improving over time. The most recent survey for 2006 to 2007 found that 42.0% of complainants were dissatisfied or very dissatisfied with the outcome of their complaint, although this marked a slight improvement from 44.4% in the previous year. The percentage satisfied or very satisfied increased slightly from 38.0% in 2005–2006 to 39.6% in 2006–2007. Mixed views were held by 17.6% in 2005–2006 and 18.4% in 2006–2007 (PONI, 2006b, 2007b, p. 24). It must be kept in mind, however, that complainant dissatisfaction with complaints processes and outcomes in police-controlled systems is typically on the order of 75%, while overall satisfaction with police handling of complaints has been in the range 5% to 30%. The Ombudsman, in contrast, has scored well on numerous process-oriented factors. For example, for 2006–2007, 75% of complainants felt they were treated fairly, 63% were satisfied with the service they received (32% were very satisfied), and 95% to 97% thought staff were polite, friendly, easy to understand, patient, and professional. In addition, 76% said they would use the system again if they had a complaint, 70% were satisfied with how well they were kept informed, and 59% were satisfied with the time taken to resolve the matter (PONI, 2007b, pp. 3-4).

The limited data on police officer responses to external agencies show similarly mixed but promising results. A Philippines study found that 80% of police who had been investigated under a mixed police-civilian system were satisfied overall compared with 64% who had not had direct experience of the system. Both groups—82% and 80%, respectively—saw investigations as fair (de Guzman, 2007). A U.S. study (de Angelis & Kupchick, 2007) surveyed officers who had a complaint against them processed under a system where oversight agency staff were responsible for "participating in and monitoring all internal investigations." Although respondents reported higher levels of trust in internal affairs and lower levels of trust in citizen oversight, 97.6% reported overall satisfaction with the process. What appeared to be most important to officers was not whether or not a complaint was sustained, or the presence or absence of citizen oversight, but that the complaint was processed in a way that was procedurally fair with good communication and in a timely manner. In the case of the hybrid Minneapolis CRA, Walker & Herbst (1999, p. 6) found that 90% of police officers involved felt they were able to tell their side of the story, and 85% considered the outcome of their case to be fair. As noted, a study of the initial responses of police to the work of the Northern Ireland Ombudsman found that 58% felt that, in principle, complaints should be independently investigated (PONI, 2004). However,

- 54% claimed they were deterred from doing their job properly because of the potential for complaints,
- 63% thought investigators from the Ombudsman were "more likely to believe the person making the complaint than the officer being complained about," and
- 42% felt the Ombudsman was "out to get them."

Of police who had contact with the Ombudsman, 57% said they felt they had not been fairly treated, but 64% were satisfied with the outcome of the investigation.

Substantiation rates for complaints (or allegations) are also an important but highly problematic performance measure. Theoretically, all complaints against police could lack adequate evidence, either under criminal or civil standards, with the result that thorough and independent investigations result in zero substantiations. In fact, this could be considered one of the ultimate goals of integrity management. At the same time, in a transition period from a police control model to a civilian control model there is an expectation of an increase in substantiations. Reported substantiation rates in police-dominated systems are highly variable but a rough average, reported in the international literature, is around 10% (Prenzler & Ronken, 2001a). As noted, substantiation rates for matters investigated in the early years after the settling in of the Queensland CJC averaged 27%. Newer agencies with extensive independent powers, such as the Northern Ireland Ombudsman and the Victorian Office of Police Integrity, report much lower rates, more in the order of 12% of matters investigated, but they also make much greater use of informal resolution of matters (OPI, 2006, p. 67; PONI, 2007c, p. 16). In England and Wales, substantiation rates averaged around 8% from 1987 to 2001. They increased to about 12% in the 3 years prior to the introduction of the IPCC and have stayed at that rate (IPCC, 2007c, p. 37). In considering these figures it is important to keep in mind that substantiation rates are subject to the many problems of evidence gathering, and that they are only one performance measure among a variety of measures.

One important performance indicator in terms of public accountability and a scientific approach to integrity management is that external agencies are often much more open in documenting police misconduct, including complaint outcomes and de-identified detailed case study reports on exemplar investigations and their outcomes—see Sidebar 10.2 (see also PONI, 2002a). External agencies are also much more likely to engage in open inquiry processes, through public hearings, for example, and also more likely to conduct quality research and policy development (Seneviratne, 2004; e.g., CJC, 1997; Hoffman, 2003). These agencies are also more likely to have community representatives on their management boards and have community liaison and consultative processes, hold press conferences, attend or host conferences, and

Sidebar 10.2: Examples of Interventions by Police Oversight Agencies

Police Ombudsman of Northern Ireland
"A mother complained on behalf of her son, that he had been assaulted by a police officer resulting in the youth falling down steps causing injury to his head, elbows and knees. During the investigation a number of witnesses were identified but none was prepared to provide statements of evidence. When interviewed the youth involved was unable to provide the exact shoulder numeral of the officer concerned. However, following extensive enquiries, involving the transfer and enhancement of CCTV footage, the officer's identity was uncovered and he was interviewed by the Police Ombudsman investigating officer. The officer conceded that he had pushed the youth but stated that he was unaware of the proximity of the steps. Having secured all of the relevant documentary material the Ombudsman took the view that the officer's conduct fell below that expected by the Police Code of Ethics and recommended that he be given advice and guidance by his Divisional Commander. The Chief Constable subsequently informed the Office that the officer had received advice and guidance and that he had also completed personal safety program training" (PONI, 2007a, p. 25).

Independent Police Complaints Commission in Britain
"The IPCC upheld a complaint against the findings of a police investigation into a complaint by a man about the way an officer deployed his police dog during a large-scale public disturbance. Several people in the area at the time had complained of being bitten and of their clothing being damaged by a police dog, and the IPCC supervised an investigation by the force into the complaints. The force did not uphold any of the complaints and one complainant appealed against this finding to the IPCC. This appeal was upheld. The Commissioner who dealt with the case commented: 'Having examined the evidence and the circumstances of this incident very carefully, I am satisfied that the police dog was used inappropriately. This was not justified by the circumstances that the dog handler was facing and was not in line with force guidelines on the use of police dogs.' The officer received a written warning as a result of his conduct on the day of the disturbance and the force was invited to review its decisions in respect of the other complaints involving the officer. The force also implemented significantly improved dog-handling training that went beyond the guidelines of the National Police Dog Assessment Model"(IPCC, 2007a, p. 17).

work with researchers in universities. Greater openness, more community input, more research, and more information mean greater accountability.

A Model Oversight System

As noted in the introduction to this chapter, civilian oversight can be constructed in different ways, depending on local circumstances. The higher the indicators of current or recent misconduct, and the lower the levels of public trust, the stronger the case for a powerful highly interventionist agency. Police departments with long histories of good community relations, an absence of serious corruption, and a tradition of good in-house integrity management might not require close routine scrutiny. At the same time, a number of fundamentals have emerged as essential to ensure that oversight is effective in most societies. In fact, although the term "oversight" is retained here because of familiarity, it understates the level of intervention required in many cases. The establishment and acceptance of the Northern Ireland Ombudsman demonstrates that many of the practical issues associated with the civilian control model can be worked through. It is possible to create an agency that is controlled by non-police staff, that directly investigates complaints, and that has an authoritative role in discipline. At a minimum, an agency should have the capacity to do this, and one important option is to give complainants a choice about who processes their complaint. Some might be happy for police to manage their case, while others are likely to have a strong preference for an external agency. An external agency should also possess "own motion" powers to investigate any matter, and have the capacity for covert operations and responsibility for assessing all aspects of a police department's integrity management system. It should also have a legal authority to direct police departments to act on certain issues, such as introducing an early warning system or introducing drug and alcohol testing. It should also have the capacity set up its own intervention and risk management systems, either in parallel to the police department's or in lieu of police systems.

Northern Ireland represents a relatively compact policing jurisdiction. Implementation of a similar oversight model in many larger policing areas will require a regional "shop front" presence to provide a localized service. An efficient way to achieve this is by integrating police oversight within a larger, well-resourced, public sector anticorruption commission (e.g., www.cmc.gov.au). An integrated model can also be efficient in the case of very small police forces. A state- or regionally based integrity commission can provide coverage of many small police departments and associated public sector entities (e.g., see www.cacole.ca).

A difficult balancing act is also required between independence from political interference, on the one hand, and, on the other hand, accountability to citizens through parliaments. A model for democratic accountability that has emerged from the Australian experiments in police oversight, and in general has strong consensus support, is that of a cross-parliamentary oversight committee (Brown, 2006; e.g., PCMC, 2008). This is a committee with representatives from both the government and opposition parties that periodically reviews and reports on the oversight agency's performance, and responds to allegations of misconduct against the agency. Various confidential protocols are required for sensitive matters. What is vital as well is that the committee has an executive capacity. This usually takes the form of an office of inspector—parliamentary inspector or parliamentary commissioner—who has many of the agency's own powers to enter property, obtain documents, and require answers to questions. The risk in cross-parliamentary oversight is that it adds an additional layer of inefficient bureaucracy and another forum for politically charged disputes; but it appears to be the best type of institutional arrangement to maximize democratic accountability of anticorruption agencies. Figure 10.1 sets out this model system of accountability, which includes police oversight within a comprehensive system of public sector oversight.

What is also apparent is that external agencies are obligated to develop a mix of performance indicators as a way of demonstrating their effectiveness

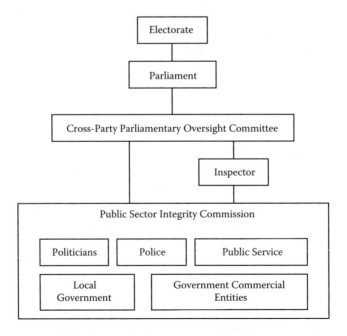

Figure 10.1 Model accountability system for police oversight.

and identifying areas that need improvement (Brereton, 2000). The more agencies conduct investigations themselves, the more they become subject to performance indicators that they should apply to police internal affairs. The following instruments and indicators have been used or recommended (Finn, 2001, pp. 127-128; Prenzler & Lewis, 2005):

- Reducing the number and seriousness of complaints
- Reducing police shootings
- Time taken to complete cases
- Stakeholder feedback
- Public confidence surveys
- Prosecution outcomes
- Successful appeals
- Case file audits
- Case study reports on activities (e.g., solving problems, resolving complaints)
- Police implementation of recommendations
- Overall assessments of police conduct using complaints, complaints dispositions, and other intelligence
- Inspector/monitor reports

Of additional note is the importance of maintaining oversight and accountability in the current War on Terror, in which policing and security agencies have come under renewed pressure to engage in process corruption, torture, and the denial of due rights. In that regard, all the principles of civilian control should apply across the wider policing complex, including secret service agencies and specialist covert units.

Conclusion

While a strong element of independence appears to be essential to improving the quality of police discipline, and for ensuring public confidence, the exact mechanics of how this should be done give rise to a variety of challenging issues. Certainly it would seem that each jurisdiction needs to work out its own arrangements, with levels of apparent misconduct being an important guide. At the same time, there is a growing convergence of opinion in favor of the view that direct external conduct of investigations is a standing requirement for all serious matters (e.g., police shootings, allegations of bribery). There would also appear to be a strong case for oversight agencies to have a free hand to investigate or research matters they consider need to be pursued on a discretionary basis (e.g., alleged police assaults revealed by the media).

Furthermore, it would appear essential that oversight agencies have direct input into disciplinary decisions, or at the very least a capacity to overturn police decisions, while police need to retain a major role in primary prevention in areas such as screening, training, risk management, and early warning systems.

Leadership for Integrity 11

Leadership is one of those obvious things required for integrity in policing, but how to generate and maintain ethical leadership is a difficult question. One point to note is that when it comes to ethical policing, inspiring good conduct by example is unlikely to be sufficient. Good leaders need to be good managers, with a detailed knowledge of the workings of their organization, facilitating and driving the successful pursuit of organizational goals. In part, this requires a figure who inspires others and sets an example of work done enthusiastically, conscientiously, and competently. More importantly, it requires a person who ensures that the right structures and systems are in place and are operating optimally. This view shifts the perspective away from a model of leadership based on a single charismatic figure toward a more sustainable systems-oriented model, and one that is also oriented toward democratic leadership (Goldsmith, 2001). A "command and control" approach is unlikely to produce ethical leadership if it insulates police from external influences, especially from the community. A greater range of democratic inputs will assist in making ethical leadership more of a shared responsibility.

A key way then to advance ethical leadership is by seeing it as something inseparable from issues of institutional structure, culture, and purpose. A comprehensive integrity system should be set up—with the right elements and written rules and duties—to be as "leadership proof" as possible. In other words, it should be built with an expectation of poor leadership and a maximum capacity to operate as effectively as possible in spite of this. At the same time, the system should include mechanisms designed to select persons with qualities of ethical leadership for leadership positions. Human will and commitment remain essential for the system to work the way it was designed to work.

Background

Inquiries and reviews into police misconduct almost invariably identify leadership as a major, if not the primary, problem. Often the failure of ethical leadership is entwined with a wider problem of general maladministration. The 1989 Fitzgerald Report declared that

[t]he Queensland Police Force is debilitated by misconduct, inefficiency, incompetence, and deficient leadership. The situation is compounded by poor organization and administration, inadequate resources, and insufficiently developed techniques and skills for the task of law enforcement in a modern complex society. Lack of discipline, cynicism, disinterest, frustration, anger and low self-esteem are the result. The culture which shares responsibility for and is supported by this grossly unsatisfactory situation includes contempt for the criminal justice system, disdain for the law and rejection of its application to police, disregard for the truth, and abuse of authority (Fitzgerald, 1989, p. 200).

One could hardly think of a more damning critique of police leadership. Unfortunately, such examples are all too common in the police inquiry literature. In the Queensland case, the commissioner was part of the core corruption racket and was sentenced to 14 years in jail. In many other cases the police chief is not found to be directly involved in corruption. Culpability occurs more in the form of tolerance of corruption or neglect of basic corruption prevention measures. Either way, judicial inquiries have also repeatedly shown that in corrupt departments, support for corruption has come down from the top. Denial and defensiveness have most frequently been the responses to allegations of corruption in these contexts (Fleming & Lafferty, 2000; Newburn, 1999; Wood, 1997).

The problem of deficient leadership is not of course confined to the police chief. It can involve the whole senior and middle levels of management. And here it is often the case that assessments reveal multilevel deficiencies. This can occur even in relatively advanced police departments in robust democracies, with long histories of good community policing and professional standards. For example, a 1999 report by the Inspectorate of policing in England and Wales made the following observation:

Of all the factors which might lead to a lack of integrity in the Service put forward by those visited by the Inspection Team, an absence of good supervision, management and leadership was by far the most prominent (HMIC, 1999a, p. 61).

Unfortunately, too, one of the problems with external oversight of police—a partial antidote for poor leadership—is that many leaders in these agencies display a peculiar enthusiasm for devolution of complaints handling to police, being seemingly content simply to review police processes and periodically criticize their deficiencies. In other words, they appear reluctant to do their job, that is, to *do* independent complaints investigations and adjudication, and to direct police regardiing corruption prevention initiatives (Prenzler, 2004).

Despite this gloomy picture, there are some grounds for optimism. The reforming commissioner is a staple of police studies—figures like August

Vollmer and Patrick Murphy. Visionary leaders are potentially there to be found. But while there is always a chance that committed leaders will be selected to drive accountability, what is now apparent is that there is a clear set of structural requirements that must be put in place so that leaders with commitment and the will to do the job properly can work unimpeded by structural constraints (for example, legal protections against a requirement for police to answer questions). And, as far as possible, ethical leadership needs to be structured into the whole system of police operations. Most importantly, close supervision of front-line officers needs to be an operational requirement (Mollen, 1994). Ethical leadership needs to be built progressively into the in-service training curriculum. Evaluations of performance in integrity related to an officer's field of responsibility also must be built into the system of performance appraisal, retention, deployment, and promotion. Ethical leadership, in Goldsmith's words, requires both "symbolism" and "systems" (2001).

Types of Leadership

Leadership is usually thought of in terms of the ability to get other people to follow. There are, of course, many different styles of leadership that are advocated for different purposes. Sometimes "hands-off" leadership is considered appropriate, for example, if staff are self-motivated and doing well largely on their own. Sometimes "hands-on" leadership is required, especially when staff are lazy and there are competency problems. Depending on the context, leaders sometimes need to be revolutionary. In other circumstances they need to maintain a good system and not destroy it because of a personal agenda, i.e., "If it ain't broken don't fix it." Readers will also be familiar with the concepts of "authoritarian" and "charismatic" leadership, both of which have fallen out of favor as leading to slavish devotion and disasters such as wars and holocausts. The traditional policing model of a hierarchical, bureaucratic, and paramilitary organization has been rejected by many contemporary theorists of policing (e.g., Bayley, 1994; Goldstein, 1990). Corruption and misconduct have been prominent among the negative outcomes of this system. "Transformational leadership" entered the policing lexicon partly as a result of the innumerable reform agendas arising from inquiries. But something more than transformational leadership is required to sustain reforms. Precisely which model is best for ethical policing is a matter of debate, and the danger perhaps is that any label put forward as encapsulating the ideal will be misused.

One concept that readers might find useful is that of "democratic leadership," advocated by Andrew Goldsmith (2001). Contrary to what might be expected from the term, Goldsmith does not advocate that police vote in their leaders or vote on policy directions. Some kind of command and control structure is still required to ensure a direct line of accountability up through the police hierarchy, through the chief to the parliament, and through the parliament to the electorate. What Goldsmith advocates is the buttressing of that main line of accountability through other lines of input, including the types of local consultative committees advocated under the community policing banner. In addition, Goldsmith argues that a police board, with cross-cultural citizen representation, should have a key role in appointing senior police, providing critical input into policy directions and performance evaluations, and generally curbing the authoritarian tendencies of police chiefs.

Assessing the Impacts of Ethical Leadership

One question that needs to be addressed is, can ethical leadership really improve police conduct? And, if so, how? The value of leadership in police corruption prevention is supported in theory by criminological research. For example, Hollinger and Clark (1983) studied occupational deviance in terms of organizational climate. In surveys and interviews with retail, manufacturing, and hospital staff, they found that diverse corrupt practices, such as employee theft, tardiness, drug and alcohol abuse on the job, and sick-leave abuse, were strongly influenced by factors within workplace cultures. Workers who felt exploited and dissatisfied were more likely to engage in deviance. Additionally, companies experiencing the least misconduct were those communicating a clear and consistent message of intolerance of misconduct. Consistent application of formal sanctions was also important in shaping the more effective peer-based informal social controls of gossip and shame.

Judicial inquiries have repeatedly shown that in corrupt departments, support for corruption has come down from the top in various forms. Historical analyses by inquiries, and post-inquiry studies, show that corruption levels, although often difficult to precisely measure, fluctuate with different leaderships, including periods of relatively high integrity that result from a combination of expressive or symbolic commitment; support for, or the creation of, well-resourced internal investigations units; innovation and experimentation with integrity technologies; and zeal in pursing investigations and discipline. In some cases the drive comes from the very top, the police chief or commissioner, or even the mayor or police minister (Fitzgerald, 1989; Fleming & Lafferty, 2000; Gelb, 1983; Henry, 1994; Knapp, 1972; Newburn, 1999; Wood, 1997). In other cases, it may come from a particularly committed Internal Affairs commander. There is also a wider field of research showing the importance of the attitudes and interest of the police chief, or a particularly progressive director of human resources, in improving equity or affirmative action in recruitment, for example, in employing and supporting women police officers (Prenzler & Hayes, 2000) or minority groups (Holdaway, 1991).

The period following the discovery of major corruption is a particularly testing time for leaders, especially given they are often new in the job. One of the innovations introduced by Police Chief Patrick Murphy in New York, based on Knapp Commission diagnostics, was much closer supervision of front-line officers. Supervisors were expected to be present at arrests for crimes where corruption had been a common problem (Newburn, 1999, p. 34). Supervisors were also expected to be involved in corruption patrols or corruption probes, where they observed police behavior in areas where corruption commonly occurred, such as night club areas (Barker, 1996, p. 75; Sherman, 1978b, p. 162). More generally, Murphy

> strengthened and re-deployed [anti-corruption units], consolidating the agency's corruption investigation mechanism at the central Internal Affairs Division, at the same time creating a subsidiary network of 17 decentralized Field Internal Affairs Units (FIAUs) throughout the Department's 10 Bureaus and 7 Patrol Borough commands. Although each was technically a sub-unit of the Bureau or Borough command, the FIAUs were modeled after the central Internal Affairs Division and acted as liaison between it and their commanding officer. Police commanders were expected to manage the specific corruption hazards existing within their part of the organization, and FIAUs gave them the capability to conduct their own corruption investigations or to conduct integrity tests of their subordinates (Henry, 1990, p. 53).

Some managers complained that they could not observe officers all the time. In reply, Murphy asserted that

> We won't assume you are automatically guilty, if something happens under your command. But, if something happens, *we will thoroughly investigate the methods you used to prevent it*, and make a judgment as to whether you were *careless*, or not using your resources effectively (Gelb, 1983, pp. 299-300).

In policing, like many occupations, managers easily become preoccupied with administration (financial accounting, rostering, etc.) at the expense of supervision, despite the fact that working with staff, including monitoring their performance, appears to be a more productive management technique (Brewer, 1991; HMIC, 1999a, p. 61). There is also some research evidence that close supervision produces lowers levels of use of force and misconduct (Walker, 2007). In New York City a study was conducted of two precincts that went against the trend of rising citizen complaints during the 1990s crackdown on crime: "Large reductions in crime occurred while complaints against officers declined" (Davis, Mateu-Gelabert & Miller, 2005, p.

229). Complaints declined by 54% in the 42nd Precinct and 64% in the 44th Precinct over several years as a number of initiatives were introduced. The researchers attributed reduced complaints to the implementation of a "courtesy, professionalism, and respect policy" (CPR), a verbal judo course, and close supervisor monitoring of staff with complaints histories. Part of the close supervision strategy was to pair experienced officers with less experienced officers deemed to have "attitude problems." The researchers observed that the leadership styles of the commanders were quite different, but the levels of commitment to ensuring integrity were similar, as were the results:

> One was described as a hands-on administrator who made a point of getting to know his officers and who encouraged a team approach. The other ran his precinct in a more traditional, hierarchical fashion. But both commanders shared a particularly strong commitment to respectful policing. Both made it clear to the officers in their charge that they considered attention to civilian complaints a high priority to comply with the new NYPD policies. Both made it clear to their supervisors and to their officers that civilian complaints were to be kept to a minimum (p. 239).

An adequate management/staff ratio appears essential to ensure that supervisors, especially field supervisors, can be properly informed of the activities of their staff, appropriately monitor their activities, and attend on the scene when necessary (Parks, 2000). An Oakland Police Department Consent Decree, for example, stipulates that there should be no more than eight members under a supervisor's control (OPD, 2004, p. 16). In fact, a supervisor-to-staff ratio of 1 to 7 or 1 to 8 appears to be an optimal arrangement (Parks, 2000, p. 341).

There are other social science studies on the topic of ethical leadership indicating that leadership by example can be effective, but that it needs to be strongly buttressed by close supervision. In the Netherlands, Huberts, Lamboo, and Punch (2003) conducted in-depth interviews with police regarding major reform efforts. Their main finding was that "there was unanimity that the Dutch police have undergone significant changes concerning integrity." A key part of this was transformational leadership:

> Police chiefs and police management ... are far more than in the past presenting a "good example," and there is little doubt about the integrity of management. ... Officers most often mentioned the following causes for the changing importance of integrity: governmental and force integrity policies, the reorganization of the police (which opened up working teams to more scrutiny) and changing values and norms in the wider environment (society) (2003, p. 229).

Note here the combination of factors. There is leadership by example in terms of both apparent personal commitment to organizational values and goals, and also role modeling of desired behaviors—setting a good example. There is attention to better structures, with a focus on greater scrutiny of operations, and there is the influence of a shift in community values, with greater expectations of accountability and ethical conduct.

Another Dutch study, utilizing a survey of police, analyzed the influence of leadership styles in terms of "role modeling," "strictness," and "openness." The influences on types of police misconduct were assessed in the following terms:

> Role modeling is especially significant in limiting unethical conduct in the context of interpersonal relationships. Employees appear to copy the leader's integrity standards in their daily interaction with one another. Strictness is important as well, but appears to be particularly effective in controlling fraud, corruption and the misuse of resources. The impact of openness is less evident (Huberts et al., 2007, p. 587).

The study related respondents' perceptions of their supervisor's leadership style to the respondents' perceptions of colleagues' violations of ethical standards. These were colleagues who worked under the same supervisor. To elaborate, the study found that "[r]ole modeling appears to have a significant influence [in positive terms] on all types of misconduct, with a relatively strong effect on internal corruption (favoritism), types of ill-treatment (discrimination, harassment, gossiping, bullying) and falsely calling in sick" (p. 599). Openness was also identified as having a positive influence on 15 of the 20 types of unethical conduct used in the study, with a particularly strong influence on "internal favoritism and discriminatory remarks to citizens and suspects" (p. 599).

Governmental promotion of ethics and a political agenda concerned with accountability appear to positively influence cultural support for integrity. This view has been supported in cross-national studies of police attitudes, most notably in the book *The Contours of Police Integrity*, which reported ethical climate survey results from Austria, Quebec, Croatia, Britain, Finland, Hungary, Japan, the Netherlands, Pakistan, Poland, Slovenia, Sweden, and the United States (Klockars et al., 2004). The book identified a problem with "the world-wide prevalence of the code of silence" (p. 17), but showed that police views about the seriousness of breaches of ethical standards, or "level(s) of intolerance for misconduct," are not uniform. Country-specific factors, such as cultural tolerance of violence and misconduct or government commitment to integrity, appear to affect police attitudes (Kutnjak Ivkovic, 2005)

In a study sponsored by the U.S. National Institute of Justice, researchers surveyed officers in 30 police departments using an ethical climate survey. From the results they selected three highly ranked departments in terms of their "integrity environment." In-depth follow-up research, including field observations, identified the following key factors in organizational integrity:

> Officers learned to gauge the seriousness of various types of misconduct by observing their department's diligence in detecting it and disciplining those who engage in police misconduct. ... The rules governing misconduct should be specified and officers trained in their application ... an effective way to educate both the police and the public is to disclose the entire disciplinary process to public scrutiny. How police manage, investigate, and discipline misconduct will show officers how serious they consider the misconduct to be. In choosing levels of discipline, police administrators should understand the educational consequences of their disciplinary acts (Klockars et al., 2005, pp. 3, 8).

Overcoming the Internal Cultural Divide

Policing is well known for a sharp disjunction between management rhetoric and rank-and-file practices: the "two cultures of policing" (Reuss-Ianni, 1983). The formal culture is concerned with due process, crime reduction, and public service standards. The informal culture is generally concerned with cutting corners, avoiding work, and engaging in petty or more serious corruption. This division is partly inevitable in any organization. Some workers are always likely to resent demands imposed on them, even reasonable work demands. At the same time, the divide can be fostered by management indifference to the genuine implementation of policies and standards. Employees constantly assess informal clues from supervisors about what is and what is not acceptable behavior in an organization. They then tend to behave within a zone of perceived permissible behaviors, regardless of formal rules.

A sense of unfairness among the rank-and-file is also likely to motivate them toward deviance. Employees are highly sensitive to hypocrisy. Role modeling, as we have seen, is usually cited as a major aspect of good leadership. Positive role modeling involves subordinates emulating leaders' behavior out of respect and admiration, and because they can see examples of career rewards for ethical behavior. Hypocrisy is part of a process of inverted role modeling. Perceived hypocrisy can provide rationalizations and incentives for workplace deviance (Hollinger & Clark, 1983), resulting in deteriorating work standards and the eventual loss of good officers (see Sidebar 9.3 in Chapter 9).

Gratuities exemplify an area vulnerable to hypocrisy. If the department's code of conduct prohibits gratuities this needs to be enforced at all levels. Tolerance of petty gratuities, such as half-price burgers or free nightclub entry, blurs the line and sends confusing messages to rank-and-file officers. The situation is greatly exacerbated if senior officers accept corporate donations from companies vying for police business. When senior officers are seen sitting in corporate boxes at sporting stadiums with executives from companies submitting tenders for police vehicle fleets or computer supplies, then a mixed message is sent out and front-line officers can only be resentful. The discipline system is another area with a high potential for hypocrisy. The Rampart Board of Inquiry in Los Angeles recommended that regular audits be done of disciplinary outcomes to stop the widespread practice of a double standard in discipline that favored management (Parks, 2000, p. 339; see also Mollen, 1994).

One of the potential obstacles to ethical leadership is the restless career-ism evident in larger police departments. This involves constant strategizing by officers about their next promotion. Everything is done, not for its intrinsic value or value to the organization's goals, but to facilitate the next move up the ladder. A police officer may undertake country service, not because they care about the security of rural communities, but because it is seen as a good career move. They will take in-service courses, in ethics, for example, simply because this will enhance their resumé and promotion prospects. Improved in-service training can lead to the complaint that some officers are "always doing courses." The pressure to build up a resumé also often means police are constantly changing positions, which makes continuity in leadership positions difficult to sustain. Good ethical leadership will involve clamping down on this kind of instability to ensure adequate continuity in the personnel and management profiles of squads and stations.

Ethical Leadership and Integrity Mechanisms

The key indicator of the quality of ethical leadership in a police organization is an indirect one. It is not so much the combined results of different measures of misconduct and integrity (Chapter 4), but focuses instead on the extent and quality of the integrity system itself, so far as the elements are the responsibility of different police managers. This follows from the points developed in preceding chapters about the need for a comprehensive integrity system. Quality audits of these elements constitute audits of the quality of ethical leadership. Ensuring that the integrity system is working is perhaps the key criterion for ethical leadership. For example, in regard to an effective complaints and discipline system,

> [s]upervisors and managers at all levels within the Police Service are expected to provide both leadership by example and a robust measure of quality assurance and challenge. In addition, the responsibilities of chief police officers are to:

- Keep themselves informed about complaints and conduct matters within their force;
- Ensure a timely response to complaints;
- Ensure that complaints and conduct matters are properly handled and recorded; and
- Ensure that complainants, officers and staff are regularly informed of progress (HMIC, 1999b, p. 29).

Selection and Education of Ethical Leaders

One obvious way to improve ethical leadership in policing is to include it in selection criteria for promotion, as well as making it a key criterion for all training positions and probationary supervisors. This entails building ethical leadership into all in-service courses as a way of developing the required knowledge and skills in potential leaders. The Toronto Ferguson Report (Ferguson, 2003, p. 25) argued that

> [n]o member of the Service shall be promoted to a management or supervisory position unless he or she has successfully completed a designated course on management skills required in the higher rank, in addition to training in ethics and integrity.

Following training, evidence of ethical leadership must be a requirement in promotion applications as part of a merit-based selection process. The criteria need to be clearly built into the selection process, on paper, so they cannot be bypassed. Applicants also have to be judged not just on their assertions about their ethical leadership qualities, but on real life examples where they have shown ethical leadership, in managing corruption prevention programs, for example, improving the ethical culture of a squad, or helping subordinates to manage ethical dilemmas in ways consistent with organizational principles. Community representatives on selection panels can be part of a democratic leadership agenda through external scrutiny of applicants' claims and as a check on internal biases. With more senior positions, the external oversight agency and/or a police board will play an important part in these processes.

The problem of police managers changing positions too often has already been discussed. The opposite problem is that of police managers staying in place when they are ineffective. It is essential, therefore, that a tough ongoing performance review system be in place. Senior managers need to have the courage to demote managers who have not fulfilled expectations when they were promoted. Human resource management systems need to have clear protocols that allow for the removal of underperforming managers back to operational duties. While natural justice processes need to be observed, there needs to be an efficient mechanism for replacing underachievers. The idea of a dynamic merit-based system of appointment is contrary to the traditional model of policing based on "Buggins' turn" and "a job for life." Under this model, police could expect to work through a set of promotional exams and fixed rank periods and work their way up through the hierarchy on the primary criterion of seniority. They could also stay indefinitely at any point. This approach generated a culture that resented younger "tall poppies" promoted "out of turn," and held back innovation and improvement.

One partial antidote to the problem of burnout, cynicism, and time serving is to create strategic exit points for staff. This involves a borrowing into policing of a potentially positive device from the military. Incentives can be put in place at points such as 10 years, 20 years, and 30 years for officers to resign with financial packages that will assist their transition into new careers. Ideally, the system of promotion (and deployment) and the system of early exit options will be finely tuned so that those who have become dissatisfied with a police career can make a dignified exit, while those with commitment and talent can see good reasons to stay on and progress. Again, as we have seen with numerous issues in this book, deciding that an exit and retention system is as fair and efficient as possible is inevitably a difficult judgment. But getting it right will depend significantly on the use of indicators and benchmarks derived from staff surveys and interviews, advice from unions, and other data such as personnel turnover statistics.

Ethical Leadership and the Compstat Model

A notable accountability mechanism for police managers in relation to crime control that has been introduced in one form or another in many police organizations in recent years is the so-called Compstat model (Henry, 2002). Compstat has been described as "perhaps the single most important organizational/administrative innovation in policing during the latter half of the 20th century" (Kelling & Sousa, 2001, p. 6). In its original form it was developed during the time of William Bratton, NYPD Chief of Police, in the 1990s. It involved a process by which police middle managers were held to account by their superiors for their performance, primarily in terms of crime reduction in those areas for which they were responsible. The process was heavily dependent on up-to-date comprehensive crime data by means of which performance could be measured and improved. Executive level police managers held monthly meetings with precinct commanders to discuss detailed crime statistics and crime maps that allowed police performance to be tracked in highly specific terms. Commanding officers were expected to explain what they were doing to combat crime, particularly to address problems in specific hot spots.

Compstat was attributed with affecting dramatic reductions in crime in New York City. Although academic evaluations have been very mixed (Weisburd & Braga, 2006), the method has been exported to numerous other police organizations, both in the United States and outside it. What is agreed upon by most commentators is that the narrow Compstat process must be embedded in a wider institutional context. Displacement of crime is one problem that needs to be countered by this means. Another is that of complaints against police. One of the alleged downsides of the Compstat process was that an over-reliance on arrest strategies to reduce crime generated disaffection, especially among minority groups, and increased complaints against police (Davis et al., 2005). However, many of the strategies advocated in this book entail a Compstat paradigm. Integrity-related data, such as complaints data, should be presented in Compstat-style meetings. Middle managers need to be questioned about what they are doing in relation to, for example, high or increasing levels of complaints about the officers under their command. Problem-solving strategies, such as interventions with officers with high numbers of complaints, should be expected and evaluated. Ethical climate surveys should also be used to gauge the willingness of supervisors to report, or act on, misconduct by their staff (e.g., Kutnjak Ivkovic et al., 2005). The National Institute of Justice in the United States has argued that ethical climate surveys should be a key source for police managers to understand and address issues and problems relating to integrity (NIJ, 2005, p. 1):

- Do officers in this agency know the rules? Action: If they do, fine. Where they don't, teach them.
- How strongly do they support those rules? Action: If they support them, fine. Where they don't, teach them why they should.
- Do they know what disciplinary threat this agency makes for violation of the rules? Action: If they do, fine. Where they don't, teach them.
- Do they think the discipline is fair? Action: If they do, fine. If they don't, adjust discipline or correct their perceptions.

Police Union Leaders

Police unions present a major challenge for integrity management. They often maintain very high membership levels in the face of declining union membership in other occupations. Police officers see membership as a crucial form of protection from the many dangers associated with their job. Unions provide free legal defense when police are subject to disciplinary or criminal charges, assistance with compensation for injuries, and a means for bargaining for better wages and conditions. These are all positive aspects of employee collectivism that provide a form of democratic operative input that potentially can work well with responsible leadership. Police executive managers should work closely with unions to produce "win-win" outcomes on all aspects of policing strategies and management.

Unfortunately, the history of police union–management relations varies significantly from the ideal. Police unions are frequently politically powerful and they have not always used their influence in the public interest. Politicians tend to be in awe, if not in fear, of police unions because of their capacity to marshal a large voting block. Although unions are often averse to going on strike, or legally prohibited from striking because of their essential social service role, union leaders can call out large numbers of police to rallies and demonstrations that attract media coverage. Politicians are often willing to engage in deal-making with unions, sometimes in secretive arrangements, that appear more about winning votes and achieving sectional benefits than achieving community justice or accountability (Prenzler, 2000).

Police unionism is also notably prone to charismatic leadership, sometimes to the point of demagoguery. This is particularly likely to occur when police feel under pressure and adopt a siege mentality, as in crisis and transition points during and after a commission of inquiry. This is a time when union leaders have to decide which way they will swing, and they often see it in their interests to be oppositional, ostensibly at least portraying themselves as defenders of member rights from corruption witch hunts, and as the last bastion of job security (Mollen, 1994, p. 125). Union leaders have therefore often seen it as their duty to oppose enlarged police accountability, especially many of the more intrusive anticorruption measures recommended by inquiries and oversight agencies. Inquisitorial mechanisms are often characterized at member rallies and media presentations as discriminatory, involving a double standard, and as needing to be opposed on grounds of fairness. However, these positions are often not simply rhetorical. Unions normally have substantial financial assets, with enormous capacity to contract defense lawyers to fight individual cases in the courts, using every legal loophole to delay appearances, put officers onto stress leave, or organize disability discharges with financial payouts funded by the taxpayer (Kramer & Gold, 2006; Stewart, 2006).

There are nonetheless a number of cases in the policing literature where union leaders have strongly supported reform measures, including enlarged external oversight. This support has been couched in terms of the reputations and welfare of the department and members and, above all, in terms of protecting honest police from dishonest colleagues. Unions have even worked with inquiries, professional standards units, and integrity agencies on the development of initiatives such as drug and alcohol testing, where they are able to focus attention on health and safety issues, and procedural justice (Prenzler, 2004; Prenzler & Ronken, 2001b).

A key challenge then for police ethical leadership is to engage the police union leadership in integrity management. Controls need to be in place to prevent "capture" of the integrity system by an assertive union leadership, but there also need to be opportunities for consultation on policy and some input into disciplinary decisions (without compromising confidential information). The Mollen Commission, among many inquiries, argued that union leaders' power

> ... brings the obligation to educate their members about the dangers of dishonesty and corruption. In promoting and furthering their members' interest, we strongly urge police unions to join in partnership with the Department's leadership in effectively fighting corruption. With an unequivocal voice, police unions must encourage their members to report corruption and cooperate with the Department and other law enforcement agencies when it comes time to prosecute, so long as their legitimate interest and their rights are protected (Mollen, 1994, p. 68).

Conclusion

A key task for ethical leadership is to establish ethics as a standard organizational practice. This is partly achieved by training and education. It is partly achieved by role modeling and supervision. It is also achieved by establishing and maintaining a comprehensive integrity system. Police leaders need to set the highest possible standards in their own behavior, and in corporate communications, untarnished by hypocrisy. But the most important test of ethical leadership is the extent to which police leaders have invested in the creation and maintenance of a comprehensive integrity management system.

References

3 Ex-cops get prison terms in Key West cocaine case. (1985, August 8). *News,* p. a10.

Aamodt, M. G. (2004). *Law enforcement selection: Research summaries.* Washington, DC: Police Executive Research Forum.

ACLU (1992). *Fighting police abuse: A Community action manual.* New York: American Civil Liberties Union.

ACLUT (2000). Austin community supports police oversight. *Police Accountability Project Fact Sheet #4.* Austin: American Civil Liberties Union of Texas.

Adams, D. (1997, November 7). One in two officers back existing system of complaints investigations. *Police Review,* 4.

AIC (1996). *Analysis of material derived from a survey undertaken by the Royal Commission into the NSW Police.* Canberra: Australian Institute of Criminology.

Alain, M., & Grégoire, M. (2008). Can ethics survive the shock of the job? Quebec's police recruits confront reality. *Policing and Society, 18,* 169–189.

ALRC (1995). *Under the spotlight: Complaints against the AFP and NCA.* Canberra: Australian Law Reform Commission.

Anatomy of an integrity test. (1997, December 23). *Daily Telegraph* (Australia), p. 4.

Archbold, C. (2005). Managing the bottom line: Risk management in policing. *Policing: An International Journal of Police Strategies and Management, 28*(1), 30–48.

Associated Press. (1997, April 16). Belgian Commission urges justice overhaul in wake of girls' deaths. *Houston Chronicle,* 24.

Ayling, J., & Grabosky, P. (2006). When police go shopping. *Policing: An International Journal of Police Strategies and Management, 29*(4), 665–690.

Baker, D. (2005). *Batons and blockades: Policing industrial disputes in Australasia.* Melbourne: Melbourne Publishing Group.

Baldwin, J. (1992). *Video taping police interviews with suspects: An evaluation.* London: Home Office.

Barker, T. (1978). An empirical study of police deviance other than corruption. *Journal of Police Science and Administration, 6*(3), 264–272.

Barker, T. (1983). Rookie police officers' perceptions of police occupational deviance. *Police Studies, 6*(2), 30–38.

Barker, T. (1996) *Police ethics: Crisis in law enforcement.* Springfield, IL: Charles C. Thomas.

Barron, S. (2007). *Police officer suicide: A review and examination using a psychological autopsy.* Retrieved March 10, 2008, from http://barronpsych.com.au/resource.html

Barry, D. (2000). LA Police Union calls for civilian oversight. *APBnews.com.* Retrieved July 20, 2002, from www.ipsn.org/2000-10-06.htm

Bartels, E., & Silverman, E. (2005). An exploratory study of the New York City Civilian Complaint Review Board mediation program. *Policing: An International Journal of Police Strategies and Management, 28*(4), 619–630.

Bassett, M., & Prenzler, T. (2002). Complaint profiling and early warning systems. In T. Prenzler & J. Ransley (Eds.), *Police reform: Building integrity* (pp. 131–145). Sydney: Federation Press.

Bates, S. (1998, February 3). Belgian pedophile report puts blame on "incompetent" police. *The Guardian*, 11.

Bayley, D. (1991). Preface. In A. Goldsmith (Ed.), *Complaints against the police: The trend to external review* (pp. x–xi). Oxford: Clarendon Press.

Bayley, D. (1994). *Police for the future.* New York: Oxford University Press.

Bayley, D. (2001). *Democratizing the police abroad: What to do and how to do it.* Washington, DC: National Institute of Justice.

BBC News (2002, July 10). Flashback: Rodney King and the LA riots. Retrieved May 16, 2008, from http://news.bbc.co.uk/1/hi/world/americas/2119943.stm

BBC News (2006, April 7). NY police guilty of mafia murders. Retrieved March 14, 2008, from http://news.bbc.co.uk/2/hi/americas/4885674.stm

Beach, B. (1978). *Report of the board of inquiry into allegations against members of the Victoria Police Force.* Melbourne: Government Printer.

Bennett, R. (1984). Becoming blue: A longitudinal study of police recruit occupational socialization. *Journal of Police Science and Administration, 12*(1), 47–58.

Berkow, M. (1996). Weeding out problem officers. *Police Chief, 63*(4), 22–29.

Bermúdez, M. (2005). Central America: Gang violence and anti-gang death squads. *PS News.* Retrieved March 16, 2008, from http://ipsnews.net/news.asp?idnews=30163

Berry, J. (2006, September 20) Beatings, kickings caught on secret video. *The Age*, p. 1.

Black, D. (1980). *The manners and customs of the police.* New York: Academic Press.

Board of Inquiry. (2000). *Board of Inquiry into the Rampart corruption incident: Final report.* Los Angeles: Los Angeles Police Department.

Boes, J., Chandler, C., & Timm, H. (1997). *Police integrity: Use of personality measures to identify corruption-prone officers.* Monterey, CA: Defense Personnel Security Research and Education Center.

Braithwaite, H., & Brewer, N. (1998). Differences in the conflict resolution tactics of male and female police patrol officers. *International Journal of Police Science and Management, 1*(3), 276–287.

Brereton, D. (2000). Evaluating the performance of external oversight bodies. In A. Goldsmith & C. Lewis (Eds.), *Civilian oversight of policing: Governance, democracy and human rights* (pp. 105–124). Oxford: Hart Publishing.

Brereton, D., & Ede, A. (1996). The police code of silence in Queensland: The impact of Fitzgerald inquiry reforms. *Current Issues in Criminal Justice, 8*(2), 107–129.

Brewer, N. (1991) *Identifying effective supervisory behaviors.* Adelaide: National Police Research Unit.

Brown, A. J. (2006, February). *Towards a performance measurement framework for integrity agencies: Lessons from the national integrity system assessment.* Paper presented at the 2nd National Conference of Parliamentary Oversight Committees and Anti-corruption/Crime Bodies, Sydney, Australia.

Brown, D. (1987). *The police complaints procedure: A Survey of complainants' views.* London: Home Office.

Brown, L., & Willis, A. (1985). Authoritarianism in British police recruits: Importation, socialization or myth? *Journal of Occupational Psychology, 58*, 97–108.

Brown, M. (2001). *Criminal investigation: Law and practice.* Boston: Butterworth-Heinemann.

Bryett, K., Harrison, A., & Shaw, J. (1997). *The role and functions of police in Australia.* Sydney: Butterworths.

Buerger, M. (1998). The politics of third party policing. *Crime Prevention Studies, 9,* 89–116.

Bullock, S., & Gunning, N. (2007). *Police service strength England and Wales* (2nd ed.). London: Home Office.

Burger, J., & Adonis, C. (2008, June). A watchdog without teeth? The Independent Complaints Directorate. *SA Crime Quarterly, 24,* 29–34.

Bylinsky, G. (1991). How companies spy on employees. *Fortune, 124*(11), 131–134.

Carter, D., & Sapp, A. (1992). College education and policing: Coming of age. *FBI Law Enforcement Bulletin, 61*(1), 8–14.

Carter, D., Sapp, A., & Stephens, D. (1989). *The state of police education: Policy directions for the 21st century.* Washington, DC: Police Executive Research Forum.

Catlin, D. W., & Maupin, J. R. (2002). Ethical orientations of state police recruits and one-year experienced officers. *Journal of Criminal Justice, 30*(6), 491–498.

CCRC. (1999). *Report.* Calgary: Citizen Complaints Review Committee, Calgary Police Commission.

Charette, B. (1993). *Early identification of police brutality and misconduct: The Metro-Dade Police Department model.* The Florida Criminal Justice Executive Institute. Retrieved June 12, 2008, from www.fdle.state.fl.us/FCJEI/SLP/SLP%20papers/Charette.pdf

CHRI. (2005). *Police accountability: Too important too neglect, too urgent to delay.* New Delhi: Commonwealth Human Rights Initiative.

Christopher, W. (1991). *Report of the Independent Commission on the Los Angeles Police Department.* Los Angeles: Independent Commission on the LAPD.

CJC. (1994). *Informal complaint resolution in the Queensland Police Service: An evaluation.* Brisbane: Criminal Justice Commission.

CJC. (1996a). *Informal complaint resolution in the Queensland Police Service: Follow-up evaluation.* Brisbane: Criminal Justice Commission.

CJC. (1996b). *Police recruit selection: Predictors of academy performance.* Brisbane: Criminal Justice Commission.

CJC. (1996c). *Submission to the Queensland Police Service Review Committee.* Brisbane: Criminal Justice Commission.

CJC. (1997). *Integrity in the Queensland Police Service: Implementation and impact of the Fitzgerald Inquiry reforms.* Brisbane: Queensland Criminal Justice Commission.

CJC. (2000a). *Defendants' perceptions of police treatment.* Brisbane: Criminal Justice Commission.

CJC. (2000b). *Public attitudes toward the CJC.* Brisbane: Criminal Justice Commission.

CMC. (2004a). *Handling complaints against Queensland Police: Past, present and future.* Brisbane: Crime and Misconduct Commission.

CMC. (2004b). *Listening in: Results from a CMC audit of police interview tapes.* Brisbane: Crime and Misconduct Commission.

Coble, P. (1997). Early warning systems: Identification and correction of problem behavior. *The Journal of California Law Enforcement, 31*(1), 23–27.

Cochrane, R., Tett, R., & Vandecreek, L. (2003). Psychological testing and the selection of police officers: A national survey. *Criminal Justice and Behavior, 30*(5), 511–537.

Collins, S. (2008, March 14). Assault tape detectives escape time behind bars. *The Age,* p. 3.

Corbett, C. (1991). Complaints against the police: The new procedure of informal resolution. *Policing and Society, 2,* 47–60.

Cornish, D., & Clarke, R. (Eds.). (1986). *The reasoning criminal: Rational choice perspectives on offending.* New York: Springer-Verlag.

Cozzetto, D., & Pedeliski, T. (1997). Privacy and the workplace: Technology and public employment. *Public Personnel Management, 26*(4): 515–527.

Crank, J. (1998). *Understanding police culture.* Cincinnati: Anderson.

Critchley, T. (1967). *A history of police in England and Wales 900-1966.* London: Constable & Company.

Cunningham, T. (2008). Pre-court diversion in the Northern Territory: impact on juvenile offending. *Trends and Issues in Crime and Criminal Justice, 339,* 1–6.

Daley, R. (1978). *Prince of the city.* Boston: Houghton Mifflin.

Danforth, J. (2000). *Final report to the Deputy Attorney General concerning the 1993 confrontation at the Mt. Carmel Complex, Waco, Texas.* Washington, DC: Department of Justice.

Dantkzer, M. L. (1993). An issue for policing—Educational level and job satisfaction: A research note. *American Journal of Police, 12*(2), 101–118.

Davis, R., Mateu-Gelabert, P., & Miller, J. (2005). Can effective policing also be respectful? Two examples in the South Bronx. *Police Quarterly, 8*(2), 229–247.

de Angelis, J., & Kupchick, A. (2007). Citizen oversight, procedural justice, and officer perceptions of the complaint investigation process. *Policing: An International Journal of Police Strategies and Management, 30*(4), 651–671.

de Guzman, M. C. (2007). Integrity of civilian review: A contemporary analysis of complainants' and police officers' views in the Philippines. *Police Practice and Research: An International Journal, 8*(1), 31–45.

Dias, C. F., & Vaughn, M. S. (2006). Bureaucracy, managerial disorganization, and administrative breakdown in criminal justice agencies. *Journal of Criminal Justice, 34*(5), 543–555.

Dibben, K. (2008, August 31). New vests for slim officers. *Sunday Mail.*

Dixon, D. (2006). A window into the interviewing process? The audio-visual recording of police interrogation in New South Wales, Australia. *Policing & Society, 16*(4), 323–348.

DPIC. (2008). 128th inmate exonerated and freed from death row. Death Penalty Information Center. Retrieved April 13, 2008, from www.deathpenaltyinfo.org/article.php?did=2666&scid=64

Dugan, J. R., & Bread, D. R. (1991). Complaints about police officers: A comparison among types and agencies. *Journal of Criminal Justice, 19*(2), 165–171.

Eades, D. (1995, August). Cross examination of Aboriginal children: The Pinkenba case. *Aboriginal Law Bulletin, 3,* 10–11.

Eck, J., & Weisburd, D. (Eds.). (2002). *Crime and place.* Monsey, NY: Criminal Justice Press.

Ede, A. (2000). *The prevention of police corruption and misconduct: A criminological analysis of complaints against police.* Unpublished doctoral dissertation, Griffith University, Brisbane.

Ede, A., & Barnes, M. (2002). Alternative strategies for resolving complaints. In T. Prenzler & J. Ransley (Eds.), *Police reform: Building integrity* (pp. 115–130). Sydney: Federation Press.

Ede, A., Homel, R., & Prenzler, T. (2002a). Reducing complaints against police and preventing misconduct: A diagnostic study using hot spot analysis. *Australian and New Zealand Journal of Criminology, 35*(1), 27–42.

Ede, A., Homel, R., & Prenzler, T. (2002b). Situational corruption prevention. In T. Prenzler & J. Ransley (Eds.), *Police reform: Building integrity* (pp. 210–225). Sydney: Federation Press.

Ede, A., & Legosz, M. (2002). Monitoring the ethical climate of organizations: A Queensland case study. *Crime and Misconduct Commission research & issues paper no. 2.* Brisbane: Crime and Misconduct Commission.

Farrington, D., & Welsh, B. (2007). *Saving children from a life of crime: Early risk factors and effective interventions.* Oxford: Oxford University Press.

FEC. (2001). *2000 presidential electoral and popular vote.* Washington: Federal Election Commission. Retrieved July 20, 2008, from www.fec.gov/pubrec/fe2000/elecpop.htm

Ferguson, G. (2003). *Review and recommendations concerning various aspects of police misconduct* (Vol. 1). Toronto: Toronto Police Service.

Finn, P. (2001). *Citizen review of police: Approaches and implementation.* Washington DC: National Institute of Justice.

Finnane, M. (2008). No longer a "workingman's paradise"? Australian police unions and political action in a changing industrial environment. *Police Practice and Research: An International Journal, 9*(2), 131–143.

Fitzgerald, G. (1989). *Report of a commission of inquiry pursuant to orders in council.* Brisbane: Government Printer.

Fleming, J., & Lafferty, G. (2000). New management techniques and restructuring for accountability in Australian police organizations. *Policing: An International Journal of Police Strategies and Management, 23*(2), 154–168.

Frank, M., McConkey, K., & Huon, G. (1995). *Individual perspectives on police ethics.* Adelaide: National Police Research Unit.

Gabor, T. (1994). *"Everybody does it!": Crime by the public.* Toronto: University of Toronto Press.

Gelb, B. (1983). *Varnished brass: The decade after Serpico.* New York: GP Putnam's Sons.

Gibbs, G. (2006). How assessment frames student learning. In C. Bryan & K. Clegg (Eds.), *Innovative assessment in higher education* (pp. 23–36). New York: Routledge.

Gilinsky, Y. (2005). Police and the community in Russia. *Police Practice and Research: An International Journal, 6*(4), 331–346.

Gill, P. (2000). *Rounding up the usual suspects? Developments in contemporary law enforcement intelligence.* Aldershot, UK: Ashgate.

Girodo, M. (1998). Undercover probes of police corruption: Risk factors in proactive internal affairs investigations. *Behavioral Sciences and the Law, 16*(4), 479–496.

Glenn, R., Panitch, B., Barnes-Proby, D., Williams, E., Christian, J., Lewis, M., Gerwehr, S., & Brannan, D. (2003). *Training the 21st century police officer.* Santa Monica: RAND.

Goldsmith, A. (2001). Pursuit of police integrity: Leadership and governance dimensions. *Current Issues in Criminal Justice, 13*(2), 185–202.

Goldstein, H. (1990). *Problem oriented policing.* New York: McGraw Hill.

Grabosky, P., & Braithwaite, J. (1986). Corporate crime and government response in Australia. In D. Chappell & P. R. Wilson (Eds.), *The Australian criminal justice system: The mid-1980s* (pp. 84–96). Sydney: Butterworths.

Graef, R. (1990). *Talking blues: The police in their own words.* London: Fontana.

Griswold, D. B. (1994). Complaints against the police: Predicting dispositions. *Journal of Criminal Justice, 22*(3), 215–221.

Hale, D. (2002). The looking-glass world of police integrity: The ethics and integrity of women police. In K. M. Lersch (Ed.), *Policing and misconduct* (pp. 143–155). Upper Saddle River, NJ: Prentice Hall.

Harrison, J., & Cunneen, M. (2000). *An independent police complaints commission.* London: Liberty, The National Council for Civil Liberties.

Hayes, H. (2007). Restorative justice and re-offending. In G. Johnstone & D. Van Ness (Eds.), *Handbook of restorative justice* (pp. 426–444). Devon, UK: Willan.

Hayes, H., & Prenzler, T. (2007). Victim and offender characteristics. In H. Hayes & T. Prenzler (Eds.), *An introduction to crime* (pp. 79–96). Sydney: Pearson.

Hayes, M. (1997). *A police ombudsman for Northern Ireland?* Belfast: Home Office Stationery Office.

Henry, V. (1990). Lifting the "blue curtain": Some controversial strategies to control police corruption. *National Police Research Unit Review, 6*, 48–55.

Henry, V. (1994). Police corruption: Tradition and evolution. In K. Bryett & C. Lewis (Eds.), *Un-peeling tradition: Contemporary policing* (pp. 160–176). Melbourne: Macmillan.

Henry, V. (2002). *The Compstat paradigm: Management accountability in policing, business, and the public sector.* NY: Looseleaf Law Publications.

Herzog, S. (2002). Police violence in Israel: Has the establishment of a civilian complaints board made a difference? *Police Practice and Research: An International Journal, 3*(2), 119–133.

Heymann, P. (1993). *Lessons from Waco.* Washington, DC: US Department of Justice.

Hilmer, W. (1998). *Public enemies: America's criminal past.* New York: Checkmark.

HMIC. (1999a). *Police integrity, England, Wales and Northern Ireland: Securing and maintaining public confidence.* London: Her Majesty's Inspectorate of Constabulary.

HMIC. (1999b). *Raising the standard: A thematic inspection of professional standards.* London: Her Majesty's Inspectorate of Constabulary.

Hoffman, G. (2003). *Police pursuits: A law enforcement and public safety issue for Queensland.* Brisbane: Crime and Misconduct Commission.

Holdaway, S. (1991). Race relations and police recruitment. *British Journal of Criminology, 31*(4). 365–382.

Hollinger, R., & Clark, J. (1983). *Theft by employees.* Lexington, MA: D.C. Heath and Company.

Home Office. (2007). *Guidance for the use of body-worn video devices.* London.

Homel, R. (2002). Integrity testing. In T. Prenzler & J. Ransley (Eds.), *Police reform: Building integrity* (pp. 159–171). Sydney: Federation Press.

Hoque, Z., Arends, S., & Alexander, R. (2004). Policing the police service: A case study of the "new public management" within an Australian police service. *Accounting, Auditing and Accountability Journal, 17*(1), 59–84.

Huberts, L., Kaptein, M. & Lasthuizen, K. (2007). A study of the impact of three leadership styles on integrity violations committed by police officers. *Policing: An International Journal of Police Strategies and Management, 30*(4), 587–607.

Huberts, L., Lamboo, T., & Punch, M. (2003). Police integrity in the Netherlands and the United States: Awareness and alertness. *Police Practice and Research: An International Journal, 4*(3), 217–232.

Huggins, M. (1997). From bureaucratic consolidation to structural devolutions: Police death squads in Brazil. *Policing and Society, 7,* 207–234.

Human Rights Watch. (1998). *Shielded from justice: Police brutality and accountability in the United States.* New York.

Human Rights Watch. (2007). *World report: Events of 2006.* New York.

Hunt, J. (1990). The logic of sexism among police. *Women and Criminal Justice, 1*(2), 3–30.

Huon, G., Hesketh, B., Frank, M., McConkey, K., & McGrath, G. (1995). *Perceptions of ethical dilemmas.* Adelaide: National Police Research Unit.

Hyams, M. (1990). Communicating the ethical standard. *Journal of California Law Enforcement, 24*(3), 76–82.

IACP. (2002). Law enforcement code of conduct. In *Police Chiefs Desk Reference* (pp. 34–39). Washington, DC: International Association of Chiefs of Police & Bureau of Justice Assistance.

ICAC. (1994). *Investigation into the relationship between police and criminals.* Sydney: Independent Commission Against Corruption

ICAC. (2000). *Annual report.* Hong Kong: Independent Commission Against Corruption.

ICPNI. (1999). *A new beginning: Policing in Northern Ireland.* Belfast: Independent Commission on Policing for Northern Ireland.

IPCC. (2006). *Confidence in the police complaints system: A survey of the general population.* London: Independent Police Complaints Commission.

IPCC. (2007a). *Annual report and statement of accounts 2006/07.* London: Independent Police Complaints Commission.

IPCC. (2007b). *Confidence in the police complaints system: A second survey of the general population, interim report.* London: Independent Police Complaints Commission.

IPCC. (2007c). *Police complaints: Statistics for England and Wales 2006/07.* London: Independent Police Complaints Commission.

IPCC. (2008). *Criteria for investigations.* Independent Police Complaints Commission. Retrieved June 27, 2008, from www.ipcc.gov.uk/investigations_criteria.pdf

Jauregui, B. (2007). Policing in Northern India as a different kind of political science: Ethnographic rethinking of normative "political interference" in investigations and order maintenance. *Asian Policing, 5*(1), 15–48.

Jenkins, C. (1997, October 17). Independent body to investigate police has public support in poll. *Police Review,* 4.

Johnson, D. T. (2004). Police integrity in Japan. In C. Klockars, S. Kutnjak Ivkovic, & M. Haberfeld (Eds.), *The contours of police integrity* (pp. 130–151). Thousand Oaks, CA: Sage.

Jones, B., & Mathers, S. (2006). Los Angeles County Sheriff's Department risk management and civil litigation management programs. In J. Cintron Perino (Ed.), *Citizen oversight and law enforcement* (pp. 115–126). Chicago: ABA Publishing.

Jones, D., Jones, L., & Prenzler, T. (2005). Tertiary education, commitment and turnover in police work. *Police Practice and Research: An International Journal, 6*(1), 49–63.

Jones, M. (1997, October). Police officer gratuities and public opinion. *Police Forum,* 8–11.

Kappeler, V., & Potter, G. (2005). *The mythology of crime and criminal justice.* Long Grove, IL: Waveland Press.

Kappeler, V., Sluder, R., & Alpert, G. (1998). *Forces of deviance: Understanding the dark side of policing.* Prospect Heights, IL: Waveland Press.

Kaptein, M., & van Reenen, P. (2001). Integrity management of police organizations. *Policing: An International Journal of Police Strategies and Management, 24*(3), 281–300.

Kelling, G. L., & Sousa, W. H. (2001). *Do police matter? An analysis of the impact of New York City's police reforms: Civic report no. 22.* New York: Manhattan Institute.

Kennedy, G. (2004). *Final report of the Royal Commission into whether there has been any corrupt or criminal conduct by Western Australian police officers.* Perth.

Kerner, O. (1968). *Report of the National Advisory Commission on Civil Disorder.* New York: EP Dutton & Co.

Key West Police Department called a "criminal enterprise." (1984, July 1). *The New York Times,* p. 1.

Kleinig, J. (1990). Teaching and learning police ethics: Competing and complimentary approaches. *Journal of Criminal Justice, 18,* 1–18.

Kleinig, J. (1996). *The ethics of policing.* New York: Cambridge University Press.

Kleinig, J. (2008). *Ethics and criminal justice: An introduction.* New York: Cambridge University Press.

Klockars, C., Kutnjack Ivkovic, S., & Haberfeld, M. (Eds.). (2004). *The contours of police integrity.* Thousand Oaks, CA: Sage.

Klockars, C., Kutnjack Ivkovich, S., & Haberfeld, M. (2005). *Enhancing police integrity.* Washington, DC: National Institute of Justice.

Klockars, C., Kutnjak Ivkovich, S., Harver, W., & Haberfeld, M. (2000). *The measurement of police integrity.* Washington DC: National Institute of Justice.

Knapp, W. (1972). *Report of a commission to investigate allegations of police corruption and the city's anti-corruption procedures.* New York: The City of New York.

Kolts, J. (1992). *Los Angeles County Sheriff's Department: Report by Special Counsel.* Los Angeles.

KPMG. (1996). *Report to the New York City Commission to Combat Police Corruption: The New York City Police Department random integrity testing program.* New York: NYC Commission to Combat Police Corruption.

Kramer, R., & Gold, E. (2006). Collective bargaining and labor agreements: Challenges to citizen oversight. In J. Cintron Perino (Ed.), *Citizen oversight and law enforcement* (pp. 79–87). Chicago: ABA Publishing.

Kutnjak Ivkovic, S. (2005). Police (mis)behavior: A cross-cultural study of corruption seriousness. *Policing: An International Journal of Police Strategies and Management, 28*(3), 546–566.

Landau, T. (1994). *Public complaints against the police: A view from complainants.* Toronto: Butterworths.

Landau, T. (1996). When police investigate police: A view from complainants. *Canadian Journal of Criminology, 38*(3), 291–315.

Landuyt, R., & T'Serclaes, N. (1997). *Enquete parlementaire sur la manière dont l'enquête, dans ses volets policiers et judiciaries a èté menèe dans "l'affaire Dutroux-Nihoul at consorts."* (Summary and selected translations by Brigitte Bouhours.) Brussels: Chambre des Représentants de Belgique.

Langdon, J., & Wilson, P. (2005). When justice fails: A follow-up examination of serious criminal cases since 1985. *Current Issues in Criminal Justice, 17*(2), 179–202.

Lawson, G., & Oldham, W. (2006). *The brotherhoods: The true story of two cops who murdered for the mafia*. New York: Simon and Schuster.

Legosz, M. (2007, October). *A cameo of recent research about police ethics at the Crime and Misconduct Commission*. Paper presented at the Australian Public Sector Anti-corruption Conference. Sydney, Australia.

Lersch, K. M. (1998). Police misconduct and malpractice: A critical analysis of citizens' complaints. *Policing: An International Journal of Police Strategies & Management, 21*(1), 80–96.

Lersch, K. M., Bazley, T., & Mieczkowski, T. (2006). Early intervention programs: An effective police accountability tool, or punishment of the productive? *Policing: An International Journal of Police Strategies and Management, 29*(1), 58–76.

Lersch, K. M., & Mieczkowski, T. (1996). Who are the problem-prone officers? An analysis of citizen complaints. *American Journal of Police, 15*(3), 23–44.

Liberty. (2000). *An independent police complaints commission*. London: Liberty, The National Council for Civil Liberties.

Liederbach, J., Boyd, L., Taylor, R., & Kawucha, S. (2008). Is it an inside job? An examination of internal affairs complaint investigation files and the production of nonsustained findings. *Criminal Justice Policy Review, 18*(4), 353–377.

Luna, E. (1994). Accountability to the community on the use of deadly force. *Policing by Consent, 12*, 4–6.

Maas, P. (1973). *Serpico*. New York: Viking Press.

Macintyre, S., & Prenzler, T. (1999). The influence of gratuities and personal relationships on police use of discretion. *Policing and Society, 9*, 181–201.

Macintyre, S., Prenzler, T., & Chapman, J. (2008). Early intervention to reduce complaints: An Australian Victoria Police initiative. *International Journal of Police Science and Management, 10*(2), 238–250.

Macintyre, S., Ronken, C., & Prenzler, T. (2002). The MMPI-2 as a tool for preventing police misconduct: A Victoria Police study. *International Journal of Police Science and Management, 4*(3), 213–232.

MacPherson, W. (1999). *The Stephen Lawrence Inquiry: Report of an inquiry by Sir William MacPherson of Cluny*. London: Her Majesty's Stationery Office.

Maguire, M., & Corbett, C. (1991). *A study of the police complaints system*. London: Her Majesty's Stationery Office.

Marx, G. (1988). *Undercover: Police surveillance in America*. Berkeley, CA: University of California Press.

Marx, G. (1992). When the guards guard themselves: Undercover tactics turned inward. *Policing and Society, 2*(3), 151–172.

Matthews, K. (2007, October 8). Abner Louima remembers New York police torture case on 10th anniversary. *Brooklyn Daily Express*. Retrieved May 12, 2008, from www.brooklyneagle.com/categories/category.php?category_id=4&id=14753

McCulloch, J., & Palmer, D. (2005). *Report: Civil litigation by citizens against Australian police between 1994 and 2002*. Canberra: Criminology Research Council.

McDonald, D. (1981). *Commission of inquiry concerning certain activities of the Royal Canadian Mounted Police. Second report: Freedom and security under the law*. Ottawa: Minister of Supply and Services.

McGuire Research Services. (2000). *Public satisfaction survey: New York City Police Department.* New York: New York City Council.

McKenzie, N., & Berry, J. (2006, September 23). Brute force. *The Age,* p. 1.

Mieczkowski, T. (2002). Drug abuse, corruption, and officer drug testing: An overview. In K. M. Lersch (Ed.), *Policing and misconduct* (pp. 157–192). Upper Saddle River, NJ: Prentice Hall.

Mieczkowski, T., & Lersch, K. (2002). Drug-testing police officers and police recruits. *Policing: An International Journal of Police Strategies and Management, 25*(3): 581–601.

Mollen, M. (1994). *Commission report.* New York: Commission to Investigate Allegations of Police Corruption and the Anti-Corruption Procedures of the Police Department (New York City).

Murphy, K., Hinds, L., & Fleming J. (2008). Encouraging public cooperation and support for police. *Policing and Society, 18*(2), 136–155.

Newburn, T. (1999). *Understanding and preventing police corruption: Lessons from the literature.* London, UK: Home Office.

Newton, S. (1997). Integrity testing as an anti-corruption strategy. *Australian Police Journal, 51*(4), 222–225.

NCWP. (2001). *Equality denied: The status of women in policing, 2000.* Beverly Hills, CA: National Center for Women & Policing.

NIJ. (2005). *Enhancing police integrity.* Washington, DC: National Institute of Justice.

NSW Ombudsman. (2002). *Improving the management of complaints: Identifying and managing officers with complaint histories of significance.* NSW: New South Wales Ombudsman.

NSWPS. (1999). *Annual report 1998/99.* Sydney: New South Wales Police Service.

NYCLU. (1998). *The NYCLU special report: Five years of civilian review: A mandate unfulfilled.* New York: New York Civil Liberties Union.

Ombudsman Victoria. (1998). *Operation BART: Investigation of allegations against police in relation to the shutter allocation system.* Melbourne: Ombudsman Victoria.

OPD. (2004). *Negotiated settlement agreement.* Oakland: Oakland Police Department. Retrieved October 12, 2007, from www.cdsusa.org/imt_rpts/agmt.pdf

OPI. (2006). *Annual report.* Melbourne: Office of Police Integrity.

Oppal, W. (1994). *Closing the gap: Policing and the community.* Victoria: Commission of Inquiry into Policing in British Columbia.

Padraic, S. (2006). *Sympathy for the devil: Confessions of a corrupt police officer.* Sydney: ABS Books.

Paoline, E., & Terrill, W. (2007). Police education, experience, and the use of force. *Criminal Justice and Behavior, 34*(2), 179–196.

Parks, B. (2000). *Board of Inquiry into the Rampart area corruption incident: Public report.* Los Angeles: Los Angeles Police Department.

Parks, B., & Smith, A. (1999). *The 1992 Los Angeles riots: Lessons learned, changes made.* Retrieved July 3, 2002, from www.lapdonline.org/

Pate, A. M., & Fridell, L. A. (1993). *Police use of force: Official reports, citizen complaints, and legal consequences.* Washington, DC: Police Foundation.

PCMC. (2008). *Parliamentary crime and misconduct commission (Queensland).* Retrieved June 23, 2008, from www.parliament.qld.gov.au/committees/

PEAC. (1998). *Police for the future: Review of recruitment and selection for the Queensland Police Service.* Brisbane: Police Education Advisory Council.

Perez, A., Berg, K., & Myers, D. (2003). Police and riots, 1967–1969. *Journal of Black Studies, 34*(2), 153–182.

PIC. (1998). *Annual report 1997–98.* Sydney: Police Integrity Commission.

PIC. (2000). *Special report to parliament: Project Dresden, an audit of the quality of NSW Police Service internal investigations.* Sydney: Police Integrity Commission.

PIC. (2001). *Qualitative and strategic audit of the reform process (QSARP) of the NSW Police Service.* Sydney: Police Integrity Commission.

PIC. (2004). *Police integrity commission practice guidelines.* Sydney: Police Integrity Commission.

PIC. (2005). *Operation Abelia: Research and investigations into illegal drug use by some NSW police officers, volume 1, summary report.* Sydney: Police Integrity Commission.

Pollock, J. (2007). *Ethical dilemmas and decisions in criminal justice.* Belmont CA: Wadsworth.

PONI. (2002a). *First annual report.* Belfast: Police Ombudsman for Northern Ireland.

PONI. (2002b). *Public awareness of the Northern Ireland police complaints system.* Belfast: Police Ombudsman for Northern Ireland.

PONI. (2004). *A study of the attitudes of members of the Police Service of Northern Ireland to the Office of the Police Ombudsman for Northern Ireland and the new complaints system: Main findings.* Belfast: Police Ombudsman for Northern Ireland.

PONI. (2005). *An evaluation of police-led informal resolution of police complaints in Northern Ireland.* Dublin: Police Ombudsman for Northern Ireland.

PONI. (2006a). *A report into complainant non co-operation with the complaints process.* Belfast: Police Ombudsman for Northern Ireland.

PONI. (2006b). *Complainant satisfaction survey 2005/6.* Belfast: Police Ombudsman for Northern Ireland.

PONI. (2007a). *Annual report and accounts 2007.* Belfast: Police Ombudsman for Northern Ireland.

PONI. (2007b). *Complainant satisfaction survey 2006/7.* Belfast: Police Ombudsman for Northern Ireland.

PONI. (2007c). *Developments in police complaints—7 years on.* Belfast: Police Ombudsman for Northern Ireland.

Potts, L. W. (1981). Higher education, ethics, and the police. *Journal of Police Science and Administration, 9*(2), 131–134.

Prados, J. (1986). *Presidents' secret wars: CIA and Pentagon covert operations since World War II.* New York: William Morrow.

Prenzler, T. (2000). Civilian oversight of police: A test of capture theory. *The British Journal of Criminology, 40*(4), 659–674.

Prenzler, T. (2002). Corruption and reform: Global trends and theoretical perspectives. In T. Prenzler & J. Ransley (Eds.), *Police reform: Building integrity* (pp. 3–23). Sydney: Federation Press.

Prenzler, T. (2004). Stakeholder perspectives on police complaints and discipline: Towards a civilian control model. *Australian and New Zealand Journal of Criminology, 37*(1), 85–113.

Prenzler, T. (2006). Senior police managers' views on integrity testing, and drug and alcohol testing. *Policing: An International Journal of Police Strategies and Management, 29*(3), 394–407.

Prenzler, T., & Hayes, H. (2000). Measuring progress in gender equity in Australian policing. *Current Issues in Criminal Justice, 12*(1), 20–38.

Prenzler, T., & Lewis, C. (2005). Performance indicators for police oversight agencies. *Australian Journal of Public Administration, 64*(2), 77–83.

Prenzler, T., & Mackay, P. (1995). Police gratuities: What the public think. *Criminal Justice Ethics, 14*(1), 15–25.

Prenzler, T., & Ronken, C. (2001a). Models of police oversight: A critique. *Policing and Society, 11*, 151–180.

Prenzler, T., & Ronken, C. (2001b). Police integrity testing in Australia. *Criminal Justice: The International Journal of Policy and Practice, 1*(3), 319–342.

Prenzler, T., & Sarre, R. (2009a). The criminal justice system. In H. Hayes & T. Prenzler (Eds.), *An introduction to crime and criminology* (pp. 259–273). Sydney: Pearson.

Prenzler, T., & Sarre, R. (2009b). The police. In H. Hayes & T. Prenzler (Eds.), *An introduction to crime and criminology* (pp. 274–291). Sydney: Pearson.

Punch, M. (2003). Rotten orchards: "Pestilence," police misconduct and system failure. *Policing and Society, 13*(2), 171–196.

Quinn, S. (2006). Citizen complaints and mediation. In J. Cintron Perino (Ed.), *Citizen oversight and law enforcement* (pp. 127–146). Chicago: ABA Publishing.

Ramsey, R., & Frank, J. (2007). Wrongful conviction: Perceptions of criminal justice professionals regarding the frequency of wrongful conviction and the extent of system errors. *Crime and Delinquency, 53*(3), 436–470.

Ransley, J. (2002). Miscarriages of justice. In T. Prenzler & J. Ransley (Eds.), *Police reform: Building integrity* (pp. 24–38). Sydney: Federation Press.

Ransley, J., Anderson, J., & Prenzler, T. (2007). Litigation against police in Australia: Policy implications. *Australian and New Zealand Journal of Criminology, 40*(2), 143–160.

Ratcliffe, J. (2008). *Intelligence-led policing.* Cullompton: Willan Publishing.

RCCJ. (1993). *The questioning and interviewing of suspects outside the police station (research study).* London: Royal Commission on Criminal Justice (Stationery Office Books).

Reiner, R. (1991). Multiple realities, divided worlds: Chief constables' perspectives on the police complaints system. In A. Goldsmith (Ed.), *Complaints against the police: The trend to external review* (pp. 211–231). Oxford: Clarendon Press.

Reuss-Ianni, E. (1983). *Two cultures of policing: Street cops and management cops.* New Brunswick, NJ: Transaction Books.

Richardson, J. (1987). *Review of the investigation of complaints by the Internal Investigation Department of the Victoria Police.* Melbourne: Victoria Police.

RIRP. (2000). *Report of the Rampart Independent Review Panel.* Los Angeles, CA: Los Angeles Board of Police Commissioners.

Rix, B., Walker, D., & Brown, R. (1997). *A study of deaths and serious injuries resulting from police vehicle accidents.* London: Home Office.

Rosen, P. (2000). *The Canadian Security Intelligence Service.* Retrieved April 12, 2008, from www.parl.gc.ca/information/library/PRBpubs/8427-e.htm#A.%20The%20Origins

Ross, D. (2000). Emerging trends in police failure to train liability. *Policing: An International Journal of Police Strategies and Management, 23*(2), 169–193.

Rothwell, G., & Baldwin, J. (2007). Whistle-blowing and the code of silence in police agencies: Polices and structural predictors. *Crime and Delinquency, 53*(4), 605–632.

Royal Commission. (1981). *Second report—Freedom and security under the law.* Ottawa: Commission of Inquiry Concerning Certain Activities of the RCMP, Canadian Government Publishing Centre.

Rozenberg, J. (1992). Miscarriages of justice. In E. Stockdale & S. Casales (Eds.), *Criminal justice under stress* (pp. 91–116). London: Blackstone.

Russell, K. (1978). Complaints against the police. *The Police Journal, 51*(1), 34–44.

Sarre, R. (1989). Towards the notion of policing "by consent" and its implications for police accountability. In D. Chappell & P. Wilson (Eds.), *Australian policing: Contemporary issues* (pp. 102–119). Sydney: Butterworths.

Scarman, L. G. (1986). *Scarman report.* London: Penguin.

Sced, M. (2004). *Screening for corruption using standard psychological tests of personality: A review of the research evidence.* Adelaide: Australasian Centre for Policing Research.

Scher, R., & Weathered, L. (2004). Should the United States establish a Criminal Cases Review Commission? *Judicature, 88*(3), 122–125, 145.

Schlaefli, A., Rest, J., & Thomas, S. (1985). Does moral education improve moral judgment? A meta-analysis of intervention studies using the Defining Issues Test. *Review of Educational Research, 55*(3), 319–352.

SCRGSP (Steering Committee for the Review of Government Service Provision). (2008). *Report on government services 2008.* Canberra: Productivity Commission.

Sechrest, D., & Burns, P. (1992). Police corruption: The Miami case. *Criminal Justice and Behavior, 19*(3), 294–313.

Self, D., Baldwin, D., & Olivarez, M. (1993). Teaching medical ethics to first-year students by using film discussion to develop moral reasoning. *Academic Medicine, 68*(5), 383–385.

Seneviratne, M. (2004). Policing the police in the United Kingdom. *Policing & Society, 14*(4), 329–347.

Sherman, L. (1977). Police corruption control: Environmental context versus organizational policy. In D. Bayley (Ed.), *Police and society* (pp. 143–155). Beverley Hills CA: Sage.

Sherman, L. (1978a). *Quality of police education: A critical review with recommendations for improving programs in higher education.* San Francisco: Jossey-Bass.

Sherman, L. (1978b). *Scandal and reform: Controlling police corruption.* Berkeley: University of California Press.

Sherman, L. (1983). From whodunit to who does it: Fairness and target selection in deceptive investigations. In G. Caplan (Ed.), *ABSCAM ethics: Moral issues and deception in law enforcement* (pp. 118–134). Washington, DC: The Police Foundation.

Sigler, R., & Dees, T. (1988). Public perceptions of petty corruption in law enforcement. *Journal of Police Science and Administration, 16*(1), 14–20.

Skolnick, J. (1994). *Justice without trial: Law enforcement in democratic society.* New York: Macmillan.

Smith, G. (2003). Actions for damages against the police and the attitudes of claimants. *Policing and Society, 13*(4), 413–422.

Stevens, D. (2008). Forensic science, wrongful convictions, and American prosecutor discretion. *The Howard Journal, 47*(1), 31–51.

Stevens, K. (2000). Structure interviews to hire the best people. In Locke, E., ed. *The Blackwell handbook of principles of organizational behavior: Executive handbook* (pp. 29–40). Oxford: Blackwell.

Stewart, L. (2006). What to expect of outreach: Different strategies for different stake-holders. In J. Cintron Perino (Ed.), *Citizen oversight and law enforcement* (pp. 169–188). Chicago: ABA Publishing.

Stone, A. (1993). *Report and recommendations concerning the handling of incidents such as the Branch Davidian standoff in Waco Texas.* Retrieved March 17, 2008, from www.pbs.org/wgbh/pages/frontline/waco/stonerpt.html

Strudwick, K. (2003). Is independence the only answer to complainants' satisfaction of the police complaints process? A perspective from the United Kingdom. *Police Practice and Research: An International Journal, 4*(1), 35–46.

Sviridoff, M., & McElroy, J. (1989). *Processing complaints against police in New York City: The complainant's perspective.* New York: Vera Institute.

Sykes, G., & Matza, D. (1957). Techniques of neutralization: A theory of delinquency. *American Sociological Review, 22,* 664–670.

Tarling, R., & Dowds, L. (1997). Crime and punishment. In R. Jowell, et al., (Eds.), *British social attitudes* (pp. 197–214). Aldershot: Ashgate Publishing.

Thomassen, G. (2002). Investigating complaints against the police in Norway: An empirical evaluation. *Policing and Society, 12*(3), 201–210.

Thorne, C., & Chantler, N. (2008). Process of investigations. In R. Broadhurst & S. Davies (Eds.), *Policing in context,* pp. 102–122. Melbourne: Oxford University Press.

Toch, H., & Grant, J. D. (2005). *Police as problem solvers: How frontline workers can promote organizational and community change.* Washington, DC: American Psychological Association.

Transparency International. (2004). *Report on the Transparency International Global Corruption Barometer.* Berlin.

UN. (1979). *Code of conduct for law enforcement officials.* Geneva: United Nations, Office for Democratic Institutions and Human Rights. Retrieved July 20, 2008, from www.legislationline.org/legislation.php?tid=155&lid=4519&less=false

USCCR. (1981). *Who is guarding the guardians? A report on police practices.* Washington, DC: United States Commission on Civil Rights.

USCCR. (2000). *Revisiting who is guarding the guardians? A report on police practices and civil rights in America.* Washington, DC: United States Commission on Civil Rights.

USDoJ. (1994). *Report of the Ruby Ridge Task Force.* Washington DC: United States Department of Justice. Retrieved March 15, 2008, from www.byington.org/Carl/ruby/ruby1.htm

USDoJ. (2001). *Principles for promoting police integrity: Examples of promising police practices and policies.* Washington DC: US Department of Justice.

USDoJ. (2002). *A review of allegations of a double standard of discipline at the FBI.* Washington DC: Department of Justice.

Walker, S. (2001). *Police accountability: The role of citizen oversight.* Belmont, CA: Wadsworth.

Walker, S. (2003). *The disciplinary matrix: An effective police accountability tool?* Omaha, NE: University of Nebraska.

Walker, S. (2007, November). *Police accountability: Current issues and research needs.* Paper presented at the Policing Research Workshop: Planning for the Future, National Institute of Justice, Washington, DC.

Walker, S., Alpert, G. P., & Kenney, D. J. (2001). *Early warning systems: Responding to the problem police officer.* Washington, DC: National Institute of Justice.

Walker, S., Archbold, C., & Herbst, L. (2002). *Mediating citizen complaints against police officers: A guide for police and community leaders.* Washington, DC: US Department of Justice.

Walker, S., & Bumphus, V. (1992). The effectiveness of civilian review. *American Journal of Police, 11*(4), 1–26.

Walker, S., & Herbst, L. (1999). *Citizen and police officer evaluations of the Minneapolis Civilian Review Authority.* Minneapolis: Minneapolis Civilian Review Authority.

Waters, I., & Brown, K. (2000). Police complaints and the complainants' experience. *British Journal of Criminology, 40*(2), 617–638.

Waugh, L., Ede, A., & Alley, A. (1998). Police culture, women police and attitudes towards misconduct. *International Journal of Police Science and Management, 1*(3), 288–300.

Weisburd, D., & Braga, A. (Eds.). (2006). *Police innovation: Contrasting perspectives.* Cambridge: Cambridge University Press.

Weitzer, R. (2004). Public perceptions of police misconduct and reform. In M. Hickman, A. Piquero, & J. Greene (Eds.), *Police integrity and ethics* (pp. 190–208). Belmont, CA: Wadsworth.

Wells, W., & DeLeon-Granados, W. (1998). "Do you want extra police coverage with those fries?" An exploratory analysis of the relationship between patrol practices and the gratuity exchange principle. *Police Quarterly, 1*(2), 71–85.

White, D. (2006). A conceptual analysis of the hidden curriculum of police training in England and Wales. *Policing and Society, 16*(4), 386–404.

White, R. (1998). Curtailing youth: A critique of coercive crime prevention. *Crime Prevention Studies, 9*, 17–140.

Whitton, E. (1990, March 10). Diary of a disgraced cop. *Sydney Morning Herald*, p. 71.

Wood, J. (1996). *Royal Commission into the New South Wales Police Service, interim report: Immediate measures for the reform of the Police Service of New South Wales.* Sydney: Government of the State of NSW.

Wood, J. (1997). *Royal Commission into the New South Wales Police Service: Final report.* Sydney: NSW Government Printer.

Worrall, J. (2002). If you build it they will come: Consequences of improved citizen complaint review procedures. *Crime and Delinquency, 48*(3), 355–379.

Wortley, R., & Homel, R. (1995). Police prejudice as a function of training and out-group contact: A longitudinal investigation. *Law and Human Behavior, 19*(3), 305–317.

Index

A

Abduction, 10
Academic research on corruption, 7–8
Access controls, data, 127–128
Accountability
    minimalist model of, 80–81, 113
    model oversight system, 170–172
Adams, D., 161
Administrative authority, 91–93, 179–180
ADR. *See* Alternative dispute resolution (ADR)
Affirmative action, 70–72
Agencies, oversight, 157–158, 164–170
Age of recruits, 74
Alcohol use. *See* Drug and alcohol testing
Allegations of misconduct, 52, 89–90, 168
Allocation and assessment, case, 86–87
Alpert, G., 1
Alternative dispute resolution (ADR)
    for complaints against police, 99–101
    defined, 98
    evaluations of, 101–107
    informal resolution in, 100, 104–107
    managerial resolution in, 101
    mediation in, 99–100
    movement, 97–99
    quality control, intelligence, and
        behavioral change in, 108–112
Ambiguity, 11–13
American Civil Liberties Union (ACLU),
    162
Apartheid, 3
Armed robbery, 7
Arrestee surveys, 54–56
Assault, 7, 10
Assessments
    integrity system, 62–63
    threat, 126–127
ATF. *See* U. S. Bureau of Alcohol, Tobacco,
    and Firearms
Attorneys, 60
Audits

financial, 148–149
system, 61–62
Australia, 148. *See also* Queensland Police
    Service; Victoria Police
    external oversight in, 157, 165
    leadership in, 175–176
Authority, administration, 91–93, 179–180

B

Bank robbery, 7
Barker, T., 7, 57
Barnes, M., 109
Bartels, E., 110
Bayley, David, 32, 153
Beach, B., 85
Behavioral change, 108–112
Belgium, 10
Berkow, M., 120
Birmingham Six, 9
Body-worn video (BWV), 95
Brammer, Mal, 138
Branch Davidian religious sect, 12–13
Bratton, William, 185
Bribery, 16, 38
British Social Attitudes Survey, 161
Brixton riots, 4
Brothels, 7
Brutality, 16, 22–23
Buerger, Michael, 31
Burnout, 185

C

Canada, 30, 70, 88, 164, 184
Capone, Al, 148
Caracappa, Stephen, 11
Case assessment and allocation, 86–87
Casso, Anthony, 11
Categories of police misconduct, 15–17
Causes of police misconduct, 20–25
CCTV (closed circuit television), 50, 169
Central Intelligence Agency (CIA), 3

Q

R

A Call for Authors

Introducing a New Book Series from CRC Press

Advances in Police Theory and Practice

AIMS AND SCOPE:

This cutting-edge series is designed to support strong collaboration between researchers and practitioners in police work. We are especially interested in volumes that focus on the nexus between research and practice, with the end goal of implementing innovative police programs. We will consider collections of expert contributions as well as individually authored works. Books in this series will be marketed internationally to both academic and professional audiences. This series seeks to —

- Bridge the gap in knowledge between theory and practice regarding who the police are, what they do, and how they maintain order, administer laws, and serve their communities

- Improve cooperation between those who are active in the field and those who are involved in academic research so as to facilitate the application of innovative police work

The series especially encourages the contribution of works co-authored by police practitioners and researchers that will highlight a particular subject from both points of view and offer suggestions for applications of the research. We are also interested in works comparing policing approaches and methods from one nation to another, examining such areas as the policing of international states, democratic policing, policing and social minorities, preventive policing, investigation, patrolling and response, and drug enforcement. Manuscripts should be between 200 and 600 pages. If you have a proposal for an original work or for a contributed volume, please be in touch.

Series Editor
Dilip Das, Ph.D., Editor-in-Chief, International Police Executive Symposium
Ph: 318-274-2520   E-mail: dilipkd@aol.com

Dr. Das is President of the International Police Executive Symposium. He also chairs the Criminal Justice Department at Grambling State University and serves as a human rights consultant to the United Nations. In addition to editing the *World Police Encyclopedia* (Taylor & Francis, 2006), Dr. Das has over 40 years of experience in police practice, research, writing, and education. He is founding Editor-in-Chief of *Police Practice and Research: An International Journal* (Routledge/Taylor & Francis).

Proposals for the series may be submitted to the series editor or directly to —
Carolyn Spence
Acquisitions Editor • CRC Press / Taylor & Francis Group
561-998-2515 • 561-997-7249 (fax)
carolyn.spence@taylorandfrancis.com • www.crcpress.com
6000 Broken Sound Parkway NW, Suite 300, Boca Raton, FL 33487

CRC Press
Taylor & Francis Group